MONEY AND MARKETS

MONEY AND MARKETS
ESSAYS BY ROBERT W. CLOWER

Edited by
DONALD A. WALKER
Department of Economics
Indiana University of Pennsylvania

The right of the
University of Cambridge
to print and sell
all manner of books
was granted by
Henry VIII in 1534.
The University has printed
and published continuously
since 1584.

CAMBRIDGE UNIVERSITY PRESS

Cambridge
London   New York   New Rochelle
Melbourne   Sydney

Published by the Press Syndicate of the University of Cambridge
The Pitt Building, Trumpington Street, Cambridge CB2 1RP
32 East 57th Street, New York, NY 10022, USA
10 Stamford Road, Oakleigh, Melbourne 3166, Australia

First published 1984
First paperback edition 1986

Printed in the United States of America

Library of Congress Cataloging in Publication Data
Clower, Robert W.
Money and markets.
Includes index.
1. Money – Addresses, essays, lectures.   2. Money
supply – Addresses, essays, lectures.   3. Economics –
Addresses, essays, lectures.   I. Walker, Donald A.
(Donald Anthony), 1934–   .II. Title.
HG221.C65   1984   332.4   84–1902
ISBN 0 521 26231 3 hardcovers
ISBN 0 521 33560 4 paperback

To Patricia and Valerie

CONTENTS

PART V. AFTERWORD

PREFACE

I had read some of Dr. Robert Clower's work during the late 1950s and early 1960s, and correspondence between us about it led to our meeting for the first time in 1964, on the occasion of my responding to his invitation to give a talk at Northwestern University. I felt an immediate affinity for his cast of mind and personality, and my study of his writings during the ensuing years imbued me with a deep regard for the intellectual course that he was charting. I have always found his work like a breath of fresh air. Iconolastic but constructive, he not only calls for realism and relevance—we can all do that—he also shows what those qualities are and how they can be achieved. My conviction of the value of his contributions led to my proposing, twenty years after our first meeting, that I edit a collection of them. Professor Clower not only approved of the idea, but also agreed to review my introduction and to answer my many questions. Most important, however, he agreed to write a piece for this volume. The result is an afterword in which he reflects upon his past work, evaluates current Keynesian, monetarist, and new classical models, and states his present position on the direction that monetary theory should take.

Before beginning the essays, the reader should know something about their author. Robert Wayne Clower was born in Pullman, Washington, on February 13, 1926. He received an A.B. in economics with highest distinction from Washington State University in 1948. In that same year he became an instructor in economics at WSU, and began work there on an M.A. degree, which he finished in 1949. When he was selected as a Rhodes scholar, he went to Oxford University, where he held a Nuffield College Studentship, served as chairman of the Oxford-London-Cambridge Joint Economic Seminars, and in 1952 completed a master of letters in economics. Oxford University recognized his scientific contributions by awarding him the degree of doctor of letters in economics in 1978.

Clower joined the faculty of Washington State University as an assistant professor of economics in 1952. There he concentrated on microeconomic studies, a number of which are summarized in his durable classic, *Introduction to Mathematical Economics*,[1] written with D.W.

---

[1] D. W. Bushaw and Robert W. Clower, *Introduction to Mathematical Economics* (Homewood, Ill.: Irwin, 1957).

Bushaw. From 1954 to 1956, during the first of several visits to underdeveloped countries, he taught at the University of Punjab in Lahore, West Pakistan. In 1957 he moved to Northwestern University as an associate professor of economics, an appointment that began a phase of his career notable for its scholarly productivity, particularly in the field of stock-flow analysis—which he largely created—and in the study of monetary economics. He was promoted to professor at Northwestern in 1963, and was chairman of the Department of Economics from 1958 to 1964. In 1960 he was awarded a Ford Foundation Faculty Research Fellowship. Continuing his interest in underdeveloped countries, he became director of the Northwestern University Economic Survey of Liberia in 1961 and visited Liberia during 1961 and 1962. He was ejected from Liberia in 1962 for holding opinions unpalatable to the Liberian government, and in 1966 completed, with colleagues, a book presenting those adverse findings.[2] His interest in the economics of underdeveloped countries was also manifested by his authorship with John Harris of a book on Puerto Rican shipping,[3] a number of articles and special studies,[4] and his acceptance of the position of visiting professor of economics at Makerere College in Kampala, Uganda, for the summer of 1965. He strengthened his ties with England in several ways: he visited the economics faculty of Cambridge University for the Michaelmas term in 1962; he became the John Maynard Keynes Visiting Professor at Economics at the University of Essex and a holder of a John Simon Guggenheim Memorial Foundation Fellowship in 1965; and he took the positions of dean of the School of Social Studies and professor of economics at the University of Essex during the 1968 academic year.

In 1971 Clower moved to the University of California at Los Angeles as professor of economics, the position he holds at the present time. His career at UCLA has been rich in achievement and experiences, with respect tò not only his publications, but also his teaching, asso-

    [2] Robert W. Clower, George Dalton, A. A. Walters, and M. Harwitz, *Growth Without Development: An Economic Survey of Liberia* (Evanston, Ill.: Northwestern University Press, 1966).
    [3] Robert W. Clower and John Harris, *Puerto Rican Shipping and the U.S. Maritime Laws: An Economic Appraisal* (Evanston, Ill.: Transportation Center, Northwestern University, 1965).
    [4] Robert W. Clower, "The Future of Banking in Pakistan," *Al-Iqtisad*, 9 (March 1956), 5–10; and "Review of *Problems and Practices of Development Banks*, by Shirley Boskey (1959)," *Journal of Political Economy*, 69 (October 1961), 521; Robert W. Clower, George Dalton, and A. A. Walters, "Statistics and Development Policy Decisions," *Development Research Review*, 1 (July 1962), 54–5; Robert W. Clower, "Mainsprings of African Economic Progress," Fifth Melville J. Herskovits Memorial Lecture, November 9, 1966 (Edinburgh: Centre of African Studies, University of Edinburgh, 1968).

ciations with colleagues, and editorship of two great scholarly journals.
His editorial experience began with his appointment to the editorial
board of the *American Economic Review* for the period 1963 to 1966.
In 1966 he also became a consulting editor for Penguin Books, a post
he still holds. His editorship of *Economic Inquiry* (formerly the *Western
Economic Journal*) began in 1973. In large measure in recognition of
his editorial contributions to the latter journal, he was selected as the
managing editor of the *American Economic Review* in 1980.

Clower has continued to visit other universities. In the summer of
1972 he went to Australia as visiting professor at Monash University.
During October of the following year he became visiting professor at
the Bank of Italy Research Staff Seminar in Perugia. In March of
1974 he went to the Institute for Advanced Study in Vienna as visiting
professor. In the fall of that same year, and again in the fall of 1977,
he lectured at the University of Western Ontario. From 1978 to 1980
he was adjunct professor at Washington State University. In July and
August of 1982, as holder of an Erskine Fellowship, he lectured at
Monash University and at Canterbury University in New Zealand,
and in May of 1983 he accepted an invitation to visit the Hebrew
University in Jerusalem.

Clower has also been active in professional associations. He is a
member of the American Economic Association, and served on its
Executive Committee from 1978 to 1981. He is a member of the Royal
Economic Society and was made a Fellow of the Econometric Society
in 1978. He holds membership in the American Association of Rhodes
Scholars, Phi Kappa Phi, and Phi Beta Kappa, and is an Honorary
Fellow of Brasenose College of Oxford University.

I am grateful to the staff of the Cambridge University Press for their
efforts on this book, and to Indiana University of Pennsylvania for a
grant to aid my work on it.

DONALD A. WALKER
Indiana, Pennsylvania
March 1984

ACKNOWLEDGMENTS

The editor and the Cambridge University Press wish to thank Robert W. Clower and the original publishers of the essays in this volume for permission to reprint them, and to thank M. L. Burstein, Peter W. Howitt, and Axel Leijonhufvud for permission to reprint the essays that they authored with Dr. Clower.

Chapter 1. "Keynes and the Classics: A Dynamical Perspective," *Quarterly Journal of Economics*, 74 (May 1960), 318–23. Copyright 1960 by the President and Fellows of Harvard College. Reprinted by permission of John Wiley and Sons, Inc.

Chapter 2. "Classical Monetary Theory Revisited," *Economica*, 30 (May 1963), 165–70. Reprinted by permission of the *Economica* Publishing Office.

Chapter 3. "The Keynesian Counter-Revolution: A Theoretical Appraisal," in *The Theory of Interest Rates*, ed. F. H. Hahn and F. P. R. Brechling (London: Macmillan, 1965), 103–25. Reprinted by permission of Macmillan, London and Basingstoke, and the International Economic Association. This article was first published as "Die Keynesianische Gegenrevolution: eine theoretische Kritik," *Schweizerische Zeitschrift für Volkswirtschaft und Statistik*, 99 (1963), 8–31.

Chapter 4. "Monetary History and Positive Economics," *Journal of Economic History*, 24 (September 1964), 364–80. Reprinted by permission of the Economic History Association.

Chapter 5. "A Reconsideration of the Microfoundations of Monetary Theory," *Western Economic Journal* (now *Economic Inquiry*), 6 (December 1967), 1–8. Reprinted by permission of the Western Economic Association.

Chapter 6. "Comment: The Optimal Growth Rate of Money," *Journal of Political Economy*, 76, Pt. II (July/August 1968), 876–80. Reprinted by permission of The University of Chicago Press. Copyright 1968 by The University of Chicago.

Chapter 7. Introduction to *Monetary Theory: Selected Readings*, ed. R. W. Clower (Harmondsworth: Penguin Books Ltd., 1969), 7–21. Introduction copyright held by Robert W. Clower, 1969. Reprinted and slightly abridged by permission of Penguin Books Ltd.

Chapter 8. "Theoretical Foundations of Monetary Policy," in *Monetary Theory and Monetary Policy in the 1970's: Proceedings of the 1970*

Sheffield Money Seminar, ed. G. Clayton, J. C. Gilbert, and R. Sedgwick (London: Oxford University Press, 1971), 15–28. Copyright Oxford University Press 1971. Reprinted by permission of Oxford University Press.

Chapter 9. "What Traditional Monetary Theory Really Wasn't," *Canadian Journal of Economics*, 2 (May 1969), 299–302. Reprinted by permission of the *Canadian Journal of Economics* and the Canadian Economics Association.

Chapter 10. "Is There an Optimal Money Supply?" *Journal of Finance*, 25 (May 1970), 425–33. Reprinted by permission of the *Journal of Finance*, New York University.

Chapter 11. "On the Invariance of Demand for Cash and Other Assets," by Robert W. Clower and M. L. Burstein, *Review of Economic Studies*, 28 (October 1960), 32–6. Reprinted by permission of M. L. Burstein and the Society for Economic Analysis Ltd., publishers and copyright holders of the *Review of Economic Studies*.

Chapter 12. "Say's Principle, What It Means and Doesn't Mean, Part I," by Robert W. Clower and Axel Leijonhufvud, *Intermountain Economic Review* (which became *Economic Forum* in 1979), 4 (Fall 1973), 1–16. Reprinted by permission of Axel Leijonhufvud and the *Economic Forum*.

Chapter 13. "The Transactions Theory of the Demand for Money: A Reconsideration," by Robert W. Clower and Peter W. Howitt, *Journal of Political Economy*, 86 (June 1978), 449–66. Reprinted by permission of Peter W. Howitt and The University of Chicago Press. Copyright 1978 by The University of Chicago.

Chapter 14. "Reflections on the Keynesian Perplex," *Zeitschrift für Nationalökonomie*, 35 (July 1975), 1–24. Reprinted by permission of Springer-Verlag, Wien.

Chapter 15. "The Coordination of Economic Activities: A Keynesian Perspective," by Robert W. Clower and Axel Leijonhufvud, *American Economic Review*, 65 (May 1975), 182–88. Reprinted by permission of Axel Leijonhufvud and the American Economic Association.

Chapter 16. "A Reconsideration of the Theory of Inflation," in *Resource Allocation and Public Policy*, ed. M. Allingham and M. L. Burstein (London: Macmillan, 1976), 14–25. Reprinted by permission of Macmillan, London and Basingstoke.

Chapter 17. "The Anatomy of Monetary Theory," *American Economic Review*, 67 (February 1977), 206–12. Reprinted by permission of the American Economic Association.

Chapter 18. "The Genesis and Control of Inflation," in *On the Stability of Contemporary Economic Systems: Proceedings of the Third Reisens-*

burg Symposium, ed. Oldřich Kýn and Wolfram Schrettl (Göttingen: Vandenhoeck and Ruprecht, 1979), 11–23. Reprinted by permission of Vandenhoeck and Ruprecht.

INTRODUCTION

Robert W. Clower has been contributing to our understanding of money and markets for nearly a quarter of a century, during which time he has participated in many of the central debates on those subjects. He has had an important influence on the major branches of monetary analysis, not only by identifying fundamental theoretical conditions and relationships, but also by suggesting new approaches that have altered our perception of how the economy works and enlarged our view of what aspects of monetary behavior should be studied. He has developed a major school of thought on the interpretation of Keynes's work. He has opened up the question of the nature of money to fresh examination. He has pioneered in the formulation of a microeconomic approach to understanding monetary behavior. Because of his methods, his interests, and his percipience, the papers he has contributed to monetary economics are as fresh and relevant today as when they were first published; and taken together, they constitute a well-rounded treatment of the major problems of monetary economics. It is time, therefore, that they be brought together, made easily accessible, arranged according to topic, and introduced by an essay that provides a general orientation for their study.

DOUBTS ABOUT ORTHODOXY

When Clover began his career he may have had some private doubts about the orthodox views of the economy and the ways it should be analyzed, but he was not ready to challenge the economics establishment. Much of his early work, therefore, was not critical of the corpus of received economic doctrine. Nevertheless, a fundamental characteristic of his intellectual orientation is to question the validity of established ideas, an attitude that has resulted in his creative reformulations and discoveries in a variety of areas of economic theory. One of the first manifestations of this attitude was his development in 1960 of the thesis that the Keynes of the *General Theory* was primarily concerned with disequilibrium behavior and therefore with dynamic

1

adjustments. Clower argued that Keynes identified the possibility of the economy's remaining for protracted periods of time at less than full employment, in contrast to the classical and neoclassical emphasis on the probability of an equilibrium at full employment. Clower illustrated the two alternatives with the use of aggregate supply and demand functions for labor (Chapter 1, 1960).[1] He then explained that after identifying disequilibrium states, Keynes developed tools, such as the propensity to consume and the marginal efficiency of capital, to deal with them. Although Keynes used the methods of traditional comparative statics, the disequilibrium situations he examined had a dynamic flavor. It appeared to Clower that the essential difference between Keynes and orthodox economics was therefore primarily one of subject matter, rather than of underlying postulates. The Keynesian problems, Clower asserted, require dynamic techniques of analysis. A shift from static to dynamic habits of thought must be made.

The first doubts as to the usefulness of orthodox economics had therefore begun to enter Clower's thinking. His work began to reveal divided loyalties by following neo-Walrasian lines while simultaneously urging the desirability of a change in subject matter and correspondingly in the technique of analysis. These characteristics were evidenced in his assessment of the static properties of a classical model (Chapter 2, 1963). He set out to explore the implications of classical monetary theory and to improve it, believing that it needed little more than dynamization to remedy its deficiencies and render it useful. He began by establishing a microeconomic foundation for his analysis, setting forth the supply and demand functions of each transactor for all commodities, and describing transactor equilibrium. Under the assumptions of fixed money prices, static price and income expectations, and the other characteristics of the stationary state, he demonstrated, the amount of money held for transactions is correctly indicated by the classical monetary theory as the quantity that will bridge the gaps between receipts and expenditures. One implication of the classical model is that Walras's law correctly states that, for all admissible values of commodity prices, the sum of all individual notional excess demands for commodities and money—in either equilibrium or disequilibrium—is identically equal to zero; another is that Say's law correctly states that the sum of all transactor equilibrium excess demands for commodities is identically equal to zero. Clower concluded optimistically that although the classical system does not

---

[1] The chapter number in the citation is the one assigned to the article in this volume (see Table of Contents); the year is the original date of publication of the article.

describe the disequilibrium dynamic path of the system, elementary dynamic assumptions can be introduced to validate the whole of traditional monetary theory. For instance, he observed, an important first step toward constructing a dynamic classical system and a useful theory of monetary dynamics is provided by Patinkin's treatment of the real-balance effect.

Clower's thoughts about the necessity of examining economic dynamics yielded important results in "The Keynesian Counter-Revolution," a seminal study of disequilibrium consumption adjustments (Chapter 3, 1963/1965). In this paper he dissented from the prevailing interpretation of Keynes's economics by arguing that it is different in content from neoclassical economics because he was concerned with the disequilibrium behavior of households. This is clear from the consideration that in Keynes's economics, as opposed to orthodox theory, the market excess-demand functions depend on current transactions. To examine household disequilibrium adjustments Clower developed what he called a dual-decision theory of consumption, basing his analysis upon an explicit microeconomic foundation that focuses on the behavior of individual transactors in markets. Households first predict the income that they will earn if they are fully employed and then plan purchases. Planned sales and purchases can be realized by everyone, however, only if the system as a whole is in a state of equilibrium. If there is disequilibrium, some households will discover that their anticipated income does not materialize because one or more of their members do not find employment. Those households therefore cannot fulfill their purchase and sale plans, and as a result must make a second round of consumption decisions. Clower's criticism (Chapter 19) of aspects of the dual-decision hypothesis should not be allowed to obscure the validity and importance of his essential insight, namely, that Keynes must have implicitly tried to take account of the disequilibrium behavior of households. Otherwise the consumption function does not make sense, the difference alleged to exist between speculative and transactions balances is illogical, and the liquidity preference theory of interest does not differ from the loanable funds theory.

When Clower explored the state of market excess demand and other features of disequilibrium situations, he found that orthodox price theory and the work of modern general equilibrium theorists in the manner of Patinkin are incapable of analyzing the dynamic stability of the economy. The received theory is still pervaded by the theoretical presuppositions that Keynes attacked—Walras's law, for example, which is correct with reference to notional excess demands but has no relevance when there is less then full employment. Orthodox economics provides a satisfactory theory of market equilibrium, but the economy is generally in disequilibrium. Clower therefore concluded that although much of orthodox theory passes for useful economics, in actuality much of it is worthless, and can even be a hindrance to fruitful research. Moreover, orthodox economics cannot provide a basis for practical policy formulation; Keynesian economics can.

A review of Milton Friedman's and Anna Schwartz's book[2] on monetary history afforded Clower the opportunity to reflect on his own orientation to monetary economics (Chapter 4, 1964). At the time he wrote the review he had arrived at an intellectual crossroads. He stated that he regarded himself as a neo-Walrasian. Such a theorist, according to Clower, believes that money does not matter much except in the long run, that levels of prices and money income depend ultimately on the amount of legal tender means of payment, and that the short-run effects of autonomous changes in the stock of legal tender money cannot be disentangled from other important sources of economic disturbances. A neo-Walrasian also emphasizes that most of the stock of money consists of debt instruments, the quantity of which is determined by the general public, not by the government. Clower offered some rationalizations for the form that neo-Walrasian theorizing has assumed. It is designed for its particular purposes, he observed. Neo-Walrasians use stylized facts (that is, intuition and common sense) to describe the workings of the economy, and do not pretend to be concerned with descriptive realism. They are very concerned, however, with "the intuitive plausibility of basic assumptions," and, rightly, with abstractness, elegance, and generality as relevant criteria for deciding whether a model promises empirical usefulness. The neo-Walrasians must plead guilty to the charge of using facts to illustrate preconceived hypotheses, "but only to the specification of being cautious, not to the specification of producing barren abstractions" (Chapter 4, Section VII). Neo-Walrasian models are excessively general, but economics is still young, progress in this regard is slow, and with some effort the models can be made more specialized. Neo-Walrasians are excessively patient, but patience is a better quality than are intemperance and hastiness.

Having affirmed his adherence to the neo-Walrasian tenets, however, Clower manifested the beginnings of dissatisfaction with Walrasian theorizing, and expressed his agreement with much of the

[2] Milton Friedman and Anna J. Schwartz, *A Monetary History of the United States: 1867–1960* (Princeton: Princeton University Press for the National Bureau of Economic Research, 1963).

monetarist outlook of Friedman and Schwartz. Although he questioned the evidential value and practical significance of some of Friedman's and Schwartz's historical judgments and maintained that research would invalidate some of them, he had no fundamental quarrel with any of their substantive conclusions. He found that neo-Walrasian models have not been as able to account for long-run behavior as the work of Friedman and Schwartz. Neo-Walrasian models have not led to the postulation of empirical relationships like the Phillips curve, or the accelerator principle, or the types of relationships identified by Friedman and Schwartz through their examination of empirical data. "I cannot," he wrote, "recall offhand a single instance in which neo-Walrasian research procedures have yielded *empirical* results of fundamental novelty or importance. Considered from this point of view, the neo-Walrasian approach must probably be adjudged relatively barren" (Chapter 4, Section VIII). When these remarks are put together with his criticism in 1963 (Chapter 3) of orthodox general equilibrium theory, it becomes clear that, perhaps without fully realizing it, Clower was almost ready to shed his neo-Walrasian allegiance. There remained one essential step, and that was to think through the question of the essential nature of money and to come to the realization that neo-Walrasian theory says nothing about the behavior of a monetary economy.

THE CHARACTER AND CONSEQUENCES OF MONEY

As he reflected on the essential characteristics of money, Clower developed one of his principal insights into the nature of neo-Walrasian models: Despite their ostensible concern with a monetary economy, in reality those models deal with a situation that is fundamentally the same as barter. He proceeded to develop that idea during the late 1960s and early 1970s, thus reopening the debate on the essential nature of money. The neo-Walrasian models ignore the unique property of money, which is that it can be traded directly for all other commodities in the economy. They also neglect the fact that in a monetary economy only one or a few commodities have that property (Chapter 7, 1969). The ostensibly monetary neo-Walrasian models are therefore little more than sophisticated barter systems in which money has no unique characteristics and therefore no special consequences. Whereas empirical treatments of exchange portray the unique role of money as a medium of exchange, orthodox price theory, which is based on the characteristics of a barter economy, cannot logically admit of such a role. Clower also noted that, as a part of the orthodox dichotomy between monetary and value theory, money was regarded as a veil in the short run and in the long run. Neoclassical economists consequently thought that there was no need for a separate theory to describe short-run price and quantity behavior in a monetary economy. Keynes disagreed with that view, but his emphasis on the importance of recognizing the influences that money has on the behavior of an economy has been disregarded by the neo-Walrasians, who believe that money matters only slightly in the short run.

When Clower achieved these perceptions, during the latter part of the 1960s, he resolved the question of the direction he would travel from his intellectual crossroads, and struck out on a path that was to put him in clear opposition to the neo-Walrasian tradition in certain fundamental respects. Major reconstructions were necessary, he realized, "to rescue monetary theory from the arid wastes of Post-Keynesian general equilibrium analysis" (Chapter 10, 1970, Section IV). By 1975 he was ready to state unreservedly that "strictly interpreted, Neo-Walrasian theory is descriptive only of a fairytale world of notional economic activities that bears not the slightest resemblance to any economy of record, past, present, or future. It is science fiction, pure and simple—clever and elegant science fiction, no doubt, but science fiction all the same" (Chapter 14, 1975, conclusion of Section III).

The task of reconstructing monetary theory led Clower to examine some of the consequences of money's being offered or demanded as one of the commodities in every trade (Chapter 5, 1967). Concentrating on microeconomic behavior, he identified for each individual the expenditure constraint, the income constraint, the income demand for money, and the reservation demand for money, expressing each of these relations with its own equation. He then explored some of the consequences of the model, contrasting its results with those of Patinkin-style theories. Most notably, he showed that in his model the activity of supplying goods does not create demand for goods, and the effects of parametric changes upon transactors, prices, and volumes traded differ from the effects in neo-Walrasian models. Developing this theme still further, he argued that because contemporary models of monetary economic growth represent money as merely one of many alternative means of payment, they reach erroneous results (Chapter 6, 1968). Confusion results from treating the theory of a monetary economy as if it involved nothing more than the addition of one more asset to a set of commodities available for trade in a barter economy. It is fundamentally misleading to convert a real growth model into a monetary one by simply choosing, or adding, a commodity and calling it money. In reality, money plays a central role as a means of payment, and its presence in the economy has structural effects. Money is used in place of barter transactions in order to allow resources to flow into the direct production of goods and services rather than to be dissipated in wasteful search and bargaining activities. It follows that the monetary authorities should devise means of discouraging the use of the stock of money for any but transactions purposes. Variations in the supply of money should be controlled so as to minimize changes in the general price level, for otherwise individuals will hold barren cash as a store of value instead of productive capital, or use inefficient rather than efficient trading practices.

Clower formulated even clearer concepts of money and of a monetary economy when he considered the foundations of monetary economics (Chapter 7, 1969). An individual's transaction period, he observed, is measured by the weighted average stocks of goods that he or she holds. Transactions costs vary inversely with the length of the transaction period. Waiting costs, which include storage costs and the subjective cost of postponing the acquisition of a commodity, vary directly with the length of the transaction period. The sum of the two types of cost functions yields a U-shaped curve, whose minimum point determines the optimum transaction period. In a barter economy trading costs would be high, because of the difficulty of finding trading partners and arriving at agreeable terms of trade. The introduction of different types of institutional arrangements to facilitate trade would alter the total trading-cost curve. For example, the establishment of trading centers in a barter economy would lower the curve. The development of institutions to ensure that one particular commodity is acceptable in exchange for any other commodity—its designation as money—would result in a lower trading-cost curve than could obtain in any type of barter economy. An essential feature of a monetary economy is therefore the existence of institutions that provide for the acceptability of money in exchange.

Although Clower felt that a definitive monetary theory would take a long time to develop, in 1971 he argued that the main outlines of an intellectually satisfying theory were emerging (Chapter 8, 1971). The outlines he had in mind were those of his own conception of a monetary economy, and he set himself to giving an account of his ideas and indicating some of their implications for monetary policy. He returned to his theme that it is necessary to have a definition of money that takes cognizance of the fact that only one or a few commodities are designated by custom or law as means of payment. Again contrasting his view with the neo-Walrasian tradition, which supposes that any commodity can function as money, he developed an alternative conception by recognizing that monetary exchange occurs in decentralized, organized markets, with a separate market for each commodity. As a result of neglecting the role of separate markets, monetary theory has failed to incorporate the consequences of the structure, roles, organization, and technology of marketplace processes—conditions that are particularly important in their effect upon the disequilibrium behavior of markets.

Why is money used? Unlike the many writers who have not answered that question, Clower showed that money is used because it provides a mode of exchange that is superior to other types of trading arrangements. Search and bargaining costs are extremely high in barter economies, whereas the exchange of commodities against money in organized trading centers can be relatively inexpensive because individuals can not only avoid holding inventories of most commodities, but also be assured that they will find someone with whom to trade. Individuals generally do not want to synchronize perfectly their purchases and sales, and therefore need money for transactions. The quantity they need is dependent upon the size of commodity inventories, in consequence of which monetary changes exert an important influence upon production and consumption flows. In a monetary system in which financial assets are largely made up of nonmonetary claims, changes in the demand for money influence production and consumption through affecting holdings of money and commodities, and influence investment through affecting securities markets, interest rates, and other financial variables.

In Clower's opinion, monetary policy has no theoretical foundations. The monetarist school, in particular, has not furnished an explicit account of the way in which a monetary economy makes adjustments, and so does not provide answers to questions about dynamics. His own conception of the economy did not lead him to view monetary policy as being of great value as an instrument of economic control, for to be effective, economic policy must be based upon knowledge of economic adjustment processes, knowledge which must come from detailed cross-sectional monthly or quarterly samples of microeconomic information about transactors' asset holdings, income, sales, and purchases. Without that information, models of monetary adjustments cannot be tested, nor can definitive answers be found to settle the interminable arguments about monetary questions.

Clower extended inventory analysis to the demand for money by recognizing that money balances are an alternative to the holding of inventories not only of other financial assets, but of goods as well.

The demand for money is therefore directly motivated not by utility, but by the links between money holdings and commodity inventory levels. Trade credit, including overdraft facilities, ought to be included in the total supply of money, he maintained, because of the importance of the transactions function of money. By providing purchasing power in addition to that which can proceed from a normal flow of income, it is possible for such credit to destabilize the economy. The identification of that possibility is an example of how Clower's definition of the supply of money is useful for studying the roles of the different components of the economy when it is in disequilibrium, although his definition also applies to equilibrium states.

MONEY SUPPLY AND DEMAND

Clower first broached the issue of the optimal supply of money in 1968 (Chapter 6). He developed a set of rules that the monetary authority should follow in order to ensure that the money supply is large enough for society to derive the maximum possible benefit from its use, concluding that the supply should be controlled so as to minimize changes in the price level. Shortly after Clower had considered this matter, Paul Samuelson gave a different answer.[3] In a classical model the quantity of money serves only to determine the level of money prices. Samuelson asserted that this implies a normative dichotomy between the private and social costs of holding real cash balances. Under laissez-faire with stable prices, he argued, individuals believe that to hold more cash balances would cost an excessive amount of foregone interest, even though the extra cash would buy some additional convenience. From the social point of view, if people were to hold larger cash balances that they turned over more slowly, the resulting lowering of absolute prices would make everybody better off. There would be smaller costs because of the smaller number of transactions required to provide cash, and because people would make fewer trips to their banks and brokers. The optimum quantity of balances would be reached when the marginal utility of holding money became equal to zero.

Clower objected that Samuelson's argument is wrong because there exists no simple device by which all money prices can be permanently reduced without either changing the nominal quantity of money or

[3] Paul Samuelson, "What Classical and Neoclassical Monetary Theory Really Was," *Canadian Journal of Economics*, 1 (February 1968), 1–15; and see the reply to Clower made by Samuelson, "Nonoptimality of Money Holding Under *Laissez-Faire*," *Canadian Journal of Economics*, 2 (May 1969), 303–8.

altering technological possibilities (Chapter 9, 1969). As a consequence of the classical dichotomy between real and monetary values, equilibrium real cash balances are a constant in Samuelson's system. They can be changed only as a result of parametric changes that he did not specify. The aggregate effective amount of real cash balances can in fact be altered only by increasing the efficiency of monetary institutions or by changes in technology and tastes. Laissez-faire produces the optimal amount of money holdings because each individual chooses his own cash balance on the basis of maximizing motives, and because the real amount of cash is determined by productivity and thrift, no matter what the nominal aggregate quantity of money may be.

Discussion of whether or not there is an optimal money supply cannot be illuminating, Clower maintained, so long as the question is posed in the context of conventional value theory (Chapter 10, 1970). His objections to Samuelson's treatment were based on what he had come to regard as the faulty conception of money embodied in neo-Walrasian models, one of which was used in Samuelson's analysis. In such models, Clower argued, nothing can be inferred about the connection between real money balances and transactions. It cannot even be asserted that money is necessarily used in exchange, because in those models goods can be traded directly for goods. The assumption in neo-Walrasian models that economic activities are costlessly coordinated by a central market authority renders them incapable of dealing with delivery and payment arrangements, or with the timing and frequency of market transactions, or with the costs of search, bargaining, and information. In the real world, equilibrium holdings of real money balances are linked to commodity inventories. In the real world, trading costs exist; they depend on inventory turnover rates and cannot be inferred directly from knowledge about holdings of real money balances. A transfer of commodity inventories from the trading to the production sector of the economy would therefore increase welfare by increasing aggregate output. Although this analysis did not enable Clower to solve the problem of the optimum money supply in a modern economy, by providing an understanding of the characteristics of money it strengthened the theoretical foundation upon which a solution to the problem must be based.

In their study of the transactions demand for money, Clower and his collaborator M. L. Burstein came to the conclusion that the equilibrium demand for real cash balances by traders is independent of the general price level and of the traders' initial balances, and that it is governed by tastes and real income (Chapter 11, 1960). He and

Burstein also concluded that equilibrium relative prices are invariant
with respect to changes in the aggregate quantity of money, and that
these relationships hold in many varieties of economic models. Furthermore, they showed that under certain conditions the equilibrium
distribution of real wealth and real income is invariant with respect
to changes in the nominal stock of money and is determined by tastes
and technique. In this study, as in his other early work on monetary
theory, Clower was not critical of the orthodox tradition.

As has been noted, Clower's attitude was much different by 1973,
when he and Axel Leijonhufvud analyzed Say's law and the demand
for money (Chapter 12, 1973). They began by identifying the relevant
aspects of the transactions activities of individuals in a market economy. They demonstrated that the relationship they called Say's
principle[4] is based in its simplest form on the proposition that the net
value of the amounts an individual plans to purchase at expected
prices, minus the amount of money available to him for expenditure,
is identically zero. They also emphasized that the principle deals with
notional excess demands only. In the course of taking account of
progressively more circumstances and varieties of behavior, they examined the form that the principle assumes in the case of a person
who holds positive amounts of commodities and is prepared to supply
them at some prices as well as to demand them at other prices. The
sum of such an individual's planned excess demands for each commodity and for money is identically equal to zero. It follows that the
sum of all individuals' planned excess demands for each commodity
and for money is also identically equal to zero, which is the macroeconomic version of Say's principle. The principle is true for any set
of prices, whether or not the economy is in equilibrium.

Having established an analytical framework, Clower and Leijonhufvud analyzed various interpretations of Say's principle that have
appeared in the literature. They noted in particular that the statement
that supply creates its own demand is true if it is interpreted as meaning that no one plans to supply anything without also planning some
use for the proceeds from the sale. The statement that each transactor
plans to supply commodities of sufficient value to finance all of his
planned net demands is also a correct interpretation. So also is the
statement that a general glut is impossible in the sense that a planned
excess supply cannot prevail for all commodities simultaneously. Clower
and Leijonhufvud used their formulation of the meaning of Say's

---

[4] This is the name Clower had given the relationship in 1962 (see Chapter 3).

principle to analyze aspects of general equilibrium, unemployment, deflation, and national income analysis, and to construct a devastating critique of Oscar Lange's treatment of Say's law and Walras's law.

When Clower was ready once more to examine the transactions demand for money, he did so with a critical eye. He and Peter Howitt (Chapter 13, 1978) maintained that standard theory is inadequate for analyzing interpersonal exchange. Basing their analysis on microeconomic foundations, they stressed the importance of traders' behavior. The assumption that individual economic agents determine the timing and frequency of sales and purchases leads to different conclusions than those reached by standard theory. Transactions involve stocks rather than flows, so small changes in the relative timing of transactions can produce large changes in average finance requirements and average bunching costs. The introduction of these considerations into monetary theory results in a reformulation of the theory of the transactions demand for money. Accordingly, Clower and Howitt rejected many orthodox comparative-statics propositions, reevaluated the conditions under which traders hold money, revised the theory of hyperinflation, and reformulated the analysis of the effects of the availability of trade credit and bonds on the demand for money.

GENERAL PROCESS ANALYSIS

Clower pointed out that because neo-Walrasian theory deals only with notional or *ex ante* economic phenomena, it is useless for the analysis of an ongoing economy in which disequilibrium trading and monetary exchange occur. As a result, it is irrelevant to the questions raised by Keynes. By 1975, however, Clower had also come to believe that Keynesian theory was inadequate (Chapter 14, 1975). The Keynesian revolution failed to sustain its momentum and collapsed, he argued, because it was essentially a modification of the superstructure and not of the foundations of economic analysis. It was less important and ultimately less influential than the revolution which stemmed from the work of Walras, but that too has run its course. This situation gives rise to the Keynesian perplex, which, according to Clower, is that although neo-Walrasian theory has led to a dead end, there is no clear perception of what alternative line of investigation should be followed.

The main question raised by Keynes is whether or not the economic system is self-adjusting. Clower and Leijonhufvud maintained that the question cannot be answered by neo-Walrasian or Keynesian models because they do not deal with production, consumption, and trading activities as they are found in the real economy (Chapter 15, 1975). Those models cannot be used to examine the short-run adjustment processes that economists must understand in order to be able to formulate effective policies. To remedy this deficiency, the authors began to develop a type of model that embodied what Leijonhufvud called general process analysis to distinguish it from equilibrium analysis. Having rejected many of the assumptions and much of the content of orthodox theory, Clower now therefore also rejected the traditional equilibrium method of analysis—not the concept of equilibrium itself, but the *ex ante* way in which it is used in orthodox equilibrium models. He believed that a valid theory must describe the behavior of an ongoing economy in which irrevocable disequilibrium and equilibrium trades are actually executed and in which disequilibrium and equilibrium production and consumption occur through time. Such a theory must be based on an account of how trade is actually organized.

Suppose it is assumed, following neo-Walrasian theory, that a single central coordinator facilitates the exchange of all commodities directly for each other at both disequilibrium and equilibrium prices, and acts to maximize the stability of the system. That type of model, Clower and Leijonhufvud observed, is self-adjusting, but it is not like the economy in which we live. The crucial flaw in neo-Walrasian theory is that it does not consider the execution as distinct from the scheduling of commodity trades. The character of exchange behavior and therefore the real problems of analyzing it are concealed by the neo-Walrasian auctioneer, who acts to reconcile trading plans through a process that excludes transactions at disequilibrium prices. Clower and Leijonhufvud, in contrast, assumed that trade occurs in many separate uncoordinated markets, that there is money, that there are disequilibrium transactions, and that the means of payment include trade credit—assumptions that produce a model very different from the neo-Walrasian type. In their model the temporary insolvency of trade specialists can prevent the effective coordination of economic activities. The growth of the means of payment in excess of the means of settlement, which is by cash only, can result in liquidity crises. Money, trade credit, and decentralized exchange give rise to the possibilities of inflation, deflation, and business fluctuations. Clower and Leijonhufvud concluded that their model and, by implication, the economy, may not be self-adjusting.

Pursuing this line of thought, Clower developed an account of the fundamental characteristics of a model of a middleman economy, which he called "neo-Marshallian" to emphasize its difference from the neo-Walrasian variety (Chapter 14, 1975). Keynes's economics, he observed, was absorbed into and transformed by neo-Walrasian economics, principally by J. R. Hicks. Keynes's own concept of the economy, however, was basically Marshallian, viewing economic agents as reasonable but often mistaken in their estimates of the future, and as often less than perfectly efficient and less than totally devoted to maximizing utility and profit. In accordance with that view, Clower assumed that individuals trade in a Marshallian world in which markets are separate and not closely coordinated. In such a situation, middlemen emerge naturally to provide facilities for trade only if costs of trade are positive and partially or wholly invariant with respect to the volumes traded. He then assumed that each middleman holds inventories of every commodity and determines ratios of exchange between them. Each trader selects middlemen with whom to exchange and determines the timing of trades. A common unit of account is adopted, and each middleman determines rates of exchange in terms of that unit. Stocks as well as flows enter into price determination; stocks as well as flows depend upon the cost of doing business and the cost of changing prices. In this decentralized economy natural economic forces result in uniform rates of exchange and in trading fees that yield normal profits. Because the prices fixed by middlemen depend not only upon current conditions, but also upon their perceptions of past history and their projections of the future, current conditions affect prices only after long and variable lags. The pricing system may therefore not be self-adjusting, in the sense that some prices may not be changed rapidly to eliminate excess demand.

If it is then assumed that each middleman deals in a single commodity and in an asset called money that is traded by all middlemen, a monetary economy is defined. Credit instruments can also be introduced, allowing an analysis of variations in the quantity of money, financial intermediation, speculation, and other similar phenomena that cannot be fitted into neo-Walrasian models. Those complications are the essence of Keynes's work, which can be viewed as a special case of Clower's general process type of analysis. The Keynesian perplex is resolved by the recognition that the proper path for economists to follow is to pursue those complications and thus complete the Keynesian revolution.

Turning to a consideration of general process analysis in relation to inflation, Clower concluded that disagreements about how to deal with inflation derive from a lack of a fresh perspective on the way in which individual economic activities are coordinated. Such a perspective, which Clower undertook to provide, ideally would facilitate reducing the issues to questions of either logic or fact and would thereby help to resolve them (Chapter 16, 1976). Clower felt that both monetarist and income–expenditure models contain faulty theories of exchange intermediation and, consequently, cannot deal with inflationary processes. He therefore used general process analysis to provide a more comprehensive and detailed view of a monetary economy by taking its essential features into account in an analytical framework adapted to the description of dynamic behavior. In his general process model, price and quantity adjustments are the outcome of the conscious decisions of individual economic agents. The behavior of the economy is regarded not as the preordained result of technical and structural factors but as an evolutionary consequence of the interaction of behavioral and technological forces.

In a simplified model in which he assumed that trading intermediaries hold inventories of money and commodities and stand ready to buy and sell at stated prices, Clower showed that if the stock of money is increased at a steady rate, the economy eventually settles down to a steady rate of inflation. He then added more detail to the model, identifying the processes that occur in the course of exchange in markets such as those for primary products, farm and fishery products, and securities. He recognized that future as well as spot sales occur, that prices are ordinarily determined at the time of delivery rather than on the date of order, and that payments are initially made in the form of book debits to trade accounts. Means of payment other than cash, such as trade credit and demand deposits, can expand or contract by substantial amounts even when the cash base is constant, and therefore the size of the cash base and the quantity of means of payment are not closely linked. Increases in the cash base, Clower contended, will not in all circumstances lead to immediate increases in other means of payment, and decreases in the cash base may sometimes lead to sharp reductions in other means of payment. Nevertheless, its variation can lead to Wicksellian cumulative processes in either direction. Although a steady and moderate expansion in the cash base will not necessarily ensure that the economy will be free of troubles, any other policy will lead to boom and bust or to sustained inflation. Clower therefore arrived at a qualified monetarist position on the issue of monetary policy.

Continuing his investigation of an ongoing economy in which trading activities and money are of central importance, Clower then adopted the approach of constructing a conjectural history of how the structural conditions of his model evolved from its basic properties (Chapter 17, 1977). In the course of the development of civilization, people begin to trade because they have different preference functions and own different amounts of commodities. Specialists in trade emerge because of the high cost of trying to find someone with whom to trade in the absence of institutions designed to facilitate it. Organized markets thus arise as a result of the working of economic forces. Monetary exchange develops in such markets because it facilitates the desired timing of trading and is therefore advantageous to the participants. One or a few commodities that have lower storage costs then become common mediums of exchange. If one of those commodities is also easy to identify, handle, and count, then it becomes dominant as a means of payment. Clower concluded that the costs of trading and the physical characteristics of commodities establish necessary conditions for monetary exchange, and that sufficient conditions depend on the precise characteristics of the economy.

During the late 1970s Clower focused much of his attention on the problems of inflation, economic instability, and the theoretical conditions necessary for formulating economic policy. These highly important topics were inherently appropriate subjects for the type of analysis he had been developing for many years—an analysis that deals with dynamic adjustments, disequilibrium, monetary economics, and market behavior. Reviewing the past record, Clower pointed out that economists in the 1930s, depending as they did on little more than second-rate sociology and the notion of the self-regulating character of the economy, had no theory of short-run economic processes.[5] They were therefore unable to predict the consequences of government policies or to prescribe remedies for their undesirable side effects. Economists are still unable to agree about the short-run consequences of alternative interventionistic policies. General competitive analysis, for example, is incapable of dealing with disequilibrium adjustment processes. Both monetarist and income–expenditure theories are incomplete, and are therefore inadequate as a basis for undertanding inflation. They refer in general terms to the forces of supply and demand, but do not deal with the actual workings of markets that are organized and operated by real individuals. In order to be able to analyze short-run processes and the effects of government intervention, it is necessary to construct an economic model that incorporates the mechanics of actual market exchange.

Clower therefore developed still further his general process model of an intermediary economy, a model that he argued is compatible

---

[5] Robert W. Clower, "The Economic Constitution and the New Deal: Discussion," in *Regulatory Change in an Atmosphere of Crisis: Current Implications of the Roosevelt Years*, ed. G. M. Walton (New York: Academic Press, 1979), 27–9.

with the general views of income–expenditure theorists and monetarists (Chapter 18, 1979). Taking the simple case of an economy with
a pure commodity money and one commodity, and with spot trading
only, Clower described the behavior of intermediaries in markets. As
does all his work, this model reflects his belief in the need for an
understanding of microeconomic behavior and his longstanding emphasis on the importance of such phenomena as trading activities, the
holding of balances of money and of inventories of goods, the way
in which payments are made, and the irregular timing of orders to
buy and sell. He noted also the necessity of taking into account the
complications introduced by future sales, by book debits to trade accounts that are later settled with cash or bank transfers, and by transactions actually occurring at the time of delivery rather than on the
date of order. Observing that a person can be a monetarist without
being a member of the Chicago school, he explained that his model
leads to the conclusions, which he maintained are true of the real
world, that the theory of cost-push inflation is wrong and that a sustained inflation can result only from increases in the cash base provided by the government. To control inflation it is therefore necessary
to diminish the rate of increase of the cash base. This is likely to
produce a sustained disruption of the economy and increased unemployment, the effects of which, Clower recommended, should be
mitigated by substantial increases in unemployment compensation
coverage. These views, written in the summer of 1975 and published
in 1979, were uncannily accurate predictions of what happened in
the early 1980s.

A SUMMARY

Clower has traveled a long intellectual road. He began with the belief
that the received tradition was adequate, but by degrees came to reject
some of its fundamental tenets and to replace them with his own
concepts. The seeds for his theoretical harvest were sown in the fertile
soil of stock-flow analysis, an analysis that developed out of his desire
to devise a way of examining phenomena that were not considered
in neoclassical theory: the dynamics of adjustment processes and disequilibrium behavior in a non-*tâtonnement* market economy. With his
interest increasingly focused on these matters, it was natural for him
to begin to question the neo-Walrasian tradition of general competitive analysis and the subsumption of Keynesian economics within the
methodological and analytical characteristics of that tradition.

One of his most important contributions was to open for reexamination the question of the nature of money and its functions and consequences. Money, he insisted, is not like other commodities, and therefore monetary economies are not like barter economies. Money is used by transactors—professional traders, businesses, consumers, and governmental units—because of the nonsynchronization of receipts and expenditures, because of the need to avoid excessive inventories, and because of the desire to eliminate the search and bargaining costs entailed by barter. Monetary exchange and the holding, depletion, and augmentation of inventories give rise to trade credit, which is part of the money supply and an important factor in monetarily induced economic instability. Another source of instability is the exchange of commodities for money in separate markets, for there is, in fact, no central auctioneer who coordinates trade by setting a vector of prices at which excess demands for all commodities are simultaneously equal to zero.

With his creative intellect, once Clower had questioned the static equilibrium analysis of orthodox theory, and once he had identified important types of economic behavior that were not treated in existing theory, it was natural that he should begin to develop a new type of model to enable those phenomena to be examined. Instead of regarding the economy as a harmonious equilibrating system, he developed a vision of an economy with many features that give rise to endogenous instability. Those features stem from the characteristics of economic agents, money, and a market economy. In the long run, under the action of given economic forces, money may be neutral. In reality, however, we live from short run to short run in an economy in which the flow of events reflects the impact of changing economic forces. In the short run there are frictions, lags, uncertainty, lack of coordination of economic activities, and changes in variables such as the total means of payment and in parameters such as the monetary base. Thus Clower long ago identified the problems of short-run fluctuations generated by monetary phenomena, and he long ago observed that orthodox theory—Keynesian and otherwise—does not have an understanding of those problems. What is lacking in orthodox theory? Clower's answer is that its analytical methods, perspective, and tools are incapable of dealing with dynamics and disequilibrium, which are the essence of short-run processes, and that its analytical building blocks—the economic behavior and institutions it identifies—do not correspond to the significant features of a monetary market economy. For some time the economics profession has been realizing with increasing clarity that he is right.

PART I

DOUBTS ABOUT ORTHODOXY

1

KEYNES AND THE CLASSICS:
A DYNAMICAL PERSPECTIVE

Although it is possible to draw various purely technical distinctions between modern and pre-Keynesian economics, it is mainly with respect to matters of intellectual orientation that the two are strikingly different. Many and diverse reasons have been advanced to explain why this should be so, most of them plausible, all of them fairly elaborate. The purpose of this note is to add an element of unity and simplicity to these explanations by suggesting a straightforward dynamical interpretation of the foundations of Keynesian and classical thought.

I

The entire discussion is developed in terms of the market for labor in a pure consumption economy of the sort described by Keynes in his preliminary skirmish with classical theory in Chapter 2 of the *General Theory*.[1] Omitting background details for the sake of brevity, let us begin with the relevant labor supply and demand functions, represented in the accompanying diagram by the curves S_L and D_L, respectively. Any point in the diagram corresponds to a pair of values of employment, N, and the real wage rate, w/p. From the standpoint of *some* dynamical system, moreover, every point in the diagram may be presumed to represent a potentially attainable "state" of the labor market or, alternatively, a potentially observable *employment situation*. On casual empirical grounds, however, it is plausible to restrict attention to situations described by a more narrowly circumscribed set of points, obtained as follows.

First, notice that any point on the demand curve for labor defines an employment situation which, if attained, is optimal for firms; i.e., any such state satisfies the (maximum profit) condition of equality between the marginal physical product of labor and the real wage rate.[2] Similarly, any point on the supply curve represents an employ-

[1] J. M. Keynes, *General Theory of Employment, Interest, and Money* (New York, 1936).
[2] *Ibid.*, p. 5, Postulate I.

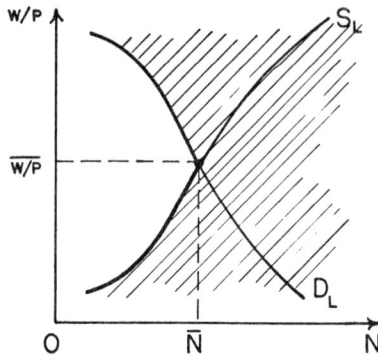

ment situation which, if attained, is optimal for households; i.e., any such point satisfies the (utility maximization) condition of equality between the marginal utility of the real wage and the marginal disutility of labor.[3] On the other hand, points in the diagram to the *right* either of the demand curve or of the supply curve (the shaded area in the diagram) represent employment situations that are nonoptimal for firms, nonoptimal for households, or nonoptimal for both. Assuming that a "short demand" always dominates a "long supply" and that a "short supply" always dominates a "long demand," situations defined by such points cannot occur in a system of voluntary trading and may be ignored accordingly.[4]

Points to the *left* both of the demand and of the supply curves (the unshaded area of the diagram) represent employment situations that are acceptable (though not optimal) for both firms and households; i.e., situations in which the real wage is less than the marginal product of labor and in which, simultaneously, the marginal utility of the real wage is greater than the marginal disutility of work. Situations of this kind are plausibly considered to be dynamically attainable, hence potentially observable; but they cannot be maintained more than momentarily because households and firms share a *mutual* desire to increase employment and output under these circumstances. In short, such states represent situations of "frictional" underemployment (and underproduction) which, on grounds of transiency, may be ignored.[5]

We are left with states represented by points (i) on the supply curve and to the left of the demand curve; (ii) on the demand curve and to the left of the supply curve; (iii) on the supply curve *and* on the demand curve.

[3] *Ibid.*, p. 5, Postulate II.
[4] *Ibid.*, p. 12.
[5] *Ibid.*, p. 6.

Taking these in reverse order, any situation defined by the inter-section of the demand and supply curves (the point $(\overline{N}, \overline{w/p})$ in the diagram, for example) corresponds to a classical (and Keynesian) state of full employment. On the basis of elementary empirical consider-ations, it is clearly plausible to suppose that states of this sort, if at-tained, tend to be maintained indefinitely in the absence of exogenous "shocks." (By Walras' Law applied to a "labor and goods" econo-my, supply–demand equality in the labor market necessarily implies supply–demand equality in the goods market.)

On the other hand, any point which lies on the demand curve but above the supply curve (case (ii), above) refers to a state of *involuntary unemployment* in the sense of Keynes; i.e., at a lower level of the real wage rate, the demand for and supply of labor both exceed the level of employment associated with the given point.[6] Under the latter circumstances, the marginal utility of the real wage exceeds the mar-ginal disutility of labor, whereas the marginal product of labor is equal to the real wage; hence *households alone* have an incentive to expand employment. By analogy with situations of a similar sort experienced in practice, it is natural to regard these as "depression" states of the model.

The interesting thing about "depression" states is that it is not di-rectly plausible to say that they cannot persist indefinitely. No doubt it can be asserted, with good reason, that any particular "depression" state will tend to be transitory; the relevant question, however, is whether the transition is towards a state of "full employment" or whether one "depression" state tends to be followed by another "depression" state, and so on, *indefinitely*. This is clearly a dynamical stability question, and casual empirical considerations might be used to support either point of view. To say anything useful about such "conflict of interest" situations, therefore, everyday knowledge has to be supplemented by a fairly detailed specification of the dynamical assumptions underlying the market adjustment process.[7] Provided one is willing to admit the existence of multiperiod planning horizons, for example, it is easy to formulate a dynamical model of a pure consumption economy in which the presence of excess supply in the labor market is associated with a tendency for the real wage, and so excess supply, either to fall or to rise over time. In slightly more general models, moreover, one does not need to resort to expecta-tional phenomena to get similar results.

So much for "depression" states. Proceeding finally to situations

---

[6] *Ibid.*, p. 15.
[7] *Ibid.*, pp. 15–19. The issue seems obvious now, but it was not so clear in 1936.

defined by points on the supply curve but below the demand curve (case (i), above), we have to do with what might be called states of *involuntary underproduction*. All such states describe situations of "full employment" in the Keynesian sense (i.e., no "involuntary unemployment");[8] since the real wage rate is less than the marginal product of labor in these cases, however, labor is in short supply from the standpoint of business firms. One might be inclined to argue that situations of this kind will soon be eliminated through a competitive "bidding up" of money wages by employers; but matters are not so simple. For we have to deal once more with a conflict of interest situation in which the reactions of employees to the actions of employers cannot be specified on the basis of casual empirical considerations. One possibility (and it is nothing more than this) is that competitive bidding for labor will entail continually rising money prices along with continually rising money wages. On this ground, and to emphasize the analogy with "depression" states of involuntary unemployment, it is natural to regard situations of involuntary underproduction as "inflation" states of our model.

II

The preceding discussion of alternative possible employment situations is basically neutral in its assignment of "probabilities of occurrence" to states of full employment, states of involuntary unemployment, and states of involuntary underproduction. In effect, it is based on the assumption that probable employment states are distributed more or less symmetrically about a mean position of full employment equilibrium.

By contrast, classical doctrine rests on the assumption that the entire probability distribution is concentrated at a single point. This might be weakened slightly; e.g., it is consistent with the general tenor of classical thought to admit that other than full employment positions are possible, but to assert that the equilibrium state of full employment is stable and so heavily damped that the probability of observing a nonequilibrium employment situation is almost negligible. Nevertheless, it is hard to deny the essential correctness of the Keynesian view that "... the postulates of the classical theory are applicable to a special case only and not to the general case, the situation it assumes being a limiting point of the possible positions of equilibrium."[9]

[8] *Ibid.*, pp. 15–16.
[9] *Ibid.*, p. 3.

The Keynesian assignment of "probabilities of occurrence" is motivated by the conviction that "depression" states are the rule rather than the exception, and the Keynesian distribution of probable employment states is correspondingly skewed to give major weight to situations of involuntary unemployment. In the light of recent history, this view has lost some of the plausibility that it had during the years of the Great Depression; but that is largely beside the point. The important thing is that the Keynesian perspective, unlike that of the classics, leads naturally to an analysis of the "...dynamical development [of output and employment] as distinct from the instantaneous picture ..."[10] For the most part, therefore, Keynes dealt with *disequilibrium* states; with states which, if recognized at all by classical writers, were never systematically analyzed. He was encouraged accordingly to create new analytical tools (the "consumption function," the "marginal efficiency of capital schedule," the "liquidity preference function"), better suited—at least in his opinion—to deal with disequilibrium phenomena. To make the probability of occurrence of disequilibrium states seem vastly greater than that of full employment equilibrium states, moreover, Keynes emphasized volatile factors like expectations and concentrated attention on speculative aspects of asset-holding phenomena. To be sure, the analytical methods adopted were those of traditional comparative statics rather than those of modern dynamics; but the situations studied had an obvious dynamical "flavor," and that is what has counted in the long run.

On this interpretation, *the essential formal difference between Keynes and the classics is more one of subject matter than of underlying postulates.* Classical theory is mainly concerned with equilibrium states, but does not specifically deny the existence of other possibilities; Keynesian theory is mainly concerned with disequilibrium states, but allows for the (very slight) possibility of "full employment." To say only this, however, would be to overlook the ultimate source of the Keynesian Revolution. Although Keynes himself never made a complete transition from statical to dynamical modes of thought, his work prompted many of his near contemporaries to do precisely this,[11] and so wrought a fundamental change in intellectual perspective in the space of a few years. Nor was this aspect of his work lost to Keynes: "The ideas which [I have] expressed so laboriously are extremely simple and should be obvious. The difficulty lies, not in the new ideas, but in escaping from

[10] *Ibid.*, Preface, p. vii.

[11] It is only necessary to mention such names as Harrod, Domar, Hicks, Modigliani, Samuelson, Goodwin, Duesenberry and Patinkin in order to appreciate the significance of this comment.

the old ones, which ramify, for those brought up as most of us have been, into every corner of our minds."[12]

Nothing could be simpler in principle than a shift from statical to dynamical habits of thought; neither, however, could anything be more difficult in practice. The fruits of the Keynesian Revolution have been, and are being, gathered primarily by a new generation of economists, a generation that has finally accustomed itself to thinking in terms of points and planes instead of curves and crosses.

[12] *Op. cit.*, Preface, p. viii.

2

CLASSICAL MONETARY THEORY REVISITED

In Part II of their important article on "Monetary and Value Theory: A Critique of Lange and Patinkin,"[1] Messrs. Archibald and Lipsey assert that *"the classical dichotomy consists in building a model in which Walras' Law does not hold."*[2] Since every classical economist whose writings I know clearly subscribed with full force and fervour to Walras' Law, I am unable to regard as valid either this assertion or Archibald and Lipsey's interpretation of classical monetary theory.

The purpose of this paper is to exhibit a "classical" theory in which

I. Walras' Law is an identity, valid whether or not individuals or markets are in equilibrium.

II. Say's Law is an identity, valid whether or not markets are in equilibrium.

III. All commodity excess demand functions are homogeneous of order zero in money prices alone.

IV. Absolute money prices are consistently determined by a Cambridge money equation or, equivalently, by a quantity equation of the form $KPT = M$, both relations being derivable within the theory.

V. The classical dichotomy is unreservedly valid.

The implications of these results both for Part II of Archibald and Lipsey's paper and for contemporary monetary theory will be evident to interested readers. Pertinent interpretative comments are set forth, however, at appropriate points in the discussion that follows.

I. THE MODEL

We begin with Marshall's dictum that "the amount of coins which a person cares to keep in his pocket is determined by the amount of business he has to do, and by the proportion which that part of his payments which he finds it most convenient to make in currency bears

---

[1] *Review of Economic Studies*, vol. xxvi (1958), pp. 9–17.

[2] *Ibid.*, p. 16. See also G. C. Archibald and R. G. Lipsey, "Monetary and Value Theory: Further Comments," *Review of Economic Studies*, vol. xxviii (1960), pp. 50–53.

to the whole."[3] Using d_m and d_i respectively to denote the quantity of money demanded to hold and the quantity of commodity "i" demanded for current purchase by a typical transactor, a fair interpretation of this remark is provided by writing

$$d_m \equiv k \sum_1^n p_i d_i \qquad (1)$$

where p_i represents the money price of the ith commodity and k denotes a positive constant.

Now, suppose that the decision problem confronting a typical transactor is expressed by:

Maximize $U(d_1, \ldots, d_n; s_1, \ldots, s_n)$.

Subject to the budget equation:

$$\sum_1^n p_i(d_i - s_i) + (d_m - s_m) = 0, \qquad (2)$$

Subject also to the monetary equilibrium equation:

$$d_m - s_m = 0, \qquad (3)$$

where U denotes a utility function and s_m and s_i respectively denote the quantity of money held and the quantity of commodity "i" offered for current sale by the transactor.

Carrying out the indicated maximization, we obtain a system of $(2n + 1)$ equations,

$$\left.
\begin{array}{ll}
\partial U/\partial d_i + \lambda_1 p_i(1 + k) + \lambda_2 k p_i = 0 & (i = 1, \ldots, n) \\
\partial U/\partial s_i - \lambda_1 p_i = 0 & (i = 1, \ldots, n) \\
-\lambda - \lambda_2 = 0, &
\end{array}
\right\} \quad (4)$$

which, taken in conjunction with the relations (1), (2), and (3), provides a total of $(2n + 4)$ equations to determine solution values, $\bar{d}_i, \bar{s}_i, \bar{d}_m, \bar{s}_m, \bar{\lambda}_1, \bar{\lambda}_2$, of the $(2n + 4)$ variables $d_1, \ldots, d_n, s_1, \ldots, s_n, d_m, s_m, \lambda_1$, and λ_2 in terms of the parameters $p_1, \ldots, p_n$ (k being a fixed constant, we ignore it). Subject to familiar continuity and curvature restrictions on the function U, we may suppose that a unique solution to this system exists for all admissible values of $p_1, \ldots, p_n$. On this supposition we may identify the existence of a well-defined set of transactor

---

[3] *Official Papers by Alfred Marshall*, p. 36.

demand and supply functions, $\bar{d}_i(p_1, \ldots, p_n)$, $\bar{s}_i(p_1, \ldots, p_n)$, $\bar{d}_m(p_1, \ldots, p_n)$, $\bar{s}_m(p_1, \ldots, p_n)$, with a state of *transactor equilibrium*.

It is worth emphasizing that, although the existence of these transactor demand and supply functions implies and is implied by transactor equilibrium, the absence of transactor equilibrium does not mean that such functions cannot be defined. It only means that they cannot be defined solely in terms of the statical equations (1) to (4).

One feature of the preceding argument which may appear objectionable is the assumption that money balances are an independent decision variable for the individual transactor. Intuitively, one might argue that the value of s_m at any instant of time depends on past history and should therefore be regarded as a given parameter. Strictly speaking, however, this is incorrect, for the concept of past history has no meaning in a statical context. There may also be some question about the monetary equilibrium condition (3); indeed, it must be admitted that the rationale of this condition is hard to describe without having recourse to rudimentary dynamical considerations. From a purely formal standpoint, however, we may justify our procedure by noting that the statical decision problem must provide for the determination (at least under ideal circumstances) of solution values of all variables over which the individual transactor is assumed to have direct control.

Putting formal considerations altogether on one side, we can make a good case on intuitive grounds for the present formulation of traditional monetary theory. Confronted with fixed money prices, static price and income expectations, and all the other appurtenances of a stationary state, how much money will a "rational" man decide to hold if money "may indeed be compared to oil used to enable a machine to run smoothly,"[4] and the time available for carrying decisions into effect is literally unlimited? The commonsense answer is that he will hold nothing in excess of what is needed for strictly technical reasons. Choice in any meaningful sense does not enter into the question. If in stationary conditions money balances are required solely to bridge gaps between the receipt of money income and its expenditure—and this is precisely the view of all traditional writers—the question is settled as indicated by our model. Looked at from this point of view, traditional theory seems naive, but that is only because in this particular case the problem to be solved is so transparent. A theory that holds for stationary states is not by virtue of that fact devoid of significance for a wider class of situations.

[4] A. Marshall, *Money, Credit and Commerce*, p. 38.

II.   IMPLICATIONS OF THE MODEL

Our next task is to elaborate relevant implications of our model. First, it is clear from the form of our maximization problem that transactor equilibrium implies $\bar{d}_m - \bar{s}_m \equiv \bar{x}_m \equiv 0$; hence that

$$\sum_1^n p_i(\bar{d}_i - \bar{s}_i) \equiv \sum_1^n p_i\bar{x}_i \equiv 0; \tag{5}$$

i.e., in equilibrium, both the excess demand for money balances and the aggregate money value of excess demand for commodities are identically zero for each transactor.

Second, it is evident that the commodity demand and supply functions, $\bar{d}_i$ and $\bar{s}_i$, hence the commodity excess demand functions, $\bar{x}_i$, are homogeneous of order zero in money prices alone. This may be expressed succinctly by writing these functions as

$$\left.\begin{array}{l} \bar{d}_i(r_1 , \ldots , r_{n-1}) \\[2mm] \bar{s}_i(r_1 , \ldots , r_{n-1}) \\[2mm] \bar{x}_i(r_1 , \ldots , r_{n-1}) \end{array}\right\} \quad (i = 1 , \ldots , n) \tag{6}$$

where $r_i \equiv p_i/p_n$ $(i = 1 , \ldots , n - 1; r_n \equiv 1)$.

Third, it is obvious that transactor equilibrium cannot occur unless the variables d_i and s_m assume values $\bar{d}_i$ and $\bar{s}_m$ which satisfy the condition

$$k\Sigma_1^n p_i\bar{d}_i - \bar{s}_m \equiv 0. \tag{7}$$

Regarding p_n as an index of the general price level and setting $p_n = P$ to get rid of an extraneous subscript, we may use the relation $p_i = r_iP$ to rewrite (7) as

$$kP\Sigma_1^n r_i\bar{d}_i - \bar{s}_m \equiv 0.$$

But the expression $\Sigma_1^n r_i\bar{d}_i$ may be regarded as a weighted index of planned commodity transactions. Denoting this index by $\bar{t}(r_1 , \ldots , r_{n-1})$, therefore, we arrive finally at

$$kP\bar{t}(r_1 , \ldots , r_{n-1}) = \bar{s}_m; \tag{8}$$

i.e., for any given set of relative prices, $r_1^0 , \ldots , r_{n-1}^0$, the individual transactor's equilibrium holdings of money balances vary directly with the general price level, P.

We are now in a position to establish the propositions set forth at the beginning of our argument. Suppose that the economy comprises a fixed number of individual transactors, and denote by capital letters D_i, S_i, D_m, S_m, X_i, X_m, and T, respectively, appropriate *sums* of the corresponding individual variables (or functions) d_i, s_i, d_m, s_m, x_i, x_m, and t. Then from (2) we infer that

$$\Sigma_1^n p_i X_i + X_m \equiv 0;$$

i.e., Walras' Law is valid as an identity for all admissible values, equilibrium or otherwise, of the variables p_i, x_i, and x_m.[5] This is Proposition I.

From equation (5) we infer that

$$\Sigma_1^n p_i \overline{X}_i \equiv 0;$$

i.e., Say's Law is valid as an identity for all admissible values of the variables p_i and for all values of the variables d_i and s_i satisfying the transactor equilibrium conditions (1) to (4). This is Proposition II.

In passing, it should be observed that the above statement of Say's Law is consistent with traditional thought and also with Lange's formulation of the principle.[6] Neither Lange nor later writers distinguish explicitly between situations in which transactor equilibrium conditions are satisfied and situations in which they are not. If this distinction is made, it is apparent that Walras' Law holds in either case, but that Say's Law is valid in a money economy only if the transactor equilibrium conditions (1) to (4) are met. More particularly, Walras' Law, unlike Say's Law, may be considered to hold even if the market excess demand functions $\overline{X}_i$ cannot be defined in terms of the usual statical criteria for transactor equilibrium—for Walras' Law follows from the budget equations alone. Contrary to what now appears to be accepted doctrine, however, Say's Law in the sense of Lange and Patinkin is applicable to a money economy as well as a barter economy.[7]

[5] This is Walras' Law as stated by Walras; cf. his *Elements of Pure Economics* (Jaffé translation), pp. 169–70. Lange's statement of the principle in his essay on "Say's Law: A Restatement and Correction" (*Studies in Mathematical Economics and Econometrics*, Chicago, 1942, pp. 49–50), clearly presupposes the existence of well-defined market demand and supply functions. His statement is therefore weaker than the one set forth here.

[6] Lange, *op. cit.*, p. 52.

[7] Cf. D. Patinkin, *Money, Interest, and Prices*, pp. 120–21, 257. A note of protest might be entered here against the practice of opposing a money to a barter economy. From a logical point of view, there is no objection to supposing that commodity transactions are conducted by direct barter even in an economy where money is the only possible store of value. Such an economy would appear to have all the properties usually associated with a money system, yet it would be a barter economy in the literal sense. Cf. J. M. Keynes, *General Theory*, chapter 17, especially pp. 229, 239ff.

Proceeding further, we infer from equation (6) that the market excess demand functions $\overline{X}_i$ are homogeneous of order zero in money prices alone. This is Proposition III. Since Proposition II then implies that one excess demand function follows from the remainder, equilibrium relative prices, $\overline{r}_1 , \ldots , \overline{r}_{n-1}$, may be determined independently of absolute money prices from the relations

$$\overline{X}_i(r_1 , \ldots , r_{n-1}) = 0 \quad (i = 1 , \ldots , n).$$

Finally, we infer from equation (7) that for market equilibrium to occur in the economy, the money price variables $p_1 , \ldots , p_n$ must assume values $\overline{p}_1 , \ldots , \overline{p}_n$ which satisfy the Cambridge money equation

$$k\Sigma_1^n p_i \overline{D}_i(\overline{r}_1 , \ldots , \overline{r}_{n-1}) = M, \tag{9}$$

where $M \equiv \Sigma s_m \equiv S_m$ is regarded as a given constant. This means that equilibrium money prices depend on the total quantity of money in the economy. More suggestively, we see from (8) and the argument in the preceding paragraph that the relation

$$k P \overline{T}(\overline{r}_1 , \ldots , \overline{r}_{n-1}) = M \tag{10}$$

is a necessary condition for all transactors, hence for all markets, to be in equilibrium simultaneously. Thus the general price level depends via an ordinary quantity equation on the total stock of money. These conclusions, taken in conjunction with the argument in the preceding paragraph, are equivalent to Propositions IV and V.

The price formation process underlying (9) and (10) is not described by our model. The reason is that our statical maximization criteria do not define excess demand functions except in conditions of transactor equilibrium. Relevant disequilibrium excess demand functions can be defined, of course, by introducing elementary dynamical assumptions into the theory of transactor behaviour. If this is done, the whole of traditional monetary theory may be rigorously validated; but Say's Law and the classical dichotomy then apply only in situations of monetary equilibrium. Needless to say, the real-balance effect plays a crucial rôle in the validation procedure. Indeed, to suggest that classical monetary theory might be validated without reference to real-balance effects would be to evade the issue; for this would imply that well-defined market excess demand functions, valid equally for states of transactor equilibrium and disequilibrium, are irrelevant to a full solution of the problem.

Professor Patinkin has vigorously defended the contrary point of view. His handling of disequilibrium aspects of the problem leaves much to be desired, as Archibald and Lipsey have so ably demonstrated.[8] However, in singling out the real-balance effect as the *sine qua non* of monetary theory,[9] Patinkin has correctly identified a major gap in classical doctrine. Because it has lacked an explicit dynamical framework, classical theory has long been regarded as little more than an intellectual exercise. Patinkin's treatment of the real-balance effect is an important first step towards the development of a useful theory of monetary dynamics.

[8] Archibald and Lipsey, *Review of Economic Studies*, vol. xxvi (1958), Part I.
[9] Cf. Patinkin, *op. cit.*, p. 22; also Archibald and Lipsey, *op. cit.*, p. 9. n. 1.

3

THE KEYNESIAN COUNTER-REVOLUTION:
A THEORETICAL APPRAISAL

Twenty-five years of discussion and controversy have produced a large and surprisingly harmonious literature on Keynes and the Classics. Although the series still has not converged to a point of universal agreement, the domain remaining open to dispute has contracted steadily with the passage of time. On one essential issue, however, contemporary opinion is still largely undecided: precisely what are the purely formal differences, if any, between Keynes and the Classics? Perhaps the clearest symptom of our uncertainty is the continued lack of an explicit integration of price theory and income analysis. Equally significant, however, is the ambivalence of professional economists towards the Keynesian counter-revolution launched by Hicks in 1937 and now being carried forward with such vigor by Patinkin and other general equilibrium theorists.[1] The elegance and generality of this literature makes it most alluring. At the same time, one can hardly fail to be impressed—and disturbed—by the close resemblance that some of its central doctrines bear to those of orthodox economics.

I do not presume at this late date either to improve the views of previous writers on Keynes and the Classics or to transform equivocations into certainties. Things are not that simple. However, I shall attempt to show that the same highly special theoretical presuppositions which led to Keynes' original attack on orthodox economics continue to pervade contemporary price theory and that the Keynesian counter-revolution would collapse without them. Unlike Keynes, who had to deal with doctrines of which no authoritative account had

Editor's note: This paper was presented at a conference organized by the International Economic Association and held at the Abbey of Royaumont, France, from March 28 to April 7, 1962. It was first published as "Die Keynesianische Gegenrevolution: eine theoretische Kritik," *Schweizerische Zeitschrift für Volkswirtschaft und Statistik,* 99:8–31 (1963).

[1] The 'counter-revolution' to which I refer is clearly not a conscious revolt against Keynesian economics, for all of the writers involved are, in a practical sense, strong supporters of what they conceive to be the Keynesian revolution. It is another question whether the same people are Keynesians in a theoretical sense. That is one of the issues on which this paper is intended to shed some light. See [10], [11], [17], [18], [20], and [21].

ever been given, we now have an extremely clear idea of the orthodox content of contemporary theory.[2] We thus have a distinct advantage over Keynes in describing what has been said. However, our basic problem is to discover and describe what has not but should have been said—and here we are on all fours with Keynes. Like Keynes, therefore, I must begin by asking 'forgiveness if, in the pursuit of sharp distinctions, my controversy is itself too keen' [13].

I. KEYNES AND TRADITIONAL THEORY

Our first task is to express in modern idiom those aspects of orthodox economics which were of special concern to Keynes. This may be accomplished most conveniently by considering a two-sector economy comprising households on one side and firms on the other. Corresponding to this division into sectors, we distinguish two mutually exclusive classes of commodities: (a) those which are supplied by firms and demanded by households; (b) those which are supplied by households and demanded by firms. Commodities in class (a) will be distinguished by numerical subscripts $i = 1, \ldots, m$, those in class (b) by numerical subscripts $j = m + 1, \ldots, n$. Thus, quantities supplied and demanded by firms are denoted, respectively, by variables $s_1, \ldots, s_m$, $d_{m+1}, \ldots, d_n$, while quantities demanded and supplied by households are denoted, respectively, by variables $d_1, \ldots, d_m, s_{m+1}, \ldots, s_n$. Prevailing market prices (expressed in units of commodity n) are then represented by symbols $\mathbf{p}_1, \mathbf{p}_2, \ldots, \mathbf{p}_{n-1}$ ($\mathbf{p}_n \equiv 1$), or, in vector notation, $\mathbf{P}$.[3]

For ease of exposition, we shall ignore aggregation problems and suppose that the preferences of all households in the economy are adequately characterized by a community utility function, $U(d_1, \ldots, d_m;$ $s_{m+1}, \ldots, s_n)$. Similarly, we shall assume that technical conditions confronting all business firms in the economy are adequately characterized by an aggregate transformation function $T(s_1, \ldots, s_m;$ $d_{m+1}, \ldots, d_n) = 0$. Needless to say, the functions U and T are assumed to possess all continuity and curvature properties needed to ensure the existence of unique extrema under circumstances to be specified below.

---

[2] For this, we have mainly to thank the counter-revolutionists, since it is their writings which have revived interest in general equilibrium theory.

[3] Here and throughout the remainder of the paper, boldface symbols will invariably be used to refer to magnitudes that are to be regarded as given parameters from the standpoint of individual transactors.

Dealing first with the orthodox theory of the firm, we obtain sector supply and demand functions, $\bar{s}_i(\mathbf{P})$, $\bar{d}_i(\mathbf{P})$ as solutions of the problem:[4]

maximize $$r = \sum_i^m \mathbf{p}_i s_i - \sum_j^n \mathbf{p}_j d_i$$

subject to[5] $$T(s_1, \ldots, s_m; d_{m+1}, \ldots, d_n) = 0.$$

Underlying both sets of solutions are transactor equilibrium conditions of the form

$$\mathbf{p}_k + \frac{\lambda \partial T}{\partial \bar{v}_k} = 0 \quad (\bar{v} = \bar{d}, \bar{s}; k = 1, \ldots, n).$$

In particular, if $n = 2$ and we interpret s_1 as goods and d_2 as labor, we easily establish Keynes' classical postulate I, namely, 'the [real] wage is equal to the marginal product of labour' ([13], p. 5).

In a similar fashion, the demand and supply functions of the household sector are obtained as solutions, $\bar{d}_i(\mathbf{P}, \mathbf{r})$, $\bar{s}_i(\mathbf{P}, \mathbf{r})$, of the problem:

maximize $$U(d_1, \ldots, d_m; s_{m+1}, \ldots, s_n),$$

subject to $$\sum_i^m \mathbf{p}_i d_i - \sum_j^n \mathbf{p}_j s_j - \mathbf{r} = 0,$$

the profit variable $\mathbf{r}$ being treated as a fixed parameter in this context.[6]

Underlying these solutions are transactor equilibrium conditions of the form

$$\frac{\partial U}{\partial \bar{v}_k} + \gamma \mathbf{p}_k = 0 \quad (\bar{v} = \bar{d}, \bar{s}; k = 1, \ldots, n).$$

Thus, if we consider the case $n = 2$ and adopt an appropriate interpretation of the variables d_1 and s_2, we readily derive Keynes' classical postulate II, namely, 'The utility of the [real] wage when a given

---

[4] The symbols Σ_i^m and Σ_j^n denote, respectively, the operations $\Sigma_{i=1}^m$ and $\Sigma_{j=m+1}^n$.

[5] Since $\mathbf{p}_n \equiv 1$ by assumption, we have not shown it as an explicit divisor of the price variables included in the vector $\mathbf{P}$; but it is there all the same. Thus, the demand and supply functions of the business sector are homogeneous of order zero in the n price variables $\mathbf{p}_1, \ldots, \mathbf{p}_n$. Provided $d_n \not\equiv 0$, however, the same functions are not in general homogeneous in the $n - 1$ *numéraire* prices which are contained in the vector $\mathbf{P}$.

[6] The household demand and supply functions are homogeneous of order zero in the $n + 1$ variables $\mathbf{p}_1, \ldots, \mathbf{p}_n$ and $\mathbf{r}$, but not in the n variables $\mathbf{p}_1, \ldots, \mathbf{p}_{n-1}$ and $\mathbf{r}$ (provided $s_n \not\equiv 0$).

volume of labour is employed is equal to the marginal disutility of that amount of employment' ([13], p. 5).

So much for the basic ideas of the orthodox theory of transactor behavior. Let us turn next to the theory of price formation, again seeking to express matters as Keynes might have expressed them had he been less steeped in Marshallian habits of thought.

At least since the time of Adam Smith, the market mechanism has been regarded by economists as an ingenious device for reconciling the freedom of individuals to trade as they please with the ultimate necessity for individuals in the aggregate to buy neither more nor less of any commodity than is offered for sale. To accomplish this feat, the mechanism must be supplied with information about individual sale and purchase plans, which is precisely what is supposed to be furnished by the supply and demand functions of orthodox theory.

Assuming that all business profits accrue to accounts in the household sector, we may assert first of all that the sale and purchase plans of individual transactors at any given instant of time[7] depend only on prevailing market prices.[8] We may then argue as follows.

If prevailing prices are such that demand differs from supply in any market, this means that individual trading plans, taken as a whole, are mutually inconsistent, which, in turn, means that at least some individual plans cannot be carried into effect at prevailing market prices. In these circumstances, it is plausible to suppose that prevailing prices tend to vary over time, rising in markets where demand exceeds supply, falling in markets where supply exceeds demand. Accordingly, the economy may be said to be in a state of disequilibrium. On the other hand, if prevailing market prices at any given instant happen to be such that demand is equal to supply in every market simultaneously, this means that individual trading plans, considered as a whole, are mutually consistent; hence, that all transactions planned at prevailing prices can, in principle, actually be carried out. In these circumstances, it is plausible to suppose that there are no extraneous

---

[7] I have chosen to regard 'time' as a continuous rather than a discrete variable, and to confine discussion to current values of all magnitudes, in order to discourage both myself and readers from playing meretricious games with alternative lag assumptions. No part of the present or subsequent argument is affected in any essential way if time is made discrete, lags are introduced, etc.

[8] Since we are performing market rather than individual experiments (Patinkin [21], p. 15), the parameter r which appears in the household demand and supply functions is now replaced by the function

$$\bar{r} = \sum_i^m \mathbf{p}_i \bar{s}_i - \sum_j^n \mathbf{p}_j \bar{d}_j,$$

the value of which depends only on the price vector $\mathbf{p}$.

forces at work tending to alter either individual trading plans or prevailing market prices, and the economy may be said to be in a state of equilibrium.

The only snag in this argument is the familiar one about the number of equations being one greater than the number of prices to be determined. From the theory of household behavior, however, we know that

$$\sum_i^m \mathbf{p}_i \bar{d}_i - \sum_j^n \mathbf{p}_j \bar{s}_j - \mathbf{r} = 0, \qquad (1)$$

and from the theory of business behavior, we know that

$$\sum_i^m \mathbf{p}_i \bar{s}_i - \sum_j^n \mathbf{p}_j \bar{d}_j - \bar{r} = 0. \qquad (2)$$

Subtracting 2 from 1, therefore, we have

$$\sum_{k=1}^n \mathbf{p}_k [\bar{d}_k - \bar{s}_k] \equiv \mathbf{r} - \bar{r}. \qquad (3)$$

Since in general the variables $\mathbf{r}$ and $\bar{r}$ refer to completely independent individual experiments, we cannot assume that $\mathbf{r} \equiv \bar{r}$ (see footnote 8). In the case of market experiments, however, it does seem plausible to suppose that $\mathbf{r} = \bar{r}$ provided that the variables $s_1, \ldots, s_m$ and $d_{m+1}, \ldots, d_n$ have assumed their profit-maximizing values. If this is granted, then (3) leads immediately to Walras' law in the sense of Lange ([16], pp. 49–68):[9]

$$\sum_{k=1}^n \mathbf{p}_k [\bar{d}_k(\mathbf{P}) - \bar{s}_k(\mathbf{P})] \equiv 0. \qquad (4)$$

Walras' law obviously implies that the *numéraire* value of one of the excess demands can be inferred from the values of the others, which rids us of the extra supply and demand equation. Rewritten in the form

$$\sum_k \mathbf{p}_k \bar{s}_k \equiv \sum_k \mathbf{p}_k \bar{d}_k,$$

Walras' law might also be said to assert that 'supply creates its own demand' (cf. [13], p. 18)—and we shall hear more of this in the sequel. For the time being, however, it may merely be remarked that Walras' law must be valid under the circumstances assumed here.

---

[9] The distinction drawn by Lange between Walras' law and Say's law is not relevant here; from a formal point of view, the two propositions are equivalent.

This account of orthodox doctrine accords well enough, I think, both with modern analysis and with Keynes' conception of classical theory. For the special case $n = 2$, in particular, it is apparent that Keynes' views, as expressed in chapter 2 of the *General Theory*, are exactly equivalent to what is presented above. Granted that this is so, we may reasonably assert that orthodox economics provides a general theory of equilibrium states—that is, an adequate account of the factors determining equilibrium prices and equilibrium transaction plans in a market economy. Moreover, the same analysis may be said to provide the beginnings of a theory of disequilibrium prices and disequilibrium transaction plans. Clearly, however, orthodox analysis does not provide a general theory of disequilibrium states: firstly, because it yields no direct information about the magnitude of *realized* as distinct from *planned* transactions under disequilibrium conditions; secondly, because it tacitly assumes that the forces tending at any instant to change prevailing market prices are independent of realized transactions at the same moment (this includes as a special case the assumption, made explicitly in all '*tâtonnement*', 'recontract' and 'auction' models, that no disequilibrium transactions occur).[10]

It is instructive to compare these views with those of Keynes, as represented by the following assortment of quotations (not all of them torn out of context):

I shall argue that the postulates of the classical theory are applicable to a special case only and not to the general case... ([13], p. 3).

The question...of the volume of the *available* resources, in the sense of the size of the employable population, the extent of natural wealth and the accumulated capital equipment, has often been treated descriptively [in orthodox writings]. But the pure theory of what determines the *actual employment* of the available resources has seldom been examined in any detail....I mean, not that the topic has been overlooked, but that the fundamental theory underlying it has been deemed so simple and obvious that it has received, at the most, a bare mention ([13], pp. 4–5).

A theory cannot claim to be a *general* theory unless it is applicable to the case where (or the range within which) money wages are fixed, just as much as to any other case. Politicians are entitled to complain that money wages *ought* to be highly flexible; but a theorist must be prepared to deal indifferently with either state of affairs ([13], p. 276).

...The classical theory...is wholly unable to answer the question what effect on employment a reduction in money-wages will have. For it has no method of analysis wherewith to attack the problem ([13], p. 260).

Clearly, there is nothing very novel in any of this; up to this point,

[10] J. R. Hicks [11], note to ch. 9, pp. 127 ff. Also Patinkin [21], supplementary note B, pp. 377–85.

at least, the belief that Keynes is 'saying nothing new' need not be confined to those '. . . who are not strongly wedded to. . . the classical theory' (cf. [13], p. v). Like us, Keynes does not in any way deny the generality of orthodox equilibrium analysis; he only denies that orthodox economics provides an adequate account of disequilibrium phenomena.

II. THE KEYNESIAN INDICTMENT OF ORTHODOX ECONOMICS

Grounds for theoretical controversy first begin to emerge when we come to the stage in Keynes' argument ([13], chapter 2), at which he seeks to isolate specific instances in orthodox economics of 'lack of clearness and of generality' ([13], p. v).

The first item in his bill of particulars is embedded in a lengthy discussion of wage bargains between entrepreneurs and workers ([13], pp. 1–15). Outwardly, this item represents little more than a vigorous attack on orthodox preconceptions about the stability of a market economy. For the burden of his argument seems to be that if labor is ever forced to move 'off its supply curve' it may be unable to get back on again. If this is an accurate interpretation, we may say immediately that Keynes' criticism are not of fundamental theoretical significance, for there is no reason to suppose that Keynes was more expert at stability analysis than his orthodox predecessors. However, the same argument might also be interpreted as a direct attack on the orthodox theory of household behavior. This would certainly put labor off its supply curve and would also explain Keynes' categorical rejection of classical postulate II. But if this is what Keynes intended, i.e., to deny the validity of the orthodox theory of household behavior, one can only say that he was singularly unsuccessful in providing a rationale for his attack.

The second item in Keynes' bill of particulars is essentially the same as the first: classical theory is charged with failure to recognize the existence of involuntary unemployment ([13], pp. 15–18). Again, the basic question is: Are 'involuntary unemployment' and 'chronic disequilibrium' synonymous terms for the same objective phenomenon, or is 'involuntary unemployment' a special kind of disequilibrium peculiarly associated with the breakdown of the orthodox theory of household behavior? Here there is somewhat clearer evidence that Keynes believes his objections to orthodox analysis go very deep indeed:

. . . If the classical theory is only applicable to the case of full employment, it is fallacious to apply it to the problems of involuntary unemployment—if there be such a thing (and who will deny it?). The classical theorists resemble

Euclidean geometers in a non-Euclidean world who, discovering that in experience straight lines apparently parallel often meet, rebuke the lines for not keeping straight—as the only remedy for the unfortunate collisions which are occurring. Yet, in truth, there is no remedy except to throw over the axiom of parallels and to work out a non-Euclidean geometry. Something similar is required today in economics. We need to throw over the second postulate of the classical doctrine and to work out the behaviour of a system in which involuntary unemployment in the strict sense is possible ([13], pp. 16–17).

Again, however, we are given no compelling theoretical reason to think that the proposed reconstruction of orthodox economics is really necessary.

The third and final item in Keynes' indictment is a denial of the relevance of Walras' law ([13], pp. 18–21). Most later writers (e.g., Ohlin [20], p. 230, footnote; Goodwin [7]; Patinkin [21], p. 249) have argued either that this portion of Keynes' indictment is wrong, or that the proposition which Keynes attacks is not in fact the one he thought he was attacking. Most economists have opted for the second explanation ([24], especially p. 113),[11] partly in deference to Keynes' acknowledged intellectual powers, partly because they recognize that if Keynes seriously meant to question the validity or relevance of Walras' law, he would have to reject the orthodox theory of household behavior and propose an acceptable alternative—and the alternative would have to include orthodox theory as a special case, valid under conditions of full employment. Walras' law is not, after all, an independent postulate of orthodox analysis; it is a theorem which is susceptible to direct proof on the basis of premises which are typically taken as given in contemporary as well as classical price theory.

III. THE POST-KEYNESIAN DILEMMA

The conclusion which I draw from all this may be put in one phrase: *either Walras' law is incompatible with Keynesian economics, or Keynes had nothing fundamentally new to add to orthodox economic theory.* This may seem an unnecessarily brutal way to confront one sacred cow with another. But what other conclusion is possible? In Keynes' mind, at least, the three items in his bill of particulars 'all amount to the same thing in the sense that they all stand and fall together, any one of them logically involving the other two' ([13], p. 22). As we have already seen, he could hardly hold this view seriously unless he regarded each

---

[11] But see H. Rose's note on Walras' law [25] and the reply by Patinkin [22].

of the three items as an attack on the orthodox theory of household behavior. But suppose that this is not in fact Keynes' view; suppose that Walras' law is both unreservedly valid, relevant and compatible with Keynesian economics. In this event, the recent literature on monetary theory makes it perfectly evident that Keynes may be subsumed as a special case of the Hicks–Lange–Patinkin theory of *tâtonnement* economics, which differs from orthodox theory only in being more detailed and precise. We would then have to conclude that Keynes added nothing fundamentally new to orthodox economic theory.

Thus, we are caught on the horns of a dilemma. If Keynes added nothing new to orthodox doctrine, why have twenty-five years of discussion failed to produce an integrated account of price theory and income analysis? If Keynes did add something new, the integration problem becomes explicable; but then we have to give up Walras' law as a fundamental principle of economic analysis. It is precisely at this point, I believe, that virtually all previous writers have decided to part company with Keynes. I propose to follow a different course. I shall argue that the established theory of household behavior is, indeed, incompatible with Keynesian economics, that Keynes himself made tacit use of a more general theory, that this more general theory leads to market excess-demand functions which include quantities as well as prices as independent variables, and that, except in conditions of full employment, the excess-demand functions so defined do not satisfy Walras' law. In short, I shall argue that there has been a fundamental misunderstanding of the formal basis of the Keynesian revolution.

IV. DISEQUILIBRIUM SYSTEMS: A PRELIMINARY VIEW

Before attempting to deal directly with the issues raised above, we must say something more about the mechanics of disequilibrium states. In our earlier discussion of orthodox analysis, it was pointed out that the whole of traditional price theory rests on the tacit assumption that market excess demands are independent of current market transactions. This implies that *income magnitudes do not appear as independent variables in the demand or supply functions of a general equilibrium model*; for incomes are defined in terms of quantities as well as prices, and quantity variables never appear explicitly in the market excess-demand functions of traditional theory. To be sure, income variables could be introduced by taking factor supplies as given parameters; but this would preclude the formulation of a general equilibrium model containing supply functions of all marketable factor services.[12] The importance of these propositions for Keynesian economics can hardly be over-emphasized, for they imply directly that the Keynesian consumption function and other market relations involving income as an independent variable cannot be derived explicitly from any existing theory of general equilibrium.[13]

The most lucid account of the role which current transactions *might* play in general equilibrium theory has been presented by Professor Hicks in *Value and Capital* (pp. 119 ff.). The following passages are especially significant in the present connection (pp. 127–9):

Since, in general, traders cannot be expected to know just what total supplies are available on any market, nor what total demands will be forthcoming at particular prices, any price which is fixed initially can be only a guess. It is not probable that demand and supply will actually be found to be equated at such a guessed price; if they are not, then in the course of trading the price will move up or down. Now if there is a change of price in the midst of trading, the situation appears to elude the ordinary apparatus of demand-and-supply analysis, for, strictly speaking, demand curves and supply curves give us the amounts which buyers and sellers will demand and supply respectively at any particular price, if that price is fixed at the start and adhered to throughout. Earlier writers, such as Walras and Edgeworth, had therefore supposed that demand-and-supply analysis ought strictly to be confined to such markets as permitted of 'recontract'; i.e. markets such that if a transaction was put through at a 'false' price...it could be revised when the equilibrium price was reached. Since such markets are highly exceptional, their solution of the problem (if it can be called one) was not very convincing.

...In the general case...gains and losses due to false trading only give rise to income effects—effects, that is, which are the same kind as the income effects which may have to be considered even when we suppose equilibrium prices to be fixed straight away. We have seen again and again that a certain degree of indeterminateness is nearly always imparted by income effects to the laws of economic theory. All that happens as a result of false trading is that this indeterminateness is somewhat intensified. How much intensified depends, of course, upon the extent of the false trading; if very extensive

[12] This was apparently overlooked by Patinkin when he formulated his 'general theory' of macroeconomics ([21], ch. 9). It is instructive to notice that this chapter is not supplemented by a mathematical appendix. Some of the consequences of this oversight are evident in the later discussion, see especially the argument beginning at p. 216, including the footnotes to pp. 218 and 220. I do not mean to suggest that authors may not put such variables as they please into their models. My point is that such variables as can be shown to be functionally dependent on others should not then be manipulated independently.

[13] Cf. Lange ([17], ch. 9, p. 53). Lange's usage of the phrase 'propensity to consume' is perfectly legitimate, but the concept invoked by him is not in any sense a consumption function of the sort Keynes worked with since, except on the Keynesian definition, it is not possible to talk about changes in consumption in response to changes in income without at the same time talking about changes in prices.

transactions take place at prices very different from equilibrium prices, the disturbance will be serious. But I think we may reasonably suppose that the transactions which take place at *very false* prices are limited in volume. If any intelligence is shown in price-fixing, they will be.

It is heartening to know that income effects can be ignored if they are sufficiently unimportant to be neglected; but this is hardly a solution to the problem at issue. The essential question is whether the supply and demand functions of traditional analysis are in any way relevant to the formulation of market prices in situations where disequilibrium transactions *cannot* be ignored.

To answer this question, we must first define explicit theoretical measures of disequilibrium transaction quantities. Perhaps the simplest way to define such measures is to suppose that actual transactions in any given market are always dominated by the 'short' side of the market; that is to say, market transactions are equal to planned market supply if demand is greater than supply, to planned market demand if supply is equal to or greater than demand ([15], p. 203; [5]; [21], pp. 157–8). This is , of course, the procedure which has been followed by all previous writers, insofar as they have said anything at all on the subject.

Taken by itself, this addendum to traditional theory has no logical implications; but it opens the way for further analysis. For example, some writers have suggested the desirability of supposing that actual transactions exert a more or less direct influence on price adjustment via 'spillover' effects—changes in prevailing supply and demand conditions to reflect current discrepancies between planned and realized purchases and sales. The most recent expression of this view has been voiced by Patinkin ([21], p. 157).[14] His suggestion is to redefine the usual price adjustment functions to make the rate of change of price in one market a function not of excess demand in that market alone, but also of excess demand in all other markets. That this is not an entirely satisfactory vehicle for expressing his basic views, however, is indicated by three considerations.

Firstly, it is not consistent with established preference analysis to suppose that transactors alter their sale and purchase plans before prevailing market prices have already varied in response to the pressure of excess demand somewhere in the economy. Secondly, the supposition that price movements in one market are governed by excess-demand conditions in all markets is logically equivalent to the supposition that individual traders respond not merely to absolute levels of prevailing prices but also to current rates of change of prices.

[14] Also see Hansen [9] and Enthoven [6].

This implies some basic changes in established preference analysis to allow prices as seen by transactors to differ from current market prices ([8], p. 42, n. 1). Thirdly, from Walras' law (obviously applicable in this instance), the 'money' value of potential 'spillover' from any given market is measured by the aggregate 'money' value of the market excess supply of all other commodities. Thus, if 'spillover' effects from a given market are *fully* reflected in other markets, we are left with effective excess demand in the given market (and, by induction, in all other markets also) identically equal to zero; which is to say that prices never vary. Patinkin does not go to this extreme; he relies instead on a proposition by Samuelson ([26], p. 274)[15] and supposes that 'spillover' effects in any given market are only partially reflected in transfers of demand to other markets. But this is simply *ad hoc* theorizing—inventing a solution to a problem which has actually been evaded rather than resolved.

A more promising way to bring current transactions into general equilibrium theory is by way of so-called stock-flow models. Unless we suppose that all commodities traded in the economy are highly perishable, it is clearly plausible to argue that goods will accumulate or decumulate (or both) somewhere in the economic system during periods of market disequilibrium. This forces us to consider possible extensions of traditional theory to deal explicitly with asset-holding phenomena.

There is now a reasonably adequate theoretical literature on this subject, including a number of recent papers on monetary theory and at least one important book on the theory of investment.[16] I think it is fair to say, however, that this literature has made little impression on the profession at large; which is perhaps another way of remarking that the equilibrium properties of stock-flow models are essentially the same as those of traditional pure-flow models and that few economists are deeply concerned with anything else. Here, therefore, I shall merely observe that the explicit introduction of asset-holding phenomena into traditional theory entails a redefinition of market

---

[15] In fairness to Samuelson, it should be added that his discussion does not refer to spillover effects, but instead to what I have elsewhere called 'dynamical interdependence' among market excess-demand functions. See Bushaw and Clower ([4], ch. 4, pp. 82 ff.).

[16] Vernon L. Smith, *Investment and Production* [27]. This book includes a comprehensive bibliography on the 'real' part of the stock-flow literature. For further details of the 'monetary' part, see George Horwich, 'Money, prices, and the theory of interest determination' [12]. The latest in this series are the article by Archibald and Lipsey [1], the related 'Symposium on monetary theory' [1], and Baumol's 'Stocks, flows, and monetary theory' [3]. The general theory underlying such models is developed at perhaps excessive length in Bushaw and Clower [4].

excess-demand functions to include asset as well as price arrays among the relevant independent variables and, along with this, an extension of the usual equation systems to include stock-adjustment functions. As a consequence, actual transaction quantities influence market adjustment indirectly, via their impact on existing asset stocks—which creates certain new sources of potential instability ([19]; [4], pp. 170–74). Even in this type of model, however, current transactions exercise an influence only after a certain time delay. As in more usual general equilibrium models, therefore, current incomes never appear as independent variables. Thus, this potential road to the *General Theory* also turns out to be a blind alley.

The preceding discussion probably does not exhaust the list of possible ways of introducing current transactions into excess-demand functions, but we have now gone far enough to appreciate that the problem is by no means so transparent as some writers might have us believe. At this point, therefore, let us return to the route which Keynes apparently travelled before us.

V. SAY'S PRINCIPLE AND WALRAS' LAW

In our earlier account of the theory of household behavior, we did not distinguish between planned and realized magnitudes because to have done so would not in fact have been a meaningful procedure in the context of orthodox equilibrium analysis. However, if we adopt the view that states of transactor disequilibrium are, in principle, just as admissible as states of transactor equilibrium (and how can we do otherwise?), the distinction between plans and realizations becomes both meaningful and theoretically relevant. In the discussion that follows, we shall adopt just this point of view; accordingly, we shall henceforth interpret boldface symbols $\mathbf{d}$, $\mathbf{s}$ and $\mathbf{r}$ as realized or actual magnitudes (hence, given parameters from the standpoint of individual transactors); planned or notional magnitudes will be denoted, as before, by such symbols as d, $\bar{s}$, r, etc.

For any individual household (here, we are informally modifying our discussion to recognize that the household sector comprises a multitude of independent decision units), we may clearly assume that the realized *numéraire* value of actual purchases during any given interval of time is identically equal to the aggregate *numéraire* value of realized sales and realized profit receipts during the same interval:

$$\sum_{k=1}^{n} \mathbf{p}_k[\mathbf{d}_k - \mathbf{s}_k] - \mathbf{r} \equiv 0. \tag{5}$$

Indeed, this is just a tacit definition of the concept of a transactor, since what it asserts is that commodities are acquired through market exchange rather than theft, gifts, heavenly favors, etc. The familiar household budget constraint, although similar in form to the truism, equation (5), asserts the rather different proposition that no transactor consciously *plans* to purchase units of any commodity without at the same time *planning* to finance the purchase either from profit receipts or from the sale of units of some other commodity. For later reference, I shall call the last and very general proposition *Say's principle*. This is essentially a rational planning postulate, not a bookkeeping identity nor a technical relation. Unlike the market principle known as Walras' law, moreover, Say's principle does not depend on the tacit assumption that values are calculated in terms of current market prices, or on the equally tacit assumption that market prices are independent of individual purchases and sales. Neither does it presuppose that individual behavior is in any sense optimal. Thus, Say's principle may indeed be regarded as a fundamental convention of economic science, akin in all relevant respects to such basic ideas of physical science as the second law of thermodynamics. Say's principle is not true in the nature of things; but unless we presuppose something of the sort, we have absolutely nothing upon which to build an account of individual decision processes.

Suppose now that we carry through the usual utility maximization procedure to arrive at household demand and supply functions, $\bar{d}_i(\mathbf{P}, \mathbf{r})$, $\bar{s}_j(\mathbf{P}, \mathbf{r})$, interpreting Say's principle to mean what it usually means in this context, namely,

$$\sum_i^m \mathbf{p}_i d_i - \sum_j^n \mathbf{p}_j s_j - \mathbf{r} = 0.$$

Must we then assert that any reasonable definition of market demand and supply magnitudes will necessarily make use of the functions $\bar{d}_i$, $\bar{s}_j$ so defined? Not necessarily, for the definition of these functions tacitly presupposes something more than Say's principle, namely, that every household expects to be able to buy or sell any desired quantity of each and every commodity at prevailing market prices ([2], p. 232 ff.).

Now, the rationale of the last presupposition is hardly self-evident. Keynes has been scoffed at on more than one occasion for his dichotomized account of spending and saving decisions (see [13], p. 166). As far as I can see, the only reason for making humorous comments about this view is that established preference analysis tacitly presupposes that selling, buying and saving plans are all carried out simultaneously. But what if one does not happen to consider the presuppositions of established preference analysis, tacit or otherwise, to be the final word on this subject? [23, 28]. I suggest that the question will bear further examination.

The notion that all household decisions are accomplished at a single stroke seems to be an analytically convenient and intuitively plausible procedure as long as we consider each household to be an isolated performer of conceptual experiments. When households are considered to be part of a connected market system, however, the same notion assumes a rather different aspect. What is then presupposed about planned sales and purchases cannot possibly be true of realized sales and purchases, unless the system as a whole is always in a state of equilibrium; that is to say, not every household can buy and sell just what it pleases if supply exceeds demand somewhere in the economy. Do we nevertheless suppose that the facts of life never intrude upon the thought experiments of households?

The answer to this is, I think, that the matter is not of much theoretical significance if, as is usually true when we deal with competitive supply and demand models, we are primarily interested in comparative-statics propositions. In this event, differences between realized and planned purchases and sales of individual households may properly be supposed to occur more or less at random. If we entertain the notion of developing market models that will have practical application to situations of chronic disequilibrium, however, we must surely question the universal relevance of the 'unified decision' hypothesis and, by the same token, question whether the usual household supply and demand functions provide relevant market signals.

VI. THE DUAL-DECISION HYPOTHESIS

For the moment, let us imagine ourselves to be involuntarily unemployed in the sense of Keynes. Specifically, imagine that we have a strong wish to satisfy our champagne appetites but that the demand for our services as economic consultants does not in fact allow us to gratify this desire without doing serious damage to our household finances. How do we communicate our thirstiness to producers of champagne; how can they be made aware of our willingness to solve their market research problems in exchange for copious quantities of their excellent beverage?

The answer is that we do so indirectly. We offer more favorable terms to potential buyers of our services (these may include some champagne merchants), leaving it to the market to provide us more employment and income and, in due time, more booze. Do we also signal our craving directly by drawing on money balances and savings accounts and sending our children out to work? In short, do we drink more even before we work more? Or do we become, at least temporarily, involuntarily abstemious and postpone our satisfaction to financially more propitious times? Clearly, this is to pose the question in a highly misleading way, for the issue is not, 'Which do we do?' but 'How much do we do of each?'

But if even this much is granted, we thereby affirm that the demand functions of orthodox theory do not provide relevant market signals. For if realized current receipts are considered to impose any kind of constraint on current consumption plans, planned consumption as expressed in effective market offers to buy will necessarily be less than desired consumption as given by the demand functions of orthodox analysis.

A formal statement of the problem will clarify matters at this point. Following the usual procedure of traditional theory, suppose that the preference function $U(\bar{d}_1, \ldots, d_m; \bar{s}_{m+1}, \ldots, s_n)$ is maximized subject to the budget constraint

$$\sum_i^m \mathbf{p}_i d_i - \sum_j^n \mathbf{p}_j s_j - \mathbf{r} = 0,$$

and the resulting first-order conditions are used to define the notional demand and supply functions $\bar{d}_i(\mathbf{p}, \mathbf{r})$ and $\bar{s}_j(\mathbf{p}, \mathbf{r})$. Provided that realized current income is not less than notional current income, i.e., provided

$$\sum_j^n \mathbf{p}_j s_j \geq \sum_j^n \mathbf{p}_j \bar{s}_j,$$

we may suppose that the functions $\bar{d}_i$ and $\bar{s}_j$ constitute relevant market signaling devices. For this is just to say that current income receipts do not impose an operative constraint on household spending decisions.[17]

In the contrary case, however, i.e., if

$$\sum_j^n \mathbf{p}_j s_j < \sum_j^n \mathbf{p}_j \bar{s}_j,$$

---

[17] More generally, we might argue that an excess of current income over desired income does affect current expenditure directly; compulsory overtime might be considered a case in point. But we shall not deal with situations of that kind here. In effect, we suppose that individuals are never forced to sell more factor services than they want to sell, though they may be forced for lack of buyers to sell less than they desire.

a second round of decision making is indicated: namely, maximize

$$U(d_1, \ldots, d_m; \mathbf{s}_{m+1}, \ldots, \mathbf{s}_n),$$

subject to the modified budget constraint

$$\sum_i^m \mathbf{p}_i d_i - \sum_j^n \mathbf{p}_j \mathbf{s}_j - \mathbf{r} = 0.$$

Solving this problem, we obtain a set of *constrained* demand functions,

$$\hat{d}_i(\mathbf{P}, \ \mathbf{Y}) \ (i = 1, \ldots, m),$$

where, by definition,

$$\mathbf{Y} \equiv \sum_j^n \mathbf{p}_j \mathbf{s}_j + \mathbf{r},$$

the values of the constrained functions, $\hat{d}_i$, will then be equal to those of the corresponding notional functions, $\bar{d}_i$, if and only if

$$\sum_j^n \mathbf{p}_j(\mathbf{s}_j - \bar{s}_j) \equiv 0.$$

Except in this singular case,[18] however, the constrained demand functions $\hat{d}_i(\mathbf{P}, \ \mathbf{Y})$ and the notional supply functions $\bar{s}_j(\mathbf{P}, \ \mathbf{r})$, rather than the notional functions $\bar{d}_i$ and $\bar{s}_j$, are the relevant providers of market signals.

Here and elsewhere in the argument, it may be helpful if the reader imagines that a central 'market authority' is responsible for setting all prices (using the nth commodity as an accounting unit), and that this 'authority' maintains continual surveillance over all sale and purchase orders communicated to it by individual transactors to ensure that no purchase order is 'validated' unless it is offset by a sale order that has already been executed (i.e., purchase orders are simply 'cancelled' unless the transactor has a positive balance of 'book credit' with the market authority sufficient to cover the entire value of the purchase order). It must be assumed that the market authority communicates continuously with each transactor to inform it of the precise level of its current credit balance, and further informs each transactor of the precise rate at which previously validated purchase orders currently are being executed. Sale orders are 'validated' automatically, but the rate at which such orders are executed is governed by prevailing

[18] The constrained demand functions are not even defined, of course, when realized income *exceeds* desired income.

demand conditions. It is implicit in this entire line of argument that, at some 'initial' state in the evolution of market trading arrangements, the market authority advances a nominal quantity of book credit to one or more transactors to set the trading process in motion (without such initial advances, no sale order could ever be executed since no purchase order would ever be validated).

Established preference analysis thus appears as a special case—valid in conditions of full employment—of the present *dual-decision theory*. Considered from this point of view, the other side of involuntary unemployment would seem to be involuntary under-consumption, which should have considerable intuitive appeal to those of us who really do have unsatisfied champagne appetites.

It is worth remarking explicitly that *the dual-decision hypothesis does not in any way flout Say's principle*. It would be more accurate to say that this hypothesis assigns greater force to the principle by recognizing that current income flows may impose an independent restriction on effective demand, separate from those already imposed by prevailing market prices and current transfer receipts. Indeed, it is this theory which is invariably presented in geometrical classroom expositions of the theory of consumer behavior. It is only in mathematical versions of preference analysis that we lose sight of realized current income as an operative constraint on effective demand.

It is another question whether Keynes can reasonably be considered to have had a dual-decision theory of household behavior at the back of his mind when he wrote the *General Theory*. For my part, I do not think there can be any serious doubt that he did, although I can find no direct evidence in any of his writings to show that he ever thought explicitly in these terms. But indirect evidence is available in almost unlimited quantity: in his treatment of the orthodox theory of household behavior, his repeated discussions of 'Say's law', his development of the consumption function concept, his account of interest theory, and his discussions of wage and price determination. It is also significant, I believe, that a year after the appearance of the *General Theory*, Keynes' own evaluation of the theoretical significance of the consumption function concept still differed sharply from that of his reviewers:

This psychological law was of the utmost importance in the development of my own thought, and it is, I think, absolutely fundamental to the theory of effective demand as set forth in my book. But few critics or commentators so far have paid particular attention to it [14].

Finally, it is important to notice that unless the orthodox approach to household behavior is modified (tacitly if not explicitly) to recognize the dual-decision hypothesis, the Keynesian notion of an aggregate consumption function does not make sense, the distinction between transactions and speculative balances is essentially meaningless, the liquidity-preference theory of interest is indistinguishable from the classical theory of loanable funds, fluctuations in the demand for physical assets cannot be supposed to have more impact on output and employment than fluctuations in the demand for securities, and excess supply in the labor market does not diminish effective excess demand elsewhere in the economy. In short, Keynes either had a dual-decision hypothesis at the back of his mind, or most of the *General Theory* is theoretical nonsense.

VII. FROM THE CLASSICS TO KEYNES

We remarked above that the dual-decision hypothesis already has an established position in the oral tradition of established preference analysis. We have also argued that it plays an important (if tacit) role in income analysis. Thus, it is only when we turn to contemporary general equilibrium theory that no trace of the hypothesis is anywhere to be found. Yet it is precisely in this area that the dual-decision approach is most clearly relevant—and most damaging to orthodoxy.

Referring to our previous account of traditional analysis (Part I, above), we recall that the business sector supply and demand functions may, from a market point of view, be so defined as to depend solely on the price vector $\mathbf{P}$, permitting us to write Walras' law in the form

$$\sum_{i}^{m} \mathbf{p}_i[\bar{d}_i(\mathbf{P}) - \bar{s}_i(\mathbf{P})] + \sum_{j}^{n} \mathbf{p}_j[\bar{d}_j(\mathbf{P}) - \bar{s}_j(\mathbf{P})] \equiv 0.^{[19]}$$

In the context of the present discussion, the most interesting implication of Walras' law is obtained by calling the commodities $1, \ldots, m$ 'goods' and the commodities $m + 1, \ldots, n$ 'factors'. We may then assert that excess supply of factors necessarily implies the simultaneous existence of excess demand for goods. More generally, we may assert that in any disequilibrium situation, there is always an element of excess demand working directly on the price system to offset prevailing elements of excess supply.

According to the dual-decision hypothesis, however, the market relevance of the household functions $\bar{d}_j(\mathbf{P})$ and $\bar{s}_j(\mathbf{P})$ is contingent on

---

[19] Cf. equation (4), above.

the satisfaction of the condition that realized current income be not less than planned income.[20] Suppose, however, that

$$\sum_{j}^{n} \mathbf{p}_j[\bar{d}_j - \bar{s}_j] < 0;$$

i.e., suppose that notional aggregate demand for factors is less than aggregate supply (in the sense indicated). Then involuntary unemployment may be said to exist since realized factor income cannot exceed the aggregate money value of planned demand for factor inputs; that is to say,

$$\sum_{j}^{n} \mathbf{p}_j[\bar{d}_j - \mathbf{s}_j] \geq 0.$$

In this situation, the dual-decision hypothesis requires that we replace the usual household demand functions, $\bar{d}_i$, by the constrained demand functions $\hat{d}_i(\mathbf{P}, \mathbf{Y})$, which, by definition, satisfy the condition

$$\sum_{i}^{m} \mathbf{p}_i \bar{d}_i(\mathbf{P}) \geq \sum_{i}^{m} \mathbf{p}_i \hat{d}_i(\mathbf{P}, \mathbf{Y});$$

i.e., the aggregate money value of constrained demand for goods is at most equal to the aggregate money value of planned demand for goods in the sense of traditional preference analysis. It follows immediately that, in a state of involuntary unemployment, Walras' law must be replaced by the more general condition

$$\sum_{i}^{m} \mathbf{p}_i[\hat{d}_i(\mathbf{P}, \mathbf{Y}) - \bar{s}_i(P)] + \sum_{j}^{n} \mathbf{p}_j[\bar{d}_j(P) - \bar{s}_j(\mathbf{P})] \leq 0;$$

i.e., *the sum of all market demands, valued at prevailing prices, is at most equal to zero.* Indeed, since the equality sign applies with certainty only in the absence of factor excess supply, the dual-decision hypothesis effectively implies that Walras' law, although valid as usual with reference to *notional* market excess demands, is in general irrelevant to any but full employment situations. *Contrary to the findings of traditional theory, excess demand may fail to appear anywhere in the economy under conditions of less than full employment.*

The common sense of the preceding analysis may be clarified by a

[20] Profit receipts do not concern us since we are still proceeding on the assumption that the condition $\mathbf{r} = \bar{r}$ is satisfied (this is no longer essential to the argument, but is very convenient). What we are supposing, in effect, is that household receivers of profit income have perfect information about profit prospects (they may even be producer-consumers) and react to this information precisely as if corresponding amounts of *numéraire* profit were actually being received.

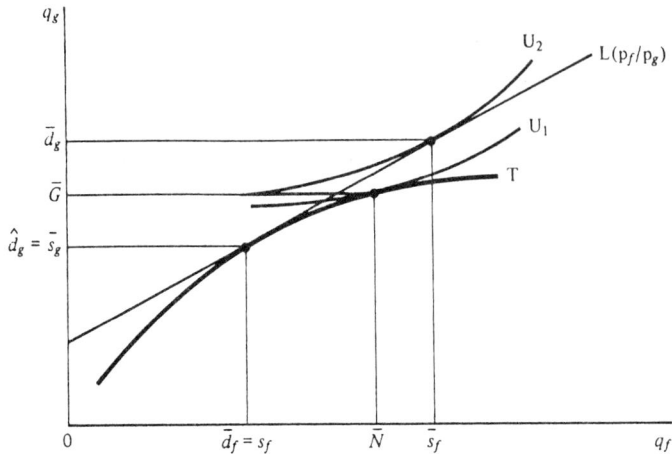

Figure 1

simple geometrical illustration. Let the curve T in the accompanying figure represent the business sector transformation function, let U_1 and U_2 represent alternative household sector indifference curves, and let $L(\mathbf{p}_f/\mathbf{p}_g)$ represent, simultaneously, the profit function of firms and the budget constraint of households. In the situation illustrated, the real wage at time t, $\mathbf{p}_f/\mathbf{p}_g$, is such that $\bar{s}_f > \bar{d}_f$; hence, factors are in excess supply. Moreover, since $\bar{d}_g > \bar{s}_g$, goods are simultaneously in a state of notional excess demand. If the real wage rate is assumed to vary inversely with notional excess demand for goods (as is assumed to be the case in orthodox analysis), $\mathbf{p}_f/\mathbf{p}_g$ will tend to fall over time at time t, and the system may therefore be said to tend towards full employment (defined by reference to the point $(\bar{N}, \bar{G})$). However, if the real wage rate is assumed to vary inversely with 'effective' excess demand for goods, no adjustment of the real wage rate will tend to occur at time t since, as indicated, constrained demand for goods, $\hat{d}_g$, is equal to planned supply of goods at prevailing price and income levels.[21]

This illustration of how effective excess demand may be insufficient to induce price adjustment, despite the obvious sufficiency of notional excess demand, says nothing, of course, about the stability of full employment equilibrium under alternative adjustment hypotheses. For example, if the real wage rate varies in response *either* to constrained excess demand for goods *or* excess demand for factors, then in the situation illustrated the system may still tend towards full em-

[21] Compare Keynes' discussion of the same model ([13], p. 261).

ployment equilibrium. The point of the example is merely to illustrate that, *when income appears as an independent variable in the market excess-demand functions—more generally, when transactions quantities enter into the definition of these functions—traditional price theory ceases to shed any light on the dynamic stability of a market economy.*[22]

This line of analysis might be carried a good deal further; but I think enough has been said to justify such conclusions as are germane to the present argument:

Firstly, orthodox price theory may be regarded as a special case of Keynesian economics, valid only in conditions of full employment.

Secondly, an essential formal difference between Keynesian and orthodox economics is that market excess demands are in general assumed to depend on current market transactions in the former, to be independent of current market transactions in the latter. This difference depends, in turn, on Keynes' tacit use of a dual-decision theory of household behavior and his consequent rejection of Walras' law as a relevant principle of economic analysis.

Thirdly, chronic factor unemployment at substantially unchanging levels of real income and output may be consistent with Keynesian economics even if all prices are flexible; this problem has yet to be investigated within the context of a Keynesian model of market price formation.

VIII. CONCLUSION

My original intention in writing this paper was simply to clarify the formal basis of the Keynesian revolution and its relation to orthodox thought. This I think I have done. In a line, Keynesian economics brings current transactions into price theory whereas traditional an-

---

[22] In an unpublished article 'A Keynesian market equilibrium model', my colleague Mitchell Harwitz considers a more general version of the rigid wages case with results that go far to anticipate the dual-decision hypothesis on which the present argument places so much weight. The following passage is particularly significant:

Suppose one market is permanently restrained from full adjustment. What does this mean in terms of the individual participants in the market? *It means that some or all of them face a binding constraint in addition to the budget constraint.* For concreteness, consider the Keynesian labor market. A worker, faced with a certain real wage, can sell *less* labor than is consistent with the usual constrained maximum. In effect, he is in equilibrium, but at a boundary [position] imposed by a quantity constraint on the labor he can sell.... It must be granted that these positions are equilibria by our definition; but their stability is a more delicate question.... A complete answer would require a theory of the dynamical behavior of economic units both in and out of equilibrium.

alysis explicitly leaves them out. Alternatively, we may say that Keynesian economics is price theory without Walras' law,[23] and price theory with Walras' law is just a special case of Keynesian economics. The bearing of my argument on the Keynesian counter-revolution is correspondingly plain: contemporary general equilibrium theories can be maintained intact only if we are willing to barter Keynes for orthodoxy.

This is not the end of the matter, for there is a choice to be made. No one can deny that general equilibrium analysis, as presently constituted, is a useful instrument for thinking about abstract economic problems, and this would hardly be so if it did not omit many realistic frills. The danger in using this instrument to think about practical problems is that, having schooled ourselves so thoroughly in the virtues of elegant simplicity, we may refuse to recognize the crucial relevance of complications that do not fit our theoretical preconceptions. As Keynes has put it, 'The difficulty lies, not in the new ideas, but in escaping from the old ones, which ramify, for those brought up as most of us have been, into every corner of our minds' ([13], p. viii).

I shall be the last one to suggest that abstract theory is useless; that simply is not so. At the same time, I am convinced that much of what now passes for useful theory is not only worthless economics (and mathematics), but also a positive hindrance to fruitful theoretical and empirical research. Most importantly, however, I am impressed by the worth of Keynesian economics as a guide to practical action, which is in such sharp contrast to the situation of general price theory. As physicists should and would have rejected Einstein's theory of relativity, had it not included Newtonian mechanics as a special case, so we would do well to think twice before accepting as 'useful' or 'general', doctrines which are incapable of accomodating Keynesian economics.

---

[23] It is vacuously true, of course, that a proposition similar to Walras' law holds even in Keynesian economics if we *define* the difference between desired sales and realized sales as an excess demand for 'money income'. But the proposition then becomes an empirically meaningless tautology. In conventional value theory, the total value of commodities (goods and money) offered for sale is always equal to the total value of commodities (goods and money) demanded for purchase because all purchase orders are presumed to be effective regardless of prevailing demand and supply conditions. But in the present discussion, purchase orders are not validated automatically, sale orders thus do not necessarily generate effective demand for other commodities (effective demands are constrained by purchase orders *executed*, not purchase orders *placed*).

REFERENCES

1. Archibald, G. C., and Lipsey, R. G., "Monetary and Value Theory: A Critique of Lange and Patinkin," *Review of Economic Studies*, 26:1–22 (1958), and "Symposium on Monetary Theory," 28:50–56 (1960).
2. Baumol, W. J., *Economic Theory and Operations Analysis* (Prentice-Hall, 1961).
3. Baumol, W. J., "Stocks, Flows, and Monetary Theory," *Quarterly Journal of Economics*, 76:46–56 (1962).
4. Bushaw, D. W., and Clower, R. W., *Introduction to Mathematical Economics* (Irwin, 1957).
5. Clower, R. W., "Keynes and the Classics: A Dynamical Perspective," *Quarterly Journal of Economics*, 74:318–320 (1960).
6. Enthoven, A. C., "Monetary Disequilibrium and the Dynamics of Inflation," *Economic Journal*, 66:256–270 (1956).
7. Goodwin, R. M., "The Multiplier as Matrix," *Economic Journal*, 59:537–555 (1949).
8. Hahn, F. A., "The Patinkin Controversy," *Review of Economic Studies*, 28:37–43 (1960).
9. Hansen, B., *A Study in the Theory of Inflation* (Allen and Irwin, 1951).
10. Hicks, J. R., "Mr. Keynes and the Classics: A Suggested Interpretation," *Econometrica*, 5:147–159 (1937).
11. Hicks, J. R., *Value and Capital* (Clarendon Press, 1939).
12. Horwich, G., "Money, Prices, and the Theory of Interest Determination," *Economic Journal*, 67:625–643 (1957).
13. Keynes, J. M., *The General Theory of Employment, Interest, and Money* (Harcourt Brace, 1936).
14. Keynes, J. M., "The General Theory of Employment," *Quarterly Journal of Economics*, 51:209–223 (1937).
15. Klein, L. R., *The Keynesian Revolution* (Macmillan, 1952).
16. Lange, O., "Say's Law: A Restatement and Criticism," in Lange, McIntyre, and Yntema (eds.), *Studies in Mathematical Economics and Econometrics* (University of Chicago Press, 1942).
17. Lange, O., *Price Flexibility and Employment* (Principia, 1944).
18. Modigliani, F., "Liquidity Preference and the Theory of Interest and Money," *Econometrica*, 12:45–88 (1944).
19. Negishi, T., "General Equilibrium Models of Market Clearing Processes in a Monetary Economy," *The Theory of Interest Rates* (Macmillan, 1965).
20. Ohlin, B., "Some Notes on the Stockholm Theory of Savings and Investment," *Economic Journal*, 47:53–69, 221–240 (1937).
21. Patinkin, D., *Money, Interest, and Prices* (Row, Peterson, 1956).
22. Patinkin, D., "Reply to R. W. Clower and H. Rose," *Economica*, 26:253–255 (1959).
23. Pearce, I. F., "A Method of Consumer Demand Analysis Illustrated," *Economica*, 28:371–394 (1961).
24. Rose, H., "Liquidity Preference and Loanable Funds," *Review of Economic Studies*, 24:111–119 (1957).
25. Rose, H., "The Rate of Interest and Walras' Law," *Economica*, 26:252–253 (1959).

26. Samuelson, P. A., *Foundations of Economic Analysis* (Harvard University Press, 1947).
27. Smith, V. L., *Investment and Production* (Harvard University Press, 1961).
28. Strotz, R. H., "The Empirical Implications of a Utility Tree," *Econometrica*, 25:269–280 (1957).

4

MONETARY HISTORY AND POSITIVE ECONOMICS

> We economists are essentially only dilettanti in the field of historical research, with the usual faults of all dilettantism: over-hasty conclusions, insufficient criticism of sources, tendentious colouring of facts, and even, on occasion, unconscious fabrication of them.
> KNUT WICKSELL

I

If successful prediction were the sole criterion of the merit of a science, economics should long since have ceased to exist as a serious intellectual pursuit. Accurate prognosis is not its forte. The real strength of the discipline lies in another direction—namely, in its apparently limitless capacity to rationalize events after they happen. This helps explain the indifference of most economic theorists to "the lessons of history"; men to whom all things are possible have little to learn from experiments conducted in the laboratory of time. It also helps explain the indifference of most economic historians to abstract theory; what have they to learn from a subject that "yields no predictions, summarizes no empirical generalizations, provides no useful framework of analysis"?[1]

Recent years have, of course, witnessed some changes in the attitude of theorists toward economic history and in the attitude of economic historians toward theory. Rummaging in attics and excavating ancient files have not yet become popular sports, but the production of historical statistics is very nearly one already. The problem is to put the data now becoming available to good use. This is hardly a novel problem; men have been debating the merits of alternative epistemologies since the dawn of time. But economic history is currently in a state

A review of *A Monetary History of the United States, 1867–1960*, by Milton Friedman and Anna Jacobson Schwartz. Princeton: published for the NBER by Princeton University Press, 1963. Pp. xxiv, 860. $15.00. Reprinted from the *Journal of Economic History*, XXIV (Sept. 1964), 364–80, by permission of the Economic History Association, the copyright holder.
[1] Milton Friedman, "The Marshallian Demand Curve," in *Essays in Positive Economics* (Chicago: University of Chicago Press, 1953), p. 92.

of flux, forced by external pressures to become less humane, torn by internal discord as to how this should be done.[2] Thus the future direction of the subject may well depend as much on the methodological views of economists playing at history as on the attitudes of economic historians. Whether this bodes well or ill for economic history, I cannot pretend to say. Much depends on just who the "dilettanti" are, for economics proper is not devoid of methodological factions either.[3]

These considerations lend peculiar interest and significance to the volume under review. To be sure, Friedman and Schwartz's *History* merits close attention in its own right; it is not every day, or even every decade, that an outstanding economic theorist joins forces with another able scholar to produce a major work in economic history. But Milton Friedman is not just an outstanding theorist. He is the leading exponent of a radical research methodology which views much of formal economic analysis as "disguised mathematics"; which regards theories as useful only if they "fit as full and comprehensive a set of related facts about the real world as it is possible to get"; which is contemptuous of any test of the validity of a hypothesis other than "comparison of its predictions with experience."[4] And he is also the author or coauthor of some highly impressive testimonials to the virtue of these views.[5] Surely this lends additional allure for both economic historians and their "dilettante" brothers to Friedman and Schwartz's venture into Clio's realm.

[2] See papers by Rostow, Meyer and Conrad, and Kuznets on "The Integration of Economic Theory and Economic History," *Journal of Economic History*, XVII (Dec. 1957), 509–53 (Kuznets' "Summary of Discussion and Postscript" is especially relevant); also Lance E. Davis, Jonathan R. T. Hughes, and Stanley Reiter, "Aspects of Quantitative Research in Economic History," *Journal of Economic History*, XX (Dec. 1960), 536–47; Douglass C. North, "Quantitative Research in American Economic History," *American Economic Review*, LIII (Mar. 1963), 128–30; and Robert W. Fogel, "Reappraisals in American Economic History—Discussion," *American Economic Review*, LIV (May 1964), 377–89.

[3] See H. Laurence Miller, Jr., "On the 'Chicago School of Economics,' " *Journal of Political Economy*, LXX (Feb. 1962), 64–69, and comments by M. Bronfenbrenner and George J. Stigler in the same issue; also G. C. Archibald, "Chamberlain *versus* Chicago," *Review of Economic Studies*, XXVIII (Oct. 1961), 2–28, and later responses by Stigler and Friedman, *ibid.*, XXX (Feb. 1963), 63–67.

[4] Friedman, "The Marshallian Demand Curve." The quoted phrases are torn out of context from Friedman's *Essays in Positive Economics*, pp. 12, 300, and 9, respectively. Friedman himself would never express views so extreme as these (compare his reply to Archibald [*Rev. Ec. St.*, XXX, pp. 65 ff.]).

[5] I refer especially to Friedman, *A Theory of the Consumption Function* (Chicago: University of Chicago Press, 1957); to Friedman and Kuznets, *Income from Independent Professional Practice* (New York: NBER, 1945); and to Friedman and Schwartz, "Money and Business Cycles," *Review of Economics and Statistics*, XLV (Feb. 1963 suppl.), 32–64. But these are just a few choice items in a long and distinguished list.

II

No brief summary can convey an accurate impression of the range and depth of Friedman and Schwartz's *History*. To be sure, the discussion is highly selective; as the authors state (p. 3): "Throughout, we trace one thread, the stock of money, and our concern with that thread explains alike which episodes and events are examined in detail and which are slighted." Nevertheless, the book reads more like a general economic history than even its authors seem to suppose. And this is as it should be; to distinguish sharply between "monetary" and "other" aspects of the history of a money economy would be artificial as well as misleading.

The book was originally conceived as a single chapter in a statistical study of monetary factors in the business cycle (Preface, p. xxi). It now covers 860 pages, comprises thirteen chapters and two appendices,[6] and appears in print in advance of the study which gave it birth.

Economic historians will probably find most to arouse their interest in the first few chapters, which cover the relatively tranquil years between 1867 and 1914. Here the authors' central theme is the untrammeled development of the economy in response to the working of natural economic forces, "avarice explaining all, always."[7] The argument is detailed, penetrating, and for the most part convincing. For sheer ingenuity in marshaling evidence, few historical narratives can match Friedman and Schwartz's discussion of "Special Problems Connected with the Greenback Period" (ch. ii, sec. 5), their analysis of the "Great Deflation" (ch. iii, sec. 1), or their account of the Panic of 1907 (ch. iv, sec. 3).

The theme of the middle portion of the *History* (chs. v through xi) is the response of the economy to the vicissitudes of international affairs and domestic politics, with special emphasis on the growing power of the Federal Reserve System as an agent of economic control. Specialists in monetary economics will find these chapters a valuable source of factual and theoretical insight into the working of financial mechanisms. Economic historians are less likely to enjoy or profit from the discussion; too much of it is concerned with technical monetary details and with lengthy accounts of the policy deliberations of the monetary authorities. Like other readers, however, they will be intrigued by Friedman and Schwartz's unconventional views on the "Great Contraction" and other episodes of the interwar period.

---

[6] Reference should also be made to the thoughtful and interesting "Director's Comment" by Albert J. Hettinger, Jr., which appears at the very end of the book (pp. 809–14).

[7] I owe this phrase to my erstwhile colleague, Meyer Burstein.

The penultimate chapter, on the post–World War II rise in the income velocity of money, seems to be more in the nature of a journal article than a contribution to monetary history, but it is of considerable interest all the same. The final chapter provides a concise but remarkably complete account of the authors' main conclusions.[8]

III

The preceding summary emphasizes the narrative rather than the analytical aspects of the *History*. Appearances to the contrary notwithstanding, the emphasis of the book is the other way around. The authors themselves do not appear to recognize the distinction; indeed, they blend analysis so effectively with narrative that one can hardly tell which of their historical judgments rest on fact and which on theoretical fancy. The difficulty lies, however, not in the authors' exposition, which is generally lucid, but rather in their failure to provide an explicit account of their methodology. My purpose in the pages that follow is to fill this gap.

The essentials of Friedman and Schwartz's analytical procedure are adumbrated in the opening paragraph of their final chapter (p. 676):

The varied character of U.S. monetary history [from 1867 to 1960] renders this century of experience particularly valuable to the student of economic change. He cannot control the experiment, but he can observe monetary experience under sufficiently disparate conditions to sort out what is common from what is adventitious and to acquire considerable confidence that what is common can be counted on to hold under still other circumstances.

I interpret this observation to say something like the following. We may view historical time-series observations as rough measures of the values assumed in various intervals of time by the variables of a general dynamic system.[9] If the values of certain variables are observed to follow some regular pattern in relation to one another, we may abstract this pattern from the data and use it as a tentative benchmark to distinguish between "equilibrium" and "disequilibrium" states of the system. The very existence of such a pattern may be taken to mean

---

[8] I omit comment on the two appendices, except to say (1) the statistical work underlying the basic tables in Appendix A and the charts and tables appearing elsewhere in the book is clearly of the highest quality (a full explanation of the estimates prepared by Friedman and Schwartz is to appear in their forthcoming study of "Trends and Cycles in the Stock of Money," another National Bureau project) and (2) the discussion of "the proximate determinants of money" in Appendix B does not add much of value to the argument in the text (most of the relevant information is already given in sec. 4 of ch. ii).

[9] Compare Friedman and Schwartz, "Money and Business Cycles," pp. 29–63.

that the economic system is basically stable.[10] Accordingly, we may assert with some confidence that departures from "equilibrium," as indicated by breaks in the pattern, will tend to be self-restoring, and we may use this stability principle as a basis for predicting the probable behavior of the economy starting from any given initial situation. Moreover, we may attribute obvious deviations from "normal" behavior to various "shocks," some of which can be identified with specific historical events. In this manner, we may assign "causal" significance to particular classes of events—"monetary," "political," "technological," etc.—and perhaps even go so far as to assess the relative importance of each as a source of economic change.

I hope this interpretation does not do serious injustice to the views actually held by Friedman and Schwartz. It portrays with reasonable accuracy a research strategy which seems to me to make some sense and with which I have considerable sympathy. And it is consistent with what I know about the methodological views of the patron saint of "positive economics," Alfred Marshall.[11] The difficulty is to put the strategy to practical use, for it is by no means clear how one is supposed to distinguish between what is "common" and what is "adventitious," between patterns that are "regular" and patterns that are not.

But here we may draw on "the methodology of positive economics." Clearly, if we are required to judge a theory not by precept but by practice, then we should judge a research strategy in the same way: that is, not by what its exponents say it can do but rather by what it enables them to accomplish. If this is our procedure, then the difficulty mentioned above may be passed over for the time being; a look at the facts may suffice to allay any doubts we have about our ability to "sort out what is common from what is adventitious."

IV

It is common knowledge that changes in money income and employment are more or less closely associated with changes in prices, financial flows, holdings of physical assets, bank deposits, etc. What is not known is the precise character of these associations, their magnitude, reliability, and causal significance. Friedman and Schwartz

[10] At least, for all practical purposes. On this, compare R. L. Basmann, "The Causal Interpretation of Non-Triangular Systems of Economic Relations," *Econometrica*, XXXI (July 1963), 442–43, 453.

[11] See Marshall, "The Present Position of Economics," in *Memorials of Alfred Marshall*, A. C. Pigou, ed. (London: Macmillan, 1925), pp. 166–69; also Friedman, "The Marshallian Demand Curve," pp. 89–92.

begin their attack on these problems by studying outwardly relevant time-series data in the hope that these will reveal patterns of association of sufficient clarity to provide a tentative foundation for further analysis.

Referring to the 93-year period from 1867 to 1960, they find that the "stock of money" (defined as currency plus commercial bank deposits) grew from less than $2 billion to more than $200 billion, while income (as measured by Kuznets' unpublished annual estimates of net national product in current prices)[12] grew from less than $6 billion to more than $200 billion (pp. 3–5 and charts 1 and 62). The income velocity of money changed substantially during the period as a whole, falling fairly steadily between 1869 and 1915 (from a value of 4.6 to a value of 2.1), oscillating around an uncertain trend from 1916 to 1946, rising to a level somewhat above that for 1915 during the years 1947–1960. Population more than quadrupled during the same period, per capita holdings of money increased more than thirtyfold, per capita income more than tenfold.

The clearest secular patterns which seem to emerge from the data involve the stock of money, on the one hand, and income and the stock of "high-powered money,"[13] on the other. All three of these magnitudes are found to display strong upward trends, money generally rising faster than high-powered money, high-powered money generally rising faster than income. The suggestion is that rates of growth of the three series have been roughly proportional to one another; but the relationship is far from exact.

Friedman and Schwartz's analysis of cyclical variations in the stock of money and in money income produces sharper results. Although the numerical value of income velocity is discovered to vary considerably from one cycle to another, velocity is found to display "a systematic and stable movement about its trend, rising during expansion and falling during contraction" (p. 682). Moreover, observed year-to-year changes in the value of velocity are "less than 10 per cent in 78 out of the 91 year-to-year changes from 1869 ... to 1960. Of the 13 larger changes, more than half came during either the Great Contraction or the two world wars, and the largest change was 17 per cent" (p. 682).

These results imply a strikingly good correlation between changes

[12] These estimates are available on request from the National Bureau of Economic Research, but are not presented in the *History*, except in charts.

[13] Defined as "the total amount of hand-to-hand currency held by the public plus vault cash plus, after 1914, deposit liabilities of the Federal Reserve System to banks" (p. 50).

in the stock of money and changes in income, comparable in important respects to the familiar time-series correlation between income and consumption.[14] Whatever view one takes of the probable causal significance of this relation, its practical importance cannot be denied. No theory of a money economy which is incapable of generating the kind of behavior required by the correlation can be taken very seriously. Conversely, any theory which is capable of generating such behavior deserves consideration, at least tentatively, as a descriptive and explanatory device. Considered from either point of view, the correlation constitutes a promising point of departure for further research.

V

Friedman and Schwartz's procedure at this stage is to ask, as it were, What is the simplest relation between the stock of money and money income that is capable of rationalizing the behavior patterns suggested by the statistical evidence? It should be emphasized that they do not concern themselves at this point with "causality" or related philosophical issues. Their question relates simply to the behavior of empirical data, not to the behavior of people or markets. How the economic system *really* works is irrelevant; what Friedman and Schwartz want to know is whether the system works *as if* its object were to ensure the maintenance of some "normal" relation between the stock of money and money income.

To cut a long story short, the answer which I interpret Friedman and Schwartz to give to their question is that, to a first approximation, the *normal* stock of money (M_n) and *normal* income (Y_n) are related by an equation of the form $M_n = KY_n^a$, where K is a constant representing the reciprocal of the "normal" income velocity of money, and a is a constant $(a > 1)$ representing the "normal" income elasticity of demand for money balances. Of course, the "normal" magnitudes M_n and Y_n are not directly observable. To connect them with corresponding *measured* magnitudes $(M$ and $Y)$, it is necessary to introduce certain "transitory" variables u_m and u_y, defined by the equations

$$M \equiv M_n + u_m$$

[14] See Friedman and David Meiselman, "The Relative Stability of Monetary Velocity and the Investment Multiplier in the United States, 1897–1958," *Stabilization Policies* (research study prepared for the Commission on Money and Credit [Englewood Cliffs, N.J.: Prentice-Hall, 1963]), pp. 165–268, especially Charts II-4 and II-6 (pp. 194 and 196). Also, Ando, Brown, Solow, and Kareken, "Lags in Fiscal and Monetary Policy," in the same volume, pp. 14–24.

and

$$Y \equiv Y_n + u_y.$$

These identities, together with the initial assumption

$$M_n = KY_n^a$$

imply that the measured stock of money and measured money income are connected by the relation

$$M = K[Y - u_y]^a + u_m.$$

Friedman and Schwartz's inquiry into monetary history is thus directed, in effect, at characterizing the general properties of the transitory magnitudes u_m and u_y, studying their interrelations, and identifying independent variations in each with specific historical events—wars, crises, international gold flows, actions by the Federal Reserve authorities, etc.

They do not couch their argument in these terms; the language and symbols that I am using are mine, not theirs, and so is the interpretation.[15] The purpose of my free translation is to suggest to the reader something that I did not begin to realize until after I started to write this review: that the conceptual framework of Friedman and Schwartz's *History* is virtually indistinguishable from that of Friedman's earlier *A Theory of the Consumption Function*. Once this analogy is grasped, the whole of Friedman and Schwartz's analytical narrative is seen to follow a purposeful pattern; what at first sight seems a slightly untidy argument is instead discovered to be a masterly mosaic of logic and facts.

But is it "history"? Most historians would probably want to reserve judgment about the non-narrative portions of the argument, on the ground that the establishment as distinct from the verification of "laws" of social development is not an essential aspect of history *qua* history. On the other hand, most economists would probably say that the entire argument is strictly history, on the ground that evidence about past human behavior, however important it may be for testing economic hypotheses, is not a necessary, sufficient, or reliable basis for formulating them.

This conflict of viewpoints raises some delicate and controversial issues. To what extent is Friedman and Schwartz's argument directed toward the establishment of causal rather than merely descriptive relations among economic phenomena? Is there any meaningful way

---

[15] For a very similar symbolic presentation, however, see Friedman and Schwartz, "Money and Business Cycles," pp. 56–58.

to distinguish between the two; that is, what objective criteria, if any, might be used to distinguish between relations that do and relations that do not have causal significance? It seems to me that these issues go to the heart of the problem with which this review is primarily concerned, which is to assess the "importance" of Friedman and Schwartz's book as a "contribution to knowledge." Accordingly, it is on these issues that I shall mainly focus in the pages that follow.

VI

As I emphasized earlier, Friedman and Schwartz do not initially concern themselves with questions of causality. However, the tenor of their argument gradually runs in that direction until it becomes the dominant note of the book. How do they accomplish this transmogrification? I shall not try to recapitulate the details of their argument, but I shall try to reproduce the main outlines.

The first step in the process is to show that the basic theoretical model is useful for summarizing the salient facts of U.S. monetary history since 1867. To be sure, the procedure used to derive the model in the first place guarantees that its fit to the original money and income series will be reasonably satisfactory; but the model works better than this remark might seem to suggest. Indeed, if one were simply confronted with the model and told to fit it to the data (using moving averages of measured money and measured income as estimates of the corresponding "normal" variables), I daresay he would be amazed at the results.[16]

The second step is to show that where the model does not perform almost perfectly (as during the two depression decades, 1870–1880 and 1930–1940, and during the post–World War II period of rising income velocity), this is attributable not to any basic inadequacy of the model but rather to exceptional variations in the transitory components of money or income, the "causes" of which can be at least tentatively identified. Thus, the imperfections of the model for describing monetary experience during the period 1870–1880 are explained in part by errors in Kuznets' estimates of net national product for this period (pp. 36–41). Similarly, the partial breakdown of the model during the period 1930–1940 is traced to the ineptitude of the Federal Reserve authorities in failing to take adequate measures to

---

[16] But perhaps not. On this, see Ames and Reiter's fascinating sampling experiment involving time series drawn at random from *Historical Statistics of the U.S.*, "Distributions of Correlation Coefficients in Economic Time Series," *Journal of the American Statistical Association*, LVI (Sept. 1961), 637–56.

stem the tide of the Great Contraction (pp. 693–94). And the failure of the model to account for the rise in income velocity after 1946 is attributed (after lengthy evaluation of other possible explanations, such as rising interest rates, the growth of financial intermediaries, etc.) to "changing patterns of expectations about economic stability" (p. 673).

The third and final step is to conduct some "crucial" thought experiments with historical data, the argument being that "the examination of a wide range of qualitative evidence . . . provides a basis for discriminating between [alternative] possible explanations of observed statistical covariation [so that one can] go beyond the numbers alone and, at least on some occasions, discern the antecedent circumstances whence arose the particular movements that become so anonymous when we feed the statistics into the computer" (p. 686). This technique is applied to a number of cases (including the Gold Inflation of 1897–1914, the monetary expansions accompanying World Wars I and II, the resumption and silver episodes, and the recessions of 1920, 1931, and 1937). In every instance, it is concluded that "the major channel of influence is from money to business" (p. 694), although "there have clearly also been influences running the other way" (p. 695).

Whether or not one considers the evidence and arguments introduced at each of these steps to be completely persuasive (and I do not), he can hardly fail to be jolted by their cumulative impact (as I was). True, the entire demonstration rests in the final analysis on the assumption that the original theoretical model is basically valid, which is the point at issue. True, it is one thing to use a model to summarize facts, another to use it as a basis for positive judgments about "what might have been" or "what is to be." True, Friedman and Schwartz nowhere provide an explicit statement of the manner in which changes in the stock of money are linked with changes in income.[17] Hence, Friedman and Schwartz cannot be said to have explained the nature of the causal mechanism whose existence seems to be implied by their historical judgments. Nevertheless, they make a case that is not easy to answer, and one which strongly supports the view to which they effectually commit themselves in their final chapter; that is, that *income and prices will typically be found "dancing to the tune called by independently originating monetary changes"* (p. 686, my italics).[18]

[17] An account of sorts is given in Friedman and Schwartz, "Money and Business Cycles," and criticized in the same issue by Hyman P. Minsky and Arthur Okun (pp. 68–72, 74).

[18] See also Friedman and Schwartz, "Money and Business Cycles"; Milton Friedman, "The Quantity Theory of Money: A Restatement," *Studies in the Quantity Theory of Money* (ed. Milton Friedman; Chicago: University of Chicago Press, 1956), pp. 3–21; Friedman and Meiselman, "Relative Stability," pp. 166–70.

Such a conclusion—particularly when it is backed up by over six hundred pages of detailed evidence—is bound to be a bit upsetting to those whose vision of the working of the economic system is informed by neo-Walrasian theoretical conceptions, which is to say, to all but a small handful of contemporary economists.[19] For it is an essential feature both of post-Keynesian income analysis and of contemporary monetary theory that *money does not matter much except in the long run.* More specifically, neo-Walrasians typically argue[20] that, in a closed economy, the absolute levels of money prices and aggregate money income depend *ultimately* on the quantity of *legal tender means of payment* as determined by the fiscal and monetary operations of government; but that the *impact* effects of autonomous changes in the stock of legal-tender money cannot be disentangled from other and equally important sources of economic disturbance—technological, psychological, etc.—not, at least, by visual inspection of historical time-series data and casual study of related events.[21] More pointedly, legal-tender money—which does not include either demand or time deposits—is merely one of many generally acceptable means of payment. The great bulk of objects which people regard as "money" at any given point in time[22] consists of debt instruments, the amounts of which are determined in the short run not by government authorities but by the general public. Facts and arguments to the contrary notwithstanding, therefore, it is absurd to assign a prominent role in

[19] The term "neo-Walrasian" refers to the general point of view underlying such modern classics as Hicks' *Value and Capital* and Samuelson's *Foundations of Economic Analysis.* The distinctive characteristic of this point of view as contrasted with that of Marshall, the neoclassicals, and Friedman and Schwartz, is that market demand and supply relations are explicitly defined in terms of underlying microeconomic decision processes. This aspect of the neo-Walrasian literature stands out with particular clarity in recent contributions to the general equilibrium theory of money. See, for example, Don Patinkin, *Money, Interest, and Prices* (Evanston: Row, Peterson, 1956); G. C. Archibald and R. G. Lipsey, "Monetary and Value Theory: A Critique of Lange and Patinkin," *Review of Economic Studies,* XXVI (Oct. 1958), 1–22.

[20] See M. L. Burstein, *Money* (Cambridge: Schenkman Publishing Co., 1963), pp. 749 ff.; P. A. Samuelson, "Reflections on Central Banking," *National Banking Review,* I (Sept. 1963), 15–28.

[21] For a clear statement of representative views, see H. G. Johnson, "Monetary Theory and Policy," *American Economic Review,* LII (June 1962), 335–84; also, R. G. Lipsey and F. P. R. Brechling, "Trade Credit and Monetary Policy," *Economic Journal,* LXXIII (Dec. 1963), 618–41.

[22] The time qualification is important; for example, in times of prosperity practically any asset may be regarded as "money," whereas in times of "panic" even demand deposits may sell at a discount (compare *History,* p. 161). What constitutes "legal tender" is also a problem: greenbacks were " 'lawful money' and legal tender for all debts, public and private, except customs duties and interest on the public debt, both of which were to be payable in coin," to quote Alonzo Barton Hepburn, *A History of Currency in the United States* (New York: Macmillan Co., 1915), p. 185.

cyclical movements to variations in the stock of legal-tender money, and it is even more absurd to treat the total "stock of money," however one might define it, as an independent variable. So the issue is joined.

The difference between Friedman and Schwartz and those whom I have called neo-Walrasians may at first sight appear to turn on questions of fact. If the neo-Walrasians are right (it may be said), they should be able to produce a better explanation of historical experience than that offered by Friedman and Schwartz. If they cannot do this, they should give up the game. But who is to decide if one model is "better" than another? And what does "better" mean if the purposes of alternative models are significantly different—for example, if one model is intended roughly to summarize experience covering nearly a century, and the other is intended to predict with a high degree of accuracy what will happen during a period of a few weeks or months if a certain policy action is taken now? I think there can be no doubt about the answer: *there are no objective standards for evaluating the descriptive validity of theoretical hypotheses; standards that serve for one purpose or period may not do at all for others.* This is quite sufficient to show that the real point at issue cannot be settled by appealing to "facts."

The question whether there exist objective criteria for distinguishing between relations that are "causal" and relations that are "merely descriptive" remains to be decided. This is obviously a matter for philosophers of science rather than for economists. However, since philosophers have now been debating the issue for more than two millennia, we may sensibly infer that "facts" will never resolve it. To date, the only thing on which all philosophers seem agreed is that most scientists have a strong psychological propensity to regard all correlations that are not known to be spurious as manifestations of some underlying causal process. Whether or not this propensity has a solid foundation in fact is beside the point; what is important is that the propensity itself drives scientists to think and act in certain interesting ways.[23]

VII

Thus we come at last to methodological differences as the ultimate basis for the revulsion of neo-Walrasians from the "monetomania" of Friedman and Schwartz. These differences are, I think, greater in practice than they appear to be in principle. No judicious writer on

[23] For an elaborate discussion of "causality" and its various behavior manifestations, see Ernest Nagel, *The Structure of Science* (New York: Harcourt, Brace and World, 1961), ch. x.

methodology ever takes a completely unqualified stand on any basic issue, knowing full well that some arcanum of science will be dredged up by opponents and used to show him wrong. Real methodological differences are aired in private, usually by groups of people who have fault to find with approaches used by other groups. I propose to be injudicious: to say bluntly and without qualification some things about the methodology of Friedman and Schwartz and that of the neo-Walrasians that I would normally not commit to print.

Friedman and Schwartz, like all other economists, start with certain vague notions about the working of a money economy: banks and businesses act "as if" they want to make money; households act "as if" they want to eat and work; markets act "as if" their object is to arrive at prices that equate demands with supplies. They then proceed *immediately* to give these notions definite form by shaping them in the light of empirical knowledge. There is no sharp distinction in their world between "theory" and "fact"; theory is simply an organized description of consilient inductions drawn from related sets of empirical observations. Nor is there any question of using facts to "illustrate" rather than "test" hypotheses, for this would be to illustrate facts with more facts. Whether or not Friedman and Schwartz regard personal intuitions as "facts" is uncertain; but my hunch is that they do not. If they did, they would have to pay at least some attention to the intuitive plausibility (that is, "realism") of their assumptions, and this would violate a fundamental tenet of the "methodology of positive economics."[24]

The neo-Walrasians (like Friedman and Schwartz) start with certain vague notions about the working of the economic system. However, these notions are shaped initially not in the light of concrete experience but rather with reference to *stylized facts* (that is, intuition and common sense). There is no pretense of "descriptive realism" in this procedure, but there is a very real concern with the intuitive plausibility of basic assumptions. Personal reflections about one's own objective responses to external stimuli are, after all, as real and reliable as are any observations of external events.[25]

The *crucial* test of the empirical validity of a model, for the neo-

[24] See Friedman, "The Methodology of Positive Economics," *Essays*, pp. 16–23; and more significantly, *Consumption Function*, p. 231. I should remark explicitly that my interpretation of Friedman and Schwartz's methodological position is based not so much on what they say, here or elsewhere, jointly or singly, as on what they do—and similarly for the neo-Walrasians.

[25] This is an important reason for attaching significance to so-called scientific paradoxes; see my "Permanent Income and Transitory Balances," *Oxford Economic Papers*, XV (July 1963), 177 ff.

Walrasians just as for Friedman and Schwartz, is the conformity of its predictions with experience.[26] But one of the major objectives of theorizing is to avoid having to perform needless experiments. Why put to factual test a model that is logically inconsistent or trivial, analytically unmanageable, intuitively absurd, or devoid of empirical implications even under ideal conditions? Abstractness, elegance, and generality are *not* irrelevant criteria for evaluating the potential empirical fruitfulness of a theoretical model; all have an immediate bearing on one or more of the preliminary tests listed above.

As for the familiar indictment that facts are typically used not to test but merely to illustrate preconceived hypotheses, the neo-Walrasians must certainly plead "guilty"—but only to the specification of being cautious, not to the specification of producing barren abstractions. No doubt most neo-Walrasian models are excessively general (whatever that may mean). The proper way to specialize models is gradually to modify them by reference to results obtained by refined statistical analysis of empirical data *and by reference to other relevant critical procedures.*[27] Economics is an unsettled research science, not a systemized body of established truths. It is still relatively youthful, its subject matter is complex, and its procedure is largely nonexperimental. Progress in shaping economic hypotheses to bring them to bear on concrete problems is bound to be uncertain and slow. Accordingly, neo-Walrasians may be justly charged with being excessively patient—"like highly trained athletes who never run a race,"[28] but men who are passionately "anxious to do good," who have a "burning interest in pressing issues of public policy, ... who desire to learn how the economic system really works in order that that knowledge may be used,"[29] are perhaps better employed in politics than in basic scientific research.

These remarks are not intended to settle anything; only to clarify some issues and clear some air. I have so far stressed points of apparent disagreement between the neo-Walrasians and Friedman and

[26] I should emphasize once more the inherent ambiguity of the "prediction" criterion (see last paragraph of preceding section). For a concise but exceptionally lucid discussion of the problems involved, see H. Theil, *Economic Forecasts and Policy* (Amsterdam: North-Holland Publishing Company, 1958), pp. 204–7.

[27] On this, see Karl R. Popper, *Conjectures and Refutations* (London: Routledge and Kegan Paul, 1963), ch. i; also K. Klappholz and J. Agassi, "Methodological Prescriptions in Economics," *Economica*, N. S. XXVI (Feb. 1959), pp. 60–74.

[28] Samuelson, *Foundations of Economic Analysis* (Cambridge: Harvard University Press, 1947), p. 4.

[29] Friedman, "Lange on Price Flexibility and Employment: A Methodological Criticism," *Essays*, p. 300.

Schwartz. I should now like to emphasize two points of fundamental importance on which there is clearly complete accord: first, *the essential art of the empirical scientist is that of inventing conjectures*; second, *this art is bound by no fixed rules*. There are countless "patterns of plausible inference," all potentially fruitful, none capable of *proving* anything.[30] Methodological disputes are generally idle because they are concerned with means rather than ends; the scientific worth of a conjecture does not depend on its methodological pedigree. Methodological differences are nevertheless worthwhile, because diversities of intellectual perspective are a mainstay of vigorous scientific criticism. Whether Friedman and Schwartz are right or wrong, their views, as expressed in the *History* and elsewhere, will invite attention and promote much worthwhile research. Failing the will or the ability to produce equally provocative works, neo-Walrasians will have to take such comfort as they can from the maxim that "the path to useful knowledge is paved with false conjectures."

VIII

As a general rule, every historical narrative may be expected to display one or more instances of each of Wicksell's "faults of dilettantism"; and the longer and more elaborate the narrative, the easier it is likely to be for a critic to spot them. Friedman and Schwartz's *History* is no exception to the rule, but neither is it an easy mark; the range is too great and the target too small for even a diligent critic to accumulate anything but a pitiful score. Nuances aside, I have no fundamental quarrel with any of Friedman and Schwartz's substantive conclusions. My only doubts concern the evidential force and practical significance of some of their historical judgments. The comments that follow are therefore confined to certain general aspects of Friedman and Schwartz's argument that have influenced my assessment of their work.

Research strategies may be considered effective in roughly the same measure as they help us formulate and solve worthwhile problems. The strategy implicit in "the methodology of positive economics" strikes me as being especially effective for uncovering important empirical regularities, directing attention to useful and intellectually challenging areas of research, and posing problems in a clear and forceful manner. It is not irrelevant in this connection to mention that the consumption function, the accelerator relation, and the "Phillips Curve," were all

[30] For details, see G. Polya, *Patterns of Plausible Inference* (Princeton: Princeton University Press, 1954).

products of research procedures similar to that espoused by Friedman and Schwartz. By contrast, I cannot recall offhand a single instance in which neo-Walrasian research procedures have yielded *empirical* results of fundamental novelty or importance. Considered from this point of view, the neo-Walrasian approach must probably be adjudged relatively barren.

Of course, procedures that are efficient for formulating problems may or may not be efficient for solving them. As concerns the latter criterion, however, I do not myself see any objective grounds for preferring the strategy of the neo-Walrasians to that of Friedman and Schwartz. It is perhaps more natural to associate modern techniques of econometric research with neo-Walrasian economics; and there can be no doubt about the value of these techniques for evaluating the quantitative significance of regularities discovered by other means. But econometric analysis is hardly a monopoly of the neo-Walrasians.[31]

In the final analysis, the real strengths and weaknesses of the *History* depend not on its authors' research strategy but rather on their inferential tactics. Since my outlook on economics is basically that of a neo-Walrasian (though not, I think, to the point of fanaticism), I should be the last to claim that my appraisal of this aspect of Friedman and Schwartz's book is devoid of bias. Readers may therefore place more than usual credence in my acknowledgment that Friedman and Schwartz's tactical performance is superbly ingenious and effective. This theme merits further elaboration.

Those who view the economic system through neo-Walrasian spectacles will be quick to find fault with such assertions in the *History* as:

... The stock of money shows larger fluctuations after 1914 than before 1914 and this is true even if the large wartime increases in the stock of money are excluded. The blind, undesigned, and quasi-automatic working of the gold standard turned out to produce a greater measure of predictability and regularity—perhaps because its discipline was impersonal and inescapable—than did deliberate and conscious control exercised within institutional arrangements intended to promote monetary stability (pp. 9–10);

or:

The monetary collapse [following 1929] was not the inescapable consequence of other forces, but rather a largely independent factor which exerted a powerful influence on the course of events.... Prevention or moderation of the decline in the stock of money, let alone the substitution of monetary expansion, would have reduced the contraction's severity and almost as certainly its duration. The contraction might still have been relatively severe. But it is hardly conceivable that money income could have declined by over

---

[31] However, see Friedman, "Methodology," n. 11, pp. 12–13. For some interesting observations on a related topic, see Polya, *Plausible Inference*, pp. 40–41.

one-half and prices by over one-third in the course of four years if there had been no decline in the stock of money (pp. 300–1);

or, more generally:

While the influence running from money to economic activity has been predominant, there have clearly also been influences running the other way, particularly during the shorter-run movements associated with the business cycle.... Changes in the money stock are therefore a consequence as well as an independent source of change in money income and prices, though, once they occur, they produce in their turn still further effects on income and prices. Mutual interaction, but with money rather clearly the senior partner in longer-run movements and in major cyclical movements, and more nearly an equal partner with money income and prices in shorter-run and milder movements—this is the generalization suggested by our evidence (p. 695).

But how does one respond to propositions of this character?

Clearly not by referring to bodies of evidence other than those considered by Friedman and Schwartz, for they have already covered this flank in a prefatory acknowledgment:

A full-scale economic and political history would be required to record at all comprehensively the role of money in the United States in the past century. Needless to say, we have not been so ambitious. Rather, we have kept in the forefront the initial aim: to provide a prologue and background for a [later] statistical analysis of the secular and cyclical behavior of money in the United States, and to exclude any material not relevant to that purpose (p. xxii).

Might one not then respond that to express firm judgments on the basis of such a limited range of evidence is to draw "over-hasty" conclusions? Again the answer must be qualified: first, because most of Friedman and Schwartz's judgments are advanced as "tentative hypotheses"; second, because a glance at the materials actually used to document major analytical themes in the *History* suffices to show that Friedman and Schwartz have spoken disingenuously about "not being so ambitious." Any young historian who managed to display a comparable "lack of ambition" could be certain of immediate professional recognition and renown upon his first venture into print!

Thus one is driven finally to resort to analytical dialectics—to oppose Friedman and Schwartz's judgments by saying that they picture the economic system as "a ship of income afloat on a sea of money." (The simile is not inapt; ocean waves not only influence but are influenced by the motions of a ship, but the ocean is clearly the "senior partner" in long and violent storms.) One can then pour scorn on this view of the world as presupposing that trading is perfectly synchronized in all markets of the economy at every instant of time and that all markets "clear" automatically even over relatively short time intervals. But alas, except that Friedman and Schwartz display a moderate antipathy to

Keynesian economics (see pp. 533–34, 626–27) and nowhere worry seriously about possible direct effects of current market transactions on current demand and supply conditions, this line of argument cannot be sustained either—except by gross prejudice. The *shading* of the argument is in the direction claimed, but the *substance* is not.

I need go no further. My conclusion is that Friedman and Schwartz's conjectures deserve to be taken very seriously indeed. Their book does not pretend to be a definitive account of the monetary experience of the United States (though in fact it comes close to being just that). However, their historical judgments about this history are based on painstaking examination of a fantastically large body of evidence and on thorough, honest, and closely reasoned analysis of its implications. My guess is that subsequent researches, provoked by Friedman and Schwartz's pronouncements, will overturn some of their bolder judgments,[32] but that is another story.

IX

My overall reaction to Friedman and Schwartz's *History* is mixed. Viewed as an intellectual accomplishment, the book has qualities of greatness. The argument is interesting, informative, intricate, and subtle; even a casual reader will recognize the extraordinary keenness of the minds which produced it. Still, the thread of money has strands which even Friedman and Schwartz have no hope of unraveling.

Nor is the volume free of scholarly blemishes. The omission of a detailed bibliography is regrettable, particularly since the authors also fail even to cite such standard works as Hepburn's *History of Currency*, Young's *Analysis of Bank Statistics*, and Harris' *Twenty Years of Federal Reserve Policy*. The book is also marred by a certain flavor of provincialism—cultural and historical as well as technical; this is reflected

---

[32] For example, a recent analysis by George Horwich casts serious doubt on the correctness of Friedman and Schwartz's explanation of the persistence of "excess reserves" during the period 1933–1939 (*History*, pp. 534 ff.); also on their interpretation of the 1937 contraction (*ibid.*, pp. 543–45). See George Horwich, "Effective Reserves, Credit, and Causality in the Banking System of the Thirties," in *Banking and Monetary Studies*, D. Carson, ed. (Homewood, Ill.: D. Irwin, 1963).

In a more general vein, Ando and Modigliani have shown (in a forthcoming paper) that changes in autonomous expenditure, suitably defined, are as closely correlated with changes in income and consumption as are changes in the stock of money, thus casting doubt on the causal significance of the money–income relation on which Friedman and Schwartz place so much emphasis. For background on this, see Friedman and Meiselman, "Monetary Velocity," and Franco Modigliani, "The Monetary Mechanism and Its Interaction with Real Phenomena," *Review of Economics and Statistics*, XLV (Feb. 1963 suppl.), 79–107 (esp. pp. 102 ff.).

in the absence from the "Author Index" of such names as Keynes, Robertson, Cassel, Robbins, Wicksell, Giffen, Harrod, and Sayers; a notable dearth of references to specialist works in economic history; and a general absence of what Collingwood would call "historical imagination."[33]

But the chief faults of the book (from the point of view of a reader) are opacity and lack of direction. These might have been avoided had the authors included an account of the conceptual framework of their argument. The *History* opens with an interesting quotation from Marshall, part of which is pertinent here: ". . . the most reckless and treacherous of all theorists is he who professes to let facts and figures speak for themselves, who keeps in the background the part he has played, perhaps unconsciously, in selecting and grouping them, and in suggesting the argument *post hoc ergo propter hoc*" (*Memorials*, p. 168). Perhaps the most puzzling question posed by the book is: Why did Friedman and Schwartz fail to heed Marshall's implied advice?

The transcendent virtue of the *History* is its unerring vision in searching out important problems and its clear delineation of areas needing further research. The book offers an almost inexhaustible supply of worthwhile conjectures. I have no doubt that it, along with a forthcoming volume on *Trends and Cycles in Economic Activity*, will be the focus of a major share of scholarly research on money and income during the coming decade. For this, if for no other reason, the book must be counted a monumental contribution to positive economics.

[33] R. G. Collingwood, *The Idea of History* (New York: Oxford University Press, 1956), pp. 231 ff.

PART II

THE CHARACTER AND CONSEQUENCES OF MONEY

5

A RECONSIDERATION OF THE
MICROFOUNDATIONS OF MONETARY THEORY

Modern attempts to erect a general theory of money and prices on Walrasian foundations[1] have produced a model of economic phenomena that is suspiciously reminiscent of the Classical theory of a barter economy.[2] My purpose in this paper is to show that the conception of a money economy implicit in these constructions is empirically and analytically vacuous, and to propose an alternative microfoundation for the pure theory of a money economy.

I

For simplicity of exposition, I shall address my critique of the general equilibrium theory of money and prices to the classic statement presented in Don Patinkin's *Money, Interest, and Prices*. Following Patinkin, suppose that we have to deal with an economy in which trading is rigidly synchronized within each of a series of discrete market periods. At the outset of every period, each transactor receives "like manna from heaven" a collection of goods that may be consumed directly,[3]

I am indebted to an embarrassingly large number of colleagues and students in both the U.S. and Great Britain for helpful comments on and criticism of earlier versions of this paper, the essential ideas of which were worked out and presented at various seminars in 1965–66 while I was Keynes Visiting Professor of Economics at the University of Essex. I particularly wish to acknowledge fruitful exchanges with my intellectual *alter ego* Meyer Burstein and with Axel Leijonhufvud, R. G. Lipsey, G. C. Archibald, W. M. Gorman, Sir John Hicks, John Williamson, Cliff Lloyd, Mitchell Harwitz, Peter Frevert, Carl Christ, Franco Modigliani, M. I. Nadiri, M. Bruce Johnson, Robert Coen, Alan Walters, Jerome Rothenberg, Robert Eisner, J. R. Harris, R. P. Armstrong, Frank Brechling, and Jurg Niehans.

[1] I refer specifically to O. Lange, *Price Flexibility and Employment* and Don Patinkin, *Money, Interest, and Prices*; but my comment applies also to certain portions of Hicks' *Value and Capital* and Samuelson's *Foundations*.

[2] Cf. Hicks, "A Rehabilitation of 'Classical' Economics?" *Econ. Jour.*, June 1957, 67, p. 278; also papers by Hahn, Negishi, and Clower in *The Theory of Interest Rates* (eds. Hahn and Brechling), New York, 1965.

[3] Manna commodities may be considered to include all goods and services supplies of which are decision parameters rather than decision variables in the current period.

or traded for a preferred collection of goods or for money at rates of exchange established by an independent market authority in accordance with prevailing conditions of market excess demand.

By hypothesis, market excess demands are defined in terms of individual demand functions for goods and money obtained as solutions to the decision problem:

Maximize $\qquad U_j(d_{1j}, \ldots, d_{nj}, M_j/P)$ $\qquad\qquad$ (1)

Subject to

$$\sum_{i=1}^{i=n} p_i(d_{ij} - s_{ij}) + M_j - \underline{M}_j = 0,$$ $\qquad$ (2)

where U_j satisfies familiar continuity and curvature conditions, s_{ij} and d_{ij} represent initial and desired quantitites of goods, $\underline{M}_j$ and M_j represent initial and desired quantities of fiat money, and P is a fixed-weight index of the money prices $p_1, \ldots, p_n$. The empirical content of the theory thus derives ultimately from behavior restrictions implicit in (1) and (2). As it happens, the implications of the continuity and curvature conditions imposed on the utility functions (1) are exhausted in certain analytically subtle but empirically trivial restrictions involving the existence of demand functions and the continuity of their partial derivatives. The factual content of the theory depends very largely, therefore, on restrictions implicit in the budget equations (2). Accordingly, the main question that we have to answer in order to appraise the empirical significance of contemporary monetary theory is: "Do the budget equations (2) constitute an appropriate definition of choice alternatives in a money economy?"

That the appropriateness of the choice alternatives defined by (2) is open to serious question may be seen most easily by conducting a few simple conceptual experiments. First, consider an economy in which all transactors but one have a violent aversion to holding money balances. Starting from any initial distribution of money balances, market trading over one or more periods will ultimately yield a situation in which the entire stock of money is held by a single individual. Changes in initial endowments of goods or in the stock of money will generate precisely the same qualitative effects in this model as would occur in a system where all transactors were willing to hold money balances in full equilibrium; hence the model differs in no essential respect from models discussed by Patinkin and other writers. But our model is so defined that, in equilibrium, money is not used in any exchange transaction. More pointedly, the fact that $\underline{M}_j = 0$ for all but one value of j in no way prevents any transactor from exerting an influence on market excess demands for goods. For the goods variables s_{ij} enter the budget equations (2) in precisely the same manner as the money variables $\underline{M}_j$, which is to say that *goods are indistinguishable from money as sources of effective demand.*

Next consider a general Patinkin model in which all money prices except that of labor services are free to vary. Suppose that the economy, starting from a state of full equilibrium, experiences a reduction in its stock of fiat money (the result, let us say, of a disastrous fire). The price level of goods other than labor will decline; hence, real wages will rise and the demand for labor will fall. When equilibrium is eventually reestablished, therefore, labor will be in excess supply. But the excess demand for all goods but labor will be zero. By Walras' Law, therefore, the money value of unsold labor will be positive and equal to the excess demand for money balances. If in this situation the quantity of labor offered for sale by any transactor increases, the immediate effect on demand for other goods will be the same as if the transactor had experienced an increase in his stock of money. An autonomous increase in unemployment will thus generate a rise in the price level of other goods, a decline in the real wage rate, and so an increase in employment and output! It can be shown, indeed, that an increase in unsold stocks of any commodity the price of which is fixed will, in a Patinkinesque world, generate an increase in the general price level and so, indirectly, a rise in sales of the good whose price is fixed.[4] Again, therefore, we arrive at a conclusion that is offensive to our intuitive conception of the working of a money economy, a conclusion that indicates that money plays no distinctive role in economic activity.

The same result may be reached more directly by noticing that the budget equations (2) admit as feasible trades every possible combination of commodities traded in the economy; i.e., any commodity, whether a good or money, can be offered directly in trade for every other commodity. But an economy that admits of this possibility clearly constitutes what any Classical economist would regard as a barter rather than a money economy.[5] The fact that fiat money is included among the set of tradeable commodities is utterly irrelevant; the role of money in economic activity is analytically indistinguishable from that of any other commodity.

---

[4] All of these conclusions are, of course, predicated on the assumption that the economic system is stable; i.e., that prices adjust so that markets for all commodities whose prices are permitted to vary ultimately clear.

[5] Cf. J. S. Mill, *Principles*, Book III, Chapter VII ("Of Money").

II

The answer to our query about the appropriateness of the budget constraints of established theory as a description of choice alternatives in a money economy is negative; what presently passes for a theory of a money economy is in truth descriptive of a barter economy. I turn now to the task of reformulating accepted theory to reflect relevant restrictions on transactor behavior in a world where "money matters."

The natural point of departure for a theory of monetary phenomena is a precise distinction between money and nonmoney commodities. In this connection it is important to observe that such a distinction is possible only if we assign a special role to certain commodities as means of payment. For any commodity may serve as a unit of account and standard of deferred payment, and every asset is, by its very nature, a potential store of value. If money is to be distinguished by the functions it performs, therefore, it is to the medium of exchange function that we must address our attention. The only difficulty is to express analytically what is meant when we assert that a certain commodity serves as a medium of exchange.

To resolve this difficulty, we proceed by associating with any set of commodities $C = |C_1, \ldots, C_n|$ an *exchange relation, E,* defined as a subset of the Cartesian product $C \times C$ of the commodity set C; i.e., a set of ordered pairs of commodity elements (C_i, C_j). We then say that a trade involving two commodities C_i and C_j is *feasible* if and only if the pair (C_i, C_j) is an element of the exchange relation, and we write $C_i E C_j$ (read, "Commodity i can be traded directly for commodity j") to indicate that this condition is met.

The exchange relation is necessarily nonempty and reflexive, for, since any commodity available for trade can be held by the individual who possesses it, the condition $C_i E C_i$ is satisfied vacuously for all possible values of i. Moreover, the exchange relation is symmetric; for if $C_i E C_j$, then by the nature of trade it must also be true that $C_j E C_i$.[6] In general, however, the exchange relation need not be transitive; that is to say, $C_i E C_j$, and $C_j E C_k$ may or may not entail $C_i E C_k$. Transitivity of the exchange relation of an economy is, in fact, characteristic of just one class of economies, namely, barter economies. This follows directly from the definition of a barter economy as one in which any commodity may be offered directly in trade for every commodity; i.e., an economy for which $C_i E C_j$ is true for all values of i and j.

---

[6] Cf. the contrary but nonsensical opening statement of Patinkin's *Money, Interest, and Prices*: "Money buys goods, and goods do not buy money."

	C_1	C_2
C_1	x	x
C_2	x	x

Barter Economy

(a)

	C_1	C_2	C_3
C_1	x	x	x
C_2	x	x	0
C_3	x	0	x

Pure Money Economy

(b)

	C_1	C_2	C_3	C_4
C_1	x	x	x	x
C_2	x	x	0	0
C_3	x	0	x	x
C_4	x	0	x	x

Nonpure Money Economy

(c)

Figure 1. Alternative exchange relations

Now define as a *money commodity* any element C_i of C for which $C_i E C_j$ is true for all values of j; i.e., any commodity that can be traded directly for all other commodities. It then follows that *a barter economy is one in which all commodities are money commodities.* This characterization of a barter economy may seem paradoxical at first sight; but if one ponders the matter it becomes clear that the peculiar feature of a money as contrasted with a barter economy is precisely that *some* commodities in a money economy *cannot* be traded directly for all other commodities; i.e., some exchanges necessarily involve inter-mediate monetary transactions. More precisely, we now define a money economy as a system involving at least one money commodity but a nontransitive exchange relation. We note in passing that the simplest money economy must contain at least three commodities as illustrated in Figure 1b (x indicates that $C_i E C_j$; O that $C_i \not{E} C_j$). For if it contains fewer than three, then as indicated in Figure 1a, the reflexivity and symmetry of the exchange relation implies that all elements of $C \times C$ are included in E. It follows—in keeping with common sense—that every two-commodity economy is a barter economy. Similarly, the simplest money economy that admits simultaneously of certain forms of barter (i.e., direct trading of certain commodities none of which are money commodities) must contain at least four commodities, as illustrated in Figure 1c. In general, the exchange relation of a money economy may contain numerous barter subsets (trade credit, blocked currencies, credit cards, demand deposits, etc.). Such *nonpure money economies* (as I shall call them) seriously complicate the task of defining relevant choice alternatives for transactors. Accordingly, I shall restrict attention in the argument that follows to *pure money economies* in which one and only one commodity can be traded directly for any other commodity.

So much for the distinction between money and other commodities and for the characterization of money as contrasted with barter economies. A commodity is regarded as money for our purposes if and only if it can be traded directly for all other commodities in the economy. Correspondingly, a money economy is one in which not all commodities are money. It should perhaps be observed that the feasibility of particular trades is tacitly assumed to be determined by institutional and environmental rather than economic considerations. That is to say, the exchange relation of an economy either does or does not assign a special role to certain commodities as money. The distinction between money and other commodities is thus a matter not of degree but of kind. One might express this thought more elliptically by saying that money is traded in all markets in a money economy, or, alternatively, by saying that transaction costs are infinite for any market exchange that does not involve the offer of money as a means of payment.

III

Having enunciated sharp definitions of relevant primitive terms, it is now a straightforward matter to characterize the choice alternatives open to transactors in a pure money economy. We begin by recalling that the peculiar feature of a money economy is that some commodities (in the present context, all but one) are denied a role as potential or actual means of payment. To state the same idea as an aphorism: *Money buys goods and goods buy money; but goods do not buy goods.* This restriction is—or ought to be—the central theme of the theory of a money economy. The task of reformulating microeconomic analysis to accommodate those aspects of experience that are commonly supposed to distinguish a money from a barter economy consists, indeed, of little more than an elaboration of the implications of this one restriction.

Our aphorism automatically rules out the standard budget constraints of neo-Walrasian equilibrium analysis as accurate descriptions of planning alternatives open to transactors in a money economy. For, as remarked earlier, the familiar budget constraint effectively admits as feasible trades all pairwise combinations of commodities that are traded in the economy. In sharp contrast, choice alternatives in a money economy must be so defined as to satisfy the requirement that money be offered or demanded as one of the commodities entering into every trade. Analytically, what this entails is a clear separation between goods demanded for purchase (offers to sell money) and goods offered for sale (offers to buy money). This condition may be met most easily by dichotomizing the budget constraint into two branches, the first representing a constraint on money expenditure, the second representing a constraint on money income. Symbolically, we have

$$\sum_{i=1}^{i=n} P_i \, x_{ij} + M_j - \underline{M}_j = 0, \quad x_{ij} \equiv d_{ij} - s_{ij}, \quad x_{ij} \geq 0 \tag{3}$$

as the *expenditure constraint*, and

$$\sum_{i=1}^{i=n} P_i \, X_{ij} + m_j = 0, \quad x_{ij} < 0 \tag{4}$$

as the *income constraint* where m_j represents desired "intra-period" receipts of money income and all other symbols are defined precisely as before.

The expenditure constraint asserts that all (net) purchase offers must be backed by a readiness to supply money in exchange. Note that the expenditure constraint cannot be satisfied for nonnegative values of all x_{ij} unless $M_j - \underline{M}_j$ is non-positive (i.e., $0 \leq M_j \leq \underline{M}_j$). Thus M corresponds to what is commonly referred to as demand for pre-cautionary money balances; i.e., total initial cash balances less pro-spective (gross) depletions of cash balances for currently scheduled purchases of goods. It follows that the *total value of goods demanded cannot in any circumstances exceed the amount of money held by the transactor at the outset of the period*. Our definition of choice alternatives thereby captures the essential meaning of the traditional (but curiously non-modern) contention that demand in a money economy is effective only if it involves a combination of desire with money purchasing power.

The income constraint asserts that all (net) sale offers involve a demand for just one other commodity, namely money, in exchange. Thus m_j corresponds to what is commonly referred to as demand for transactions balances (to replace cash currently scheduled for dis-bursement from initial holdings of money balances).[7] For convenient reference, I shall refer henceforth to m_j as the income demand for money, to M as the reservation demand for money. Such a separation of income and reservation demands has no place in accepted equilib-rium models, for these models invariably contain a budget constraint that permits but does not require that offers to purchase goods be backed by willingness to give, and that offers to sell goods be accom-panied by willingness to receive units of money in exchange. The

---

[7] The income constraint cannot be satisfied for nonpositive values of x_{ij} unless $m_j > 0$; like the variable M_j, therefore, m_j is, in general, positive.

omission of these restrictions from contemporary monetary theory is a natural consequence of the tacit presupposition, appropriate in a world of tâtonnement or recontract, that money is just one of many commodities that may be bartered directly for other commodities.

Given the budget restraints (3) and (4), we may write the utililty function of a typical transactor as

$$U_j(d_{1j}, \ldots, d_{nj}, M_j/P, m_j/P) \qquad (5)$$

and proceed as usual to define individual demand functions for goods, reservations balances, and money income as solutions to the problem of maximizing (5) subject to the expenditure and income constraints (3) and (4). The inequality conditions that determine whether a given net demand x_{ij} enters the expenditure or the income constraint preclude us from stating precise conditions that will guarantee the existence of the required solutions. Supposing that the decision problem has a solution, however, we arrive at individual demand and excess demand functions that differ in crucial respects from those of established theory.

As in established theory, so in our model the demand functions for goods and for real money income and real reservation balances are homogeneous of degree zero in money prices and initial money balances. In contrast with established theory, however, substitution effects of changes in price are asymmetrical unless both commodities are either offered for sale or demanded for purchase. Unlike established theory, moreover, a change in initial money balances has no "income" effect on goods offered for sale. More significantly, changes in initial endowments of goods have no "income" effect on commodities that are demanded for purchase; i.e., supply of goods does not create demand for other goods. All of these results are obvious consequences of dichotomizing budget constraints into separate expenditure and income branches.[8]

As in established theory, the money value of the sum of all excess demands, including the excess demand for reservation balances and for money income, is identically zero; hence a proposition analogous to what has come to be known as Walras' Law applies to transactors in a money as well as to transactors in a barter economy. As noted earlier, however, in our model the money value of the sum of *gross* demands for goods and for reservation balances is identically equal

---

[8] Certain qualifications are in order if the initial solution value of $x_{ij} = 0$, for in this case changes in M_j or s_{ij} determine which branch of the budget constraint the terminal solution value of x_{ij} enters.

to initial cash balances. Demand (and excess demand) functions in a money economy are thus subject to much more severe restrictions than are those of a barter economy—the latter category being interpreted to include all neo-Walrasian models of money and prices.

A full statement of the implications of my proposed microfoundation for monetary theory cannot be given here. For present purposes, it is sufficient to observe that the results given above ensure that the response of transactors to changes in prices or in initial endowments of goods or money will differ qualitatively from findings suggested by established theory. Correspondingly, the response of market prices and quantities traded to changes in tastes, initial endowments, or in the aggregate stock of money will differ qualitatively from findings associated with established doctrines.

IV

The tasks that I set myself in this paper were: first, to demonstrate that the conception of a money economy implicit in modern accounts of the general equilibrium theory of money and prices is formally equivalent to the Classical conception of a barter economy; second, to propose a reformulation of established microeconomic analysis suitable as a foundation for explicit analysis of the working of a money economy. The first of these tasks has, I think, been carried through to completion. The second is obviously unfinished. All I have done is to exhibit a model that is immune to the specific criticisms that can be levelled at established microeconomic analysis—a model where, in sharp contrast with established theory, money commodities play a peculiar and central role in shaping prevailing forces of excess demand. My work with this model has already yielded numerous results, including an explicit formal integration of price theory and income analysis and a wholesale reconstruction of large areas of multiple-market dynamics. These and other findings will be presented elsewhere in the near future. My central aim in this paper has been not so much to present results of finished research as to communicate to other economists what seems to me a fruitful conceptual basis for systematic theoretical analysis of large areas of experience that have hitherto eluded such treatment.

6

COMMENT: THE OPTIMAL GROWTH RATE OF MONEY

If one comes to the modern literature on money and economic growth from the general theory of money and prices, one cannot fail to notice the *ad hoc* theorizing and nonchalant empiricism that characterize virtually all contributions to the field, including the papers presented at this session by Professors Tobin and Marty.[1] As may be gathered from this observation, my reaction to this literature is distinctly negative. While the comments that follow are indirectly responsive to the papers of Tobin and Marty, the main thrust of the argument is directed not at their work but rather at the general literature on monetary aspects of neoclassical one-sector growth models.

It is well to remark at the outset that I see little point in attempts to derive optimality rules from models that bear as little relation to reality as does Aristotelian physics. Considered as a purely intellectual exercise, the elaboration of alternative growth models—with or without monetary frills—is surely worthwhile and may even offer some useful insights into the working of observable economic systems. But if one considers the literature on money and growth as a branch of positive economics, he can hardly fail to be appalled—if he takes theory seriously—by the extent to which contributors to it disregard elementary canons of scientific inquiry. The standard procedure is to convert "real" growth models, the properties of which are already established, into "monetary" growth models by simply adding a commodity called "money," the analytical characteristics of which are specified implicitly or not at all. The resulting models—if we may call them by such a name—are correspondingly devoid of logical sense or em-

Editor's note: This paper was presented at the Fifth Conference of University Professors sponsored by the American Bankers Association and Long Island University at Montauk Point, New York, September 5–8, 1967.

In the preparation of these comments, I have benefited greatly from discussions with colleagues at Northwestern University and the University of Essex, but most especially from talks with Joseph Ostroy.

[1] James Tobin, "Notes on Optimal Monetary Growth," *Journal of Political Economy*, 76, Pt. II (July/August 1968), 833–59; Alvin L. Marty, "The Optimal Rate of Growth of Money," *Journal of Political Economy*, 76, Pt. II (July/August 1968), 860–85.

pirical content. We may perhaps claim to have some knowledge about the formal properties of real growth models on the basis of established general equilibrium analysis of Walrasian systems of multilateral barter. We cannot make the same claim as regards monetary growth models, however, for the plain fact is that there exists no accepted or acceptable microeconomic foundation for the theory of an economy in which money plays an *essential* role as a means of payment. All we have is a general theory of an economy in which money is one of many alternative means of payment, which is to say that its only obvious function is as a store of value and unit of account. As is well known, serious difficulties confront any attempt to explain why money will be held at all in these circumstances, unless it is the *only* store of value in the economy. But all real one-sector growth models already involve one store of value, namely, malleable capital-consumption goods. To assign an analytically meaningful role to money in generalized versions of such models, therefore, it is necessary to begin by providing an explicit rationale for the holding of money balances by individual transactors. One cannot in good conscience discuss the working characteristics of models the conceptual foundations of which are unclear even to their authors.

Tobin, Marty, and other writers on money and growth invariably *assert* that money is used both as a medium of exchange and as a store of value. But when they consider the role of money in economic growth, only the store of value function is developed in detail. Money that bears no own rate of interest, so we are told, will be regarded as an inferior asset relative to resources that yield a positive rate of return. Thus, in Tobin's paper we read:

> Scarcity of means of payment forces individuals, firms, and other economic units to economize their cash holdings. In order to gain the earnings possible from keeping their working balances heavily invested in assets, which are not means of payment but yield higher real returns, they must make frequent transactions in and out of cash. These transactions have real costs, for example, the labor of the transactors themselves or their agents. Diversion of productive resources into the handling of in-and-out transactions is socially wasteful, because there is no cost to society in creating means of payment.
>
> The way to avoid this waste is ... [for] means of payment to bear a high enough real rate of return to remove the incentive to economize them.[2]

This chain of reasoning is both specious and fallacious. If fiat money has no special advantages as a means of payment, it will never be held as a store of value as long as any income-earning asset is available. If fiat money does have special advantages as a means of payment, then

---

[2] Tobin, op. cit., p. 846.

in equilibrium it will be used for no other purpose. Money prices will adjust to a level such that the imputed rate of return on real balances, reflecting real costs of barter that the use of money as a means of payment allows individuals to avoid, is just equal at the margin to real rates of return on income-earning assets. Individuals will not economize on transaction balances by making frequent transfers in and out of cash; they will economize by simply using all available cash for transaction purposes, thus avoiding search and other costs associated with attempts to use commodities other than money to discharge trading debts.

Let me put my point more directly by observing that it is no good to assert that money serves as a means of payment if in our theoretical analyses we are unable to assign a formal interpretation to this assertion. In the literature on money and economic growth, the means of payment function of money has not in fact been given formal expression. Failing the provision of a model in which money can be shown to play a crucial role as a means of payment, we can attach no significance even to positive, much less to normative, analyses of the economic implications of alternative growth rates of money.

My duties as a discussant do not oblige me to exhibit a model that is immune to the objections raised above. Having gone this far, however, I think it desirable to exhibit such a model if only to clarify my remarks. To this end, consider a generalized barter economy in which every commodity can be traded directly for every other commodity, that is, an economy in which all commodities are means of payment. In principle, such an economy might be so organized (for example, along the lines set out in Patinkin's version of the general equilibrium theory of money and prices) that multilateral barter with central clearing of book debits and credits was less costly for society than trading of all but one commodity in distinct markets. Suppose, however, that the latter mode of market organization was in fact more efficient. Then the members of the community might well agree to introduce a new commodity consisting of engraved pieces of paper called "cash" which, from that time forward, would be the only commodity that could be traded directly for all others. Demands for goods other than cash would then require that individuals stand ready to supply units of cash of equal value. Similarly, supplies of commodities would imply a demand for money income equal to the cash value of goods offered for sale. The introduction of this scheme of trading would involve a once-over change in institutional arrangements which, because it involves some saving of real resources, would increase social welfare. Real rates of exchange among goods would probably differ somewhat from rates prevailing before the introduction of cash trading, because certain commodities (for example, labor services) would now enter directly into production and consumption activities instead of being dissipated in pretrade search and bargaining activities. The nominal amount of money made available for transaction purposes would, in equilibrium, have no effect on relative prices; the number of pieces of cash in the economy would affect only the absolute price level. Under stationary conditions, moreover, the whole of society's stock of cash would be in continuous circulation; the demand to *hold* rather than *use* cash would be zero at every point in time, though individuals would of course find themselves holding cash balances simply because all receipts and payments would entail transfers of cash from one household to another. Even if purchase and sale transactions were perfectly synchronized, as might be true in a Schumpeterian circular flow, cash would be held by individuals in the aggregate as long as the speed of transfer of cash balances was finite (for example, equal to the speed of light).

In this kind of economy, growth of population at a constant exponential rate would introduce no essentially new complications as compared with the stationary state. An expansion of cash means of payment at a rate equal to the growth rate of population would, *ceteris paribus*, be neutral in its effects on real economic activity. If cash balances were increased less rapidly than population, prices would fall and money would come to bear a positive own rate of return that would make it attractive as a store of value; for its imputed gross rate of return would then be equal to its own rate as a payments medium *plus* the fully anticipated rate of price deflation. Society might then suffer a welfare loss because individuals would be encouraged to substitute barren cash balances for productive capital goods in their asset portfolios, thereby diminishing the future capacity of the economy to provide its members with real goods and services. Alternatively, if cash balances were increased more rapidly than population, prices would tend to rise and individuals would be encouraged to engage in direct barter of goods for goods instead of indirect trading of goods for money and money for goods. For the imputed gross rate of return on money would equal its own rate as a payments medium *less* the fully anticipated rate of price inflation. This might impose a welfare loss on society by inducing individuals to direct real resources into socially useless search and bargaining activities.

These considerations lead to an extremely simple set of rules concerning the optimal growth rate of money. The sole reason for introducing cash in place of barter market transactions is to permit a permanent diversion of resource flows from wasteful search and bargaining activities into direct production of useful goods and services. To insure full exploitation of the potential gains in social welfare made possible by this change in institutional arrangements, the monetary authorities should vary the stock of cash means of payment to discourage the use of cash for any but transactions purposes. Concretely, this means that variations in the supply of money should be so controlled as to minimize movements in the general price level, for any other policy would either induce individuals to hold barren cash in place of productive capital or to substitute inefficient for efficient trading practices.

I see no reason to modify these rules in cases where payments media consist in part or in whole of "inside" rather than "outside" money. In the simplest case where the moving force in economic growth is population increase, the real quantity of debt means of payment would be geared to productivity and abstinence in such a manner that the stock of money would tend to increase *pari passu* with population. Monetary neutrality would be built into the economic system. The optimal degree of financial intermediation—an issue raised specifically by Tobin and dealt with obliquely by Marty—seems to me to involve a range of phenomena that is utterly unrelated to the narrower question of the optimal quantity of money means of payment.

I conclude by emphasizing once more my conviction that only confusion can result from treating the theory of a money economy as if it involved nothing more than the addition of one new asset to the set of commodities available for trade in a barter economy. The difference between a money and a barter economy lies in the fact that the choice alternatives confronting individual transactors are more narrowly circumscribed in the former: goods buy money, and money buys goods, but *goods do not buy goods*. Once this central proposition is accepted, the development of an intellectually satisfying theory of a stationary or growing money economy becomes a practical possibility. If the same proposition is overlooked or ignored, however, as has been true throughout the modern literature on money and economic growth, then what passes as theorizing about a money economy consists in truth of analytically and empirically vacuous exercises in barter economics.

7

INTRODUCTION TO *MONETARY THEORY:* *SELECTED READINGS*

The literature of monetary theory overlaps or verges on virtually every other branch of economic analysis; yet it does not contain a single coherent characterization of two 'objects' the existence of which is the *sine qua non* of monetary theory itself, namely, *money commodity* and *money economy*. To attempt definitively to remedy these omissions in the space of the present introductory essay would be to confess myself a chronic sufferer from delusions of adequacy to which, in truth, I am only moderately prone. But it may be of some help to the reader to have available at least one person's conception of the foundations of the subject.

Frontal attacks on the problem of defining the terms 'money commodity' and 'money economy' traditionally have produced more heat than light. Taking a hint from the experience of mathematicians, many of whose problems can be successfully attacked only by methods of indirect proof, let us attempt to discover what money is and does by dealing first with an imaginary world in which monetary complications are non-existent—a barter economy where all exchange transactions entail simply a trade of goods for other goods.

To lend intuitive colour to our story, suppose that all individuals in our barter world live on a wooded island (perhaps in company with the odd snake or tiger) and must seek out other individuals as and when they wish to engage in commercial transactions. We need not conceive the society to be primitive in an anthropological sense; on the contrary, we may suppose that institutions for the protection of individual lives, limbs, property and the sanctity of exchange contracts, are as highly developed as might be desired by the most ardent believer in *laissez-faire*. We may further suppose that each individual is an enthusiastic trader, being impelled by talent and temperament to thirst for goods that he does not produce.

In the absence of established arrangements for organized trade, individuals will incur heavy costs (in terms of time and effort) in seeking out other individuals, establishing the existence of a double coincidence of wants (a necessary condition for barter exchange), and higgling and haggling over the terms at which proposed commodity trades shall be concluded. Accordingly, we may presume that no individual will engage in trade purely for pleasure; on the contrary, shopping expeditions will be set in motion as infrequently as can be contrived without the benefits of inaction being outweighed by psychological and other costs of having to consume one's own products.

The degree of trading inactivity of a representative individual will be reflected with fair reliability in the quantities of various goods that he holds as stocks—stocks of goods already produced and now awaiting disposal through trade, as well as stocks of goods destined for future consumption. Using some kind of weighted average of such stocks as a measure of the average length of the individual's *transaction period*, we now inquire more closely into the relation between the length of this period and total trading costs.

The total amount of time and effort that an individual spends in search and bargaining activity during any given interval of calendar time will depend directly on the length of the transaction period, for the work involved in any given shopping expedition will be much the same regardless of quantities traded; but the total amount of work required to move a given quantity of goods will be less if the individual engages in a few large transactions per unit of time than if he trades frequently in small amounts. Let us refer to this aspect of total trading expense—work devoted to search and bargaining activity—as *transaction costs*. In the nature of the case, transaction costs will vary *inversely* with the length of the transaction period.

If total trading costs consisted solely of transaction costs, rational behaviour might well induce some individuals to refrain from trade altogether—for transaction costs would surely bulk large in a world of simple barter. However, if an individual did not trade at all, he would have to consume his own produce—a subjectively abhorrent prospect, according to our earlier hypothesis. And this is just an extreme case of a general principle: subjective costs are incurred by an individual when any desired commodity trade is postponed, whether the postponement is short or long. But unlike transaction costs, subjective costs associated with delays in trade vary *directly* with the length of the transaction period. Moreover, some costs of delay are objective, for longer transaction periods involve larger costs of commodity storage and also larger costs of foregone income on earning assets whose purchase is delayed. Let us refer to all these kinds of expense—subjective and objective consequences of delayed trading—as *waiting costs*.

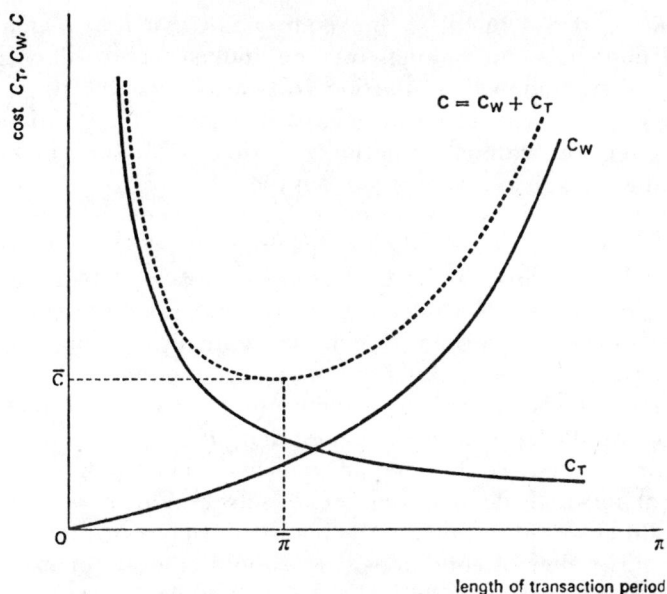

Figure 1

Since waiting costs vary directly with the length of the transaction period, whereas transaction costs vary inversely, we may be sure that somewhere between a transactions frequency of zero and a transactions frequency of infinity, there will occur a certain length of the transaction period that minimizes total trading costs per unit interval of calendar time.

The relation of transaction costs and of waiting costs to the length of the transaction period (both cost magnitudes being measured in subjectively valued units of 'work') is illustrated in Figure 1. In keeping with earlier remarks, we assume that transaction costs (per unit of calendar time) are a strictly decreasing function of the length of the transaction period, while waiting costs are a strictly increasing function of the same variable. The precise form of the two relations will depend on the mixture and amounts of commodities traded, on the individual's preferences for present as compared with future goods, on the individual's initial endowment of resources and his technical knowledge, and on various environmental conditions (including the mixture and amounts of commodities traded by *other* individuals). In any given situation of 'taste and technology', however, we may suppose that both cost relations are well defined. At any given moment of time, therefore, we may suppose that there exists for each individual an *optimal transaction period* defined by the requirement that *total trading costs* (transaction costs plus waiting costs) be minimal. This will occur, of course, where *marginal* transaction costs are just equal to *marginal* waiting costs—for at this point (($\bar{\pi}$, $\bar{C}$) in Figure 1) *any* variation in the length of the transaction period will add more to one component of trading costs than it subtracts from the other.

In barter conditions, rates of exchange among commodities would have to be settled by individual bargaining. In principle, therefore, individual choice problems would be more complicated than in a world with organized markets. Under stationary conditions, however, a barter economy presumably would settle down eventually to a long-run equilibrium in which rates of exchange among commodities were uniform for all individuals. In such an equilibrium, the usual marginal equivalencies would have to hold: that is, marginal rates of return (objective or imputed) would be equal on all assets held by an individual; marginal personal and technical rates of substitution between any two commodities would be equal to their rate of exchange, and so forth. Out of this welter of conditions there would emerge for each individual a number representing the average time elapsing between successive bouts of trading activity—the length of the optimal transaction period. In a world of barter, as in a more advanced society, what appear outwardly to be institutionally determined patterns of timing in trading activity are determined in truth by individual choices.

Total trading costs would be enormous, of course, in an economy that had no institutional arrangements for organized trade. The term 'real balances' would be anything but a euphemism for 'purchasing power'—for real commodities are precisely what people would have to use as means of payment, stores of value and units of account. We need not attempt to trace through a mythical history of the development of techniques for eliminating some of the costs and complications of barter exchange. For our purposes, it suffices to note that search and bargaining activities in our island economy would be greatly facilitated by the establishment on the island of a 'community fairground', where individuals could meet other individuals desiring to engage in commodity trade. Transaction costs could then be reduced further by establishing within the fairground a separate 'trading post' for each distinct pair of commodities traded. If provision were made for *direct* trading of each good for every other good, however, a total of $\frac{1}{2}n(n-1)$ trading posts would be required to provide enough posts for n commodities. A more convenient way to allow for *ultimate* (indirect) pairwise trading of all commodities would be to establish trading posts for all commodities *except* one, the exceptional com-

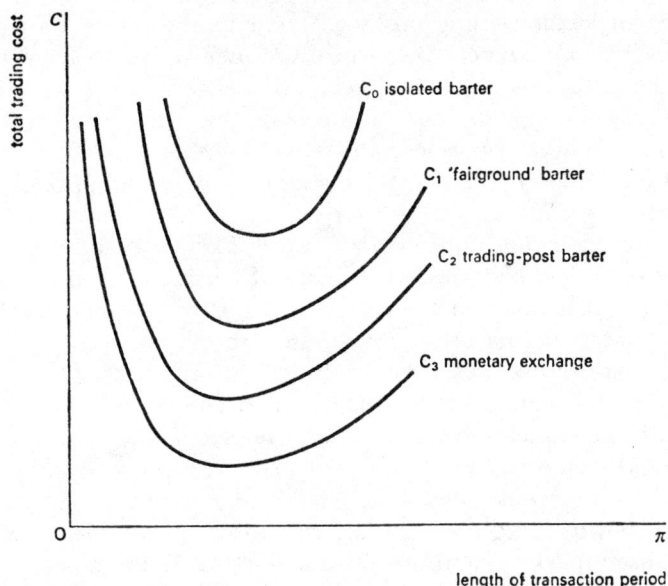

Figure 2

modity being distinguished from all others by being tradeable at all posts.

The cost implications of each of the market arrangements outlined above are illustrated in Figure 2 (the curves in this figure represent vertical sums of transaction cost and waiting cost curves such as those shown in Figure 1). We notice, first, that the total trading cost curve associated with each successive innovation lies *everywhere* below its predecessor; that is to say, there is an absolute (and possibly enormous) gap between trading costs in highly organized as compared with moderately or unorganized markets. Because market organization mainly affects transaction rather than waiting costs, however, the minimum point of each successive cost curve lies ever closer to the 'work' axis. This corresponds to a second and socially very important consequence of organized trading arrangements: transaction periods become shorter and holdings of commodity stocks become smaller as the degree of sophistication of market organization increases.

In the last of the innovations discussed above, the choice of commodities to be assigned to particular posts—hence the choice of an intermediary commodity—would be largely arbitrary. From the standpoint of minimizing transaction costs, what is important is that a prospective seller or buyer of any commodity should always be able to go to a particular trading post and know that all other individuals whose wants complement his own will sooner or later appear at the same place. However, it would evidently be wasteful of physical resources to choose as 'money' (as we may now call the intermediary commodity) a good that is a staple item of consumption. Even if such a good were chosen initially, arrangements would sooner or later be made whereby the commodity was diverted to other uses and its functions as an exchange intermediary were taken over by warehouse receipts or by socially sanctioned issues of fiat money, Giro cheques, etc. Would such 'nominal' money commodities be accepted and used? The answer is in the affirmative. The use of money in exchange transactions presupposes a certain degree of organization of trading activity. Such organization is socially beneficial because it enables individuals to channel into production or leisure labour and resources that would otherwise have to be devoted to search and bargaining activity. Barter would always be *possible* in a world with organized markets, but it would never in any circumstances be *efficient* as long as organized markets continued to function. Accordingly, we may say without hesitation that the technical characteristics of commodities chosen to serve as 'money' are of minor economic importance; what matters is the existence of social institutions condoned by either custom or law that enable individuals to trade efficiently *if they follow certain rules*—in particular, the rule that *one commodity traded in every exchange should be socially sanctioned as an exchange intermediary*. There are no specific trading rules in a world of barter; goods are simply traded for goods, and that is all that can be said. In every money economy, however, there are fairly precise rules; *goods buy money, and money buys goods—but goods do not buy goods in any organized market.*

It would appear from the preceding discussion that an essential feature of a money economy is the existence of institutional arrangements whereby at least one commodity becomes universally acceptable in exchange for all other commodities. From the standpoint of economic efficiency, however, the particular devices that are used to give effect to these arrangements are of minor concern. From a logical standpoint, indeed, the physical characteristics of *money commodities* are no more relevant to the *institution* of money than different forms of courtship are relevant to the *institution* of marriage. Possession of many commodities is, so to speak, a passport for entry into the organized sector of a money economy. No passport, no entry—but the sector exists even if some individuals do not (or cannot) visit it. The *institution of money* is a valuable social resource, fully on a par with the most advanced machines of modern industry or the richest of natural-resource endowments. But *money commodities* are another matter. Arbitrary manipulation of these, in form or quantity, clearly cannot add significantly to (but may detract substantially from) the welfare of society.

We began this discussion by asking what money is and what money does. The materials for an answer are now assembled. We observe, firstly, that the market for 'money' is surely the least thin of all markets, because the 'market' for money consists of the set of all markets for other commodities. So 'money' is the ultimate in liquidity. Secondly, 'money' must be a store of value, because one of its functions is to enable individuals to delay transactions; hence it must serve as a temporary abode of purchasing power. But these characteristics, as also the characteristic of being a unit of account, are incidental to its third and primary function, which is to give effect to institutional arrangements for organized trading. All exchangeable commodities are media of exchange by virtue of the fact that they serve to pay for at least *one* other commodity; but only money commodities are means of payment for *all* other commodities. Money differs from other commodities in being universally acceptable as an exchange intermediary by virtue not of individual choice but rather by virtue of social contrivance.

Our characterization of 'money' might be thought to have some bearing on the question as to what objects should be considered money in the real world. But this is not so; for our 'definition' of money has precise meaning only in relation to other concepts such as 'commodity' and 'organized market' that are themselves open to a variety of different factual interpretations. All of these words are primitive (undefined) concepts of monetary theory in the same sense as the words 'point' and 'line' are primitive concepts of Euclidean geometry. Considered in isolation, 'money' is just a word—as 'point' is just a word, unless we are also told that 'points' have to do with diagrams rather than verbal or written debate. Intellectual understanding of observed monetary phenomena depends not on prior 'definition' of something called 'money' (such a definition could never be more than a picturesque description in any case); what is required is prior formulation of a coherent theory of monetary phenomena.

The origins of contemporary theory are buried too deep in the past to admit of any but piecemeal excavation. The emergence everywhere of market arrangements that inhibit or preclude settlement of trading debts with any but a restricted range of socially sanctioned exchange intermediaries is no doubt attributable to private and social recognition of benefits to be realized from so organizing trading activity that only a short list of 'money commodities' are directly exchangeable for other commodities in established market-places. As such arrangements have developed, however, they have steadily eroded or altogether eliminated possibilities for engaging in trade of any kind without thereby engaging in the purchase or sale of commodities specifically designed to serve as means of payment. Thus practices that originally were matters of social convenience have hardened, with the passage of time, into legal and institutional restrictions; restrictions which ensure that virtually all market transactions involve two distinct operations—buying for money and selling for money—so that the holding of money balances for transactions purposes becomes a practical if not a physical necessity.

Early observers of this phenomenon naturally found it slightly paradoxical; for why should individuals find it advantageous to engage in *two* transactions where *one* would seem to accomplish the same final result more expeditiously? Much early writing on money was concerned directly or indirectly with analysing and resolving this paradox. To describe this literature as 'theory' would be a slight abuse of language; it might more accurately be described as systematized common sense. The scientific importance of the literature cannot be overemphasized, however, for it is from this cloth—sense evidence of the most direct and obvious kind—that the suit of formal monetary theory ultimately must be cut.

Formal theory has never managed to capture certain elements of everyday experience that 'common-sense' writers consider crucial. In all descriptive accounts of monetary exchange, for example, it is taken for granted that money commodities play a peculiar role as media of exchange—that money commodities are, in principle, distinguishable from other commodities by virtue of this role. No such distinction is logically admissible, however, within the framework of established price theory. On the contrary, the analytical (as contrasted with the verbal) content of the most general of modern statements of value and monetary theory (namely, Don Patinkin's *Money, Interest, and Prices*) is logically indistinguishable from that of the most traditional theory of a barter economy. The failure of monetary theorists adequately to express in formal language this and other aspects of their own intuitive conception of the nature of 'monetary reality' no doubt is attributable more to the complexity of monetary phenomena than to the ignorance, oversight or 'wrong-headedness' of theorists. However, the considered views of keen observers of monetary phenomena merit serious and careful study, though the observers be utterly devoid of theoretical guile.

As noted earlier, money commodities are important from the standpoint of social welfare only as devices for facilitating exchange. Individuals acquire money commodities not because such commodities are directly useful but because they can later be used to purchase other commodities that are desired for their own sake. By virtue of these devices, practical effect is given to the institution of money; the establishment of organized markets enables individuals to channel into productive activity labour and other resources that would otherwise be devoted to search and bargaining activities. But money, as money, need not be intrinsically valuable, for what matters is not the particular commodity (or commodities) that serve as money, but rather the existence of social institutions that make monetary transactions feasible and efficient.

The unimportance of the 'stuff' of which money is made is obvious enough to people who live in a world of fiat currencies; but what is obvious today was not so clear to people whose money consisted largely of gold, silver and other intrinsically valuable materials. In those circumstances, many if not most people were easily persuaded to believe that money was wealth in the same sense as, say, a cow, a field or a piece of machinery. So we find that the earliest formal analyses of monetary phenomena are directed at dispelling this illusion by examining the consequences of a once-over change in the quantity of money commodities.

The *locus classicus* of all such analyses is an essay by David Hume entitled 'Of money':

Money is nothing but the representation of labour and commodities, and serves only as a method of rating or estimating them. Where coin is in greater plenty—as a greater quantity of it is required to represent the same quantity of goods—it can have no effect, either good or bad, taking a nation within itself; any more than it would make an alteration in a merchant's books, if instead of the Arabian method of notation, which requires few characters, he should make use of the Roman, which requires a great many. . . .

Notwithstanding this conclusion, which must be allowed just, it is certain that since the discovery of the mines in America, industry has increased in all the nations of Europe, except in the possessors of those mines; and this may justly be ascribed, among other reasons, to the increase of gold and silver. Accordingly, we find that in every kingdom, into which money begins to flow in greater abundance than formerly, everything takes on a new face; labour and industry gain life; the merchant becomes more enterprising, and even the farmer follows his plough with greater alacrity and attention. . . .

To account then for this phenomenon, we must consider, that though the high price of commodities be a necessary consequence of the increase of gold and silver, yet it follows not immediately upon that increase; but some time is required before the money circulates through the whole state, and makes its effect be felt on all ranks of people. At first, no alternation is perceived; by degrees the price rises, first of one commodity, then of another; till the whole at last reaches a just proportion with the new quantity of specie which is in the kingdom. In my opinion, it is only in this interval or intermediate situation, between the acquisition of money and the rise of prices, that the increasing quantity of gold and silver is favourable to industry.*

Hume's essay provides a nicely balanced account of what has since become known as the *quantity theory of money*. Later writers have not always stated or interpreted the theory so judiciously. As construed by some writers, indeed, the propositions advanced by Hume were made to assert that the 'real' work money has to perform is determined simply by the amount of goods and services that have to be traded; hence that money, as money, is merely a 'veil', explicit consideration of which obscures the working of those *truly* important forces (and Calvinist virtues) of productivity and thrift that are the ultimate determinants of social welfare.

This bowdlerized version of Hume, or something very like it, has occupied a prominent place in the thinking of professional economists through much of modern history. It underlies what today is referred to as the *naive quantity theory*, the central proposition of which is that the total quantity of means of payment governs the absolute scale of money prices but does not affect real rates of exchange among other commodities. On this reckoning, the determination of real rates of exchange, and of quantities traded, is the business not of monetary but of value theory. Monetary theory is seen as a trivial addendum to conventional demand-and-supply analysis rather than a subject deserving systematic study in its own right. The dichotomy thus established between monetary and value theory ultimately produced two relatively distinct breeds of economist to which some wag later assigned the descriptive labels 'curve benders' and 'curve stretchers'.

There plainly is much to be said for Hume's version of the quantity theory as an *ad hoc* description of the factors that mainly govern the determination of the general level of money prices *in the long run*. Looking at the problem of price behaviour from a theoretical point of view, however, one finds it difficult to see how any significant role can be assigned to money in the long run unless money also is assumed to play an important role in short-run events; and if money is assigned an important role in short-run economic analysis, then a *separate* long-run theory of money should not be necessary. Long-run conclusions should follow from short-run assumptions. However that may be, the fact is that until the appearance in 1936 of John Maynard Keynes'

* David Hume, 'Of Money', *Essays*, Oxford University Press, 1750, pp. 292–4.

General Theory of Employment, Interest and Money, most professional economists took it for granted that all economic problems of any practical importance could be adequately handled using established techniques of demand-and-supply analysis, thereby presupposing that money was as much a 'veil' in the short run as it was in the long—for at no stage in pre-Keynesian economics was any serious attempt made to build peculiarly monetary assumptions into the micro-foundations of economic analysis.

The closest approach to such an attempt was initiated by Leon Walras (1834–1910) in his pioneering treatment of general equilibrium analysis; but it involved little more than a mechanical application of quantity theory ideas to a conceptual model, the analytical structure of which precluded assignment of a specialized role to money as a means of payment. A less formal, but ultimately more influential attack on the same problem was later undertaken by J. R. (now Sir John) Hicks in his famous 'Suggestion for simplifying the theory of money', the central theme of which was that money could be assigned a natural place in established demand-and-supply analysis by treating it as a special kind of asset. The effect of both attempts was to strengthen the already prevalent notion that economics could do without a separate theory to describe short-run price and quantity behaviour in a money economy.

Keynes' *General Theory* temporarily dispelled this illusion, firstly by raising doubts about the theoretical generality of traditional value theory and its relevance for describing *on-going* as contrasted with *virtual* economic processes; secondly by proposing an alternative scheme of analysis certain implications of which seemed inconsistent with received doctrine. I say 'temporarily dispelled' because subsequent developments in economic theory, associated mainly with the writings of Hicks, Lange, Modigliani, Samuelson and Patinkin, gradually have persuaded many and perhaps most economists that the Keynesian revolution, however beneficial may have been its *practical effects* on a nearly decadent science, added nothing novel or worthwhile to the *theoretical foundations* of economic science. As concerns monetary theory, in particular, contemporary opinion appears strongly to favour what might be described as a 'neo-Walrasian quantity theory' to the effect that money matters only slightly in the short run, and not at all in the long. No other conclusion is possible, indeed, if one adopts the conception of a money economy implicit in recent statements of the general equilibrium theory of money and prices. In all such neo-Walrasian models, money appears as just one among many analytically indistinguishable commodities in a world where trading activities are costlessly co-ordinated by a central market authority in such a manner that all feasible trades ultimately can be carried out directly, without the use of exchange intermediaries. Money indeed *is* a cipher in such a world as this, for its only apparent function is to serve as a store of value—a function that would appear to be better served by assets that have a positive income yield.

Such is the stage that monetary theory had reached by 1960. Developments since then have raised some interesting questions, generated occasional heat and produced a modicum of light on doctrinal and other issues. As a consequence, it now seems clear that neo-Walrasian monetary models are little if any better than the most orthodox of classical barter models for analysing short-run movements in economic activity. What is not yet clear, however, is how the shortcomings of accepted theory can be remedied. Most economists who are not specialists in money appear to take the view that the problem is not all that serious. Monetary specialists generally take a more serious view of the inadequacies of existing theory, but few of them have any concrete suggestions for improvement. Failing suggestions by others, they have tended to turn either to econometric study of observed behaviour (measurement with so little theory that it really does not matter), or to consciously academic exercises in the dynamics of monetary growth (theory with so little reality that it does not matter either). The theoretical rockets that accompanied the development of neo-Walrasian and Keynesian monetary theory have long since vanished, leaving behind them wispy trails of wisdom that are quite disproportionate to the original sound and fury.

8

THEORETICAL FOUNDATIONS OF MONETARY POLICY

Discussions of monetary policy traditionally have proceeded on the assumption that the distinctive feature of a money economy is the existence of institutional arrangements that assign an exclusive role to certain commodities as means of payment in organized markets. In sharp contrast with this procedure, formal treatments of monetary theory traditionally have started from premises that preclude explicit consideration of alternative technologies of exchange and related questions of market organization. Historically, therefore, specialists in monetary policy have had little intellectual guidance from specialists in monetary theory. In recent years, however, monetary theorists have become increasingly aware of the shortcomings of their conceptual tools and have taken important steps to overcome them.[1] The statement of a definitive monetary theory is still a long way off, but the main outlines of an intellectually satisfying theory seem now to be discernible in the literature. My purpose in this paper is to give a common sense account of this emerging theory and to indicate some of its implications for contemporary discussions of monetary policy.

I. THE DEFINITION OF MONEY

The most significant development in the recent literature is a growing consensus of opinion among monetary economists about the proper definition of money.[2] The main difficulty in the past has been for monetary theorists to emancipate themselves from preconceptions carried over from conventional value theory, the whole of which rests on an essentially Walrasian conception of exchange as a virtual process in which the trading plans of a set of individuals are costlessly coordinated by a central authority whose only explicit function is to determine a vector of exchange rates that will permit individuals to carry out, at least in principle, a series of mutually consistent and beneficial

---

[1] Cf. Harry G. Johnson, 'Recent Developments in Monetary Theory—A Commentary', in *Money in Britain 1959–1969*, edited by D. R. Croome and H. G. Johnson (London: Oxford University Press, 1970), pp. 95–100.

[2] See Johnson, loc. cit. My comment is based more on impressions derived from unpublished papers by Brunner and Meltzer, Niehans, Saving, Hahn, and others than on published work.

barter transactions.[3] This conception of market exchange precludes assignment of a specialized role to any single commodity as a means of payment, for its logic implies that any good may be traded directly for any other good, which is to say that all commodities are perfect substitutes as means of payment. The natural consequence is to divert attention away from the function of money as a medium of exchange and to focus attention instead on its function as a store of value. From here it is but a short step to the conclusion that all assets are 'more or less money'; hence, that the definition of money is an empirical rather than a theoretical problem and must be decided accordingly on the basis of evidence as to which of a set of alternative definitions performs best in applications.[4]

Most of these perplexities vanish if we substitute for the Walrasian paradigm a conception of the economic system that permits us to view monetary exchange as a phenomenon involving the existence of a set of independent markets in each of which units of one particular commodity can be traded directly only for units of one or more other commodities that custom or law has specifically designated as means of payment. On this view, 'money' consists of the class of all commodities that serve as means of payment in organized markets, and the definition of this class constitutes an essential preliminary in the formulation of any theoretical model.[5]

There is nothing novel in this procedure. In Walrasian equilibrium analysis, it is assumed implicitly if not explicitly that there exists just one organized market and that within this market all commodities are universally acceptable as means of payment.[6] Similarly, in traditional

[3] Cf. Sir John Hicks, *Critical Essays in Monetary Theory* (Oxford: The Clarendon Press, 1967), p. 6; Axel Leijonhufvud, *On Keynesian Economics and the Economics of Keynes* (New York: Oxford University Press, 1968), Chapter 2; E. C. H. Veendorp, 'General Equilibrium Theory for a Barter Economy', *Western Economic Journal*, Mar. 1970, pp. 1–3, 21–2; and R. W. Clower, 'Is There an Optimal Money Supply?' *Journal of Finance*, May 1970, pp. 425–7.

[4] See Milton Friedman and Anna J. Schwartz, 'The Definition of Money', *Journal of Money, Credit, and Banking*, Feb. 1969, pp. 1–14; and David Laidler, *The Demand for Money* (London: International Textbook Company, 1969).

[5] This rather obvious point seems first to have been made in my 'Reconsideration of the Microfoundations of Monetary Theory', *Western Economic Journal*, Dec. 1967. Its full significance was not clear to me, however, until I read Joseph Ostroy's *Exchange as an Economic Activity* (Ph.D. dissertation, Northwestern University, 1970), *passim*.

[6] Standard accounts of macroeconomics obscure this fact by referring not only to excess demand functions for goods, labour, bonds and money but also to 'markets' for each of these 'goods' (see, for example, Don Patinkin, *Money, Interest, and Prices*, second edition (New York: Harper and Row, 1965). Walras recognized this problem in early sections of his *Elements*, for he begins by postulating the existence of 'trading posts' for various possible pairwise combinations of exchangeable commodities; but in later lessons he anticipates modern confusion by speaking as if there were a one-to-one correspondence between 'markets' and 'commodities'.

(and modern) discussions of barter trade, it is commonly argued that a distinct market corresponds to each possible pairwise combination of individuals and commodities. Only during the past few years, however, have monetary theorists come gradually to recognize that trading arrangements in a money economy correspond more closely to the completely decentralized process envisioned in traditional treatments of barter exchange than to the completely centralized process implicit in Walrasian models.[7] Unanimity of opinion on this issue has yet to be attained, but present indications are that, in future discussions of monetary theory, 'money' will be defined theoretically in terms of explicitly postulated restrictions on trading alternatives that assign a special role to certain commodities as payment media in organized markets.[8]

It is one thing, of course, to establish a theoretical definition of money and quite another to decide what collection of objects in the real world should be considered to correspond to the definition. Two main questions arise in this connection: first, what markets in the real world are to be regarded as organized; second, what commodities routinely serve as means of payment in such markets? I do not wish to minimize the difficulty of these questions, but in my opinion both can be answered satisfactorily in relation to the objectives of any given investigation by direct inspection of trading patterns and payment procedures in various sectors of the economy. For the United States and the United Kingdom, for example, it seems clear that for most practical purposes, 'money' should be considered to include trade credit as well as currency and demand deposits.[9]

The fruitfulness of a particular definition of money will depend, of course, not only on its definition and empirical interpretation but also on the definition and empirical interpretation of other concepts of monetary theory. This point merits emphasis, for it underlies what

[7] On this, see Veendorp, op. cit.; Ostroy, *passim*; and Jurg Niehans, 'Money in a Static Theory of Optimal Payment Arrangements', *Journal of Money, Credit, and Banking*, Nov. 1969, pp. 706–25.

[8] This theme underlies virtually all work on monetary theory that I have seen in draft form over the past two years—a biased sample, no doubt, but one that includes contributions from some twenty graduate students and an even larger number of established theorists.

[9] The essential issue here is whether the tender of any given financial instrument permits a buyer to take delivery of a commodity from a seller. On this criterion, trade credit qualifies as money—trade credit being interpreted to include credit card and overdraft facilities, department store credit and travellers' checks, as well as commercial paper and book credits. On the same criterion, time deposits and other financial claims that are perfect or near-perfect substitutes for money only as stores of value unambiguously fail to qualify as money. Cf. Arthur B. Laffer, 'Trade Credit and the Money Market', *Journal of Political Economy*, Mar./Apr. 1970, pp. 239–67.

is perhaps the central theme in recent contributions to monetary theory, namely, that the main shortcomings of conventional theory derive
from faults not in empirical interpretation but in theoretical
specification.[10]

II. THE DEMAND FOR MONEY

Widespread acceptance of a definition of money that emphasizes its
role as a means of payment would be of little consequence were this
changed perspective not associated with important advances in the
theoretical understanding of market exchange processes in the real
world. Perhaps the best way to approach this subject is to observe that
the existence of organized markets in which certain commodities play
an exclusive role as means of payment does not permit us to assert
that there will exist a positive demand for such commodities for purposes of exchange. On the contrary, to establish theoretically that
there exists a positive demand for money, we must introduce a number of additional assumptions. This may be seen most easily by supposing (contrary to common sense) that it costs individuals nothing
to engage in the activity of exchange. Then an individual's choice
among alternative trading arrangements will depend simply on his
tastes and initial commodity endowment and on those of his potential
trading partners. The properties of this kind of economy have been
explored intensively by Joseph Ostroy,[11] whose findings confirm the
intuitive notion that the individual pursuit of gains from trade almost
always will lead to some indirect trading and show that informational
requirements associated with even the simplest chains of multilateral
barter are quite horrendous. But this being so, it is virtually impossible
to establish precise criteria to compare the potential efficiency of alternative sets of trading arrangements. As matters stand, therefore,
we cannot hope to make out a general case for the superiority of
monetary over other kinds of trading arrangements; that is, we cannot
assert that money *will be* used even in an economy where it *might be*
used.[12]

The most obvious way to get around this difficulty is to suppose
that it costs each individual something in terms of time or effort to

[10] Cf. R. W. Clower, *Monetary Theory: Selected Readings* (London: Penguin Books,
Ltd., 1969), Parts III and IV.

[11] Op. cit.

[12] Milton Friedman's recent attempt at formal analysis of the problem of monetary
optimality (*The Optimum Quantity of Money and Other Essays* (Chicago: Aldine Press, 1969))
is logically vitiated by his failure to recognize, much less deal with, this problem.

engage in the activity of exchange. In keeping with earlier discussions of this problem by Baumol, Tobin, Demsetz, and others, we may suppose that trading costs associated with the pairwise exchange of any two commodities generally comprise two components: a fixed charge to reflect costs of search and bargaining that are independent of quantities exchanged; a variable charge to reflect costs of storage and transport that depend directly on quantities traded. Other things being equal, individuals will have an incentive, on the one hand, to trade infrequently and in large lots in order to minimize fixed trading costs per unit of time and, on the other hand, to trade frequently in small lots in order to minimize variable trading costs. It follows that total trading costs per unit of time will be a U-shaped function of average holdings of inventories of any given commodity. The position and form of these functions will vary, depending on the mode of market organization and on the commodity pairs exchanged. In systems that admit only of direct barter, for example, search and bargaining costs are likely to be extremely high for all commodity pairs by comparison with systems that permit indirect barter; and systems that involve unorganized barter among individuals are likely to entail higher trading costs than systems that involve pairwise exchange of any two commodities at organized trading centres.[13]

It has never been demonstrated formally, but it is easy to convince oneself intuitively, that trading costs functions will be uniformly lower for all commodities if trades are carried out in markets where only a few specially designated commodities can be exchanged directly for all other commodities than if trades take place in less regimented circumstances. For only if trade is highly organized can individuals consistently avoid holding inventories of virtually all commodities and yet be sure that in any desired trade there will always be a double coincidence of wants. I shall not dwell further on this subject, for I have little to add to what has already been said in recent contributions to the transactions cost literature. Here it will suffice to suppose, albeit arbitrarily, that a 'quantum jump' in trading costs separates monetary from other systems of trade so that the mere existence of organized markets for monetary exchange effectively ensures that other possible modes are never utilized.[14]

Even on this assumption, we cannot show that there will exist a positive demand for money. As a technical matter, an individual can

[13] On this see Sir John Hicks, op. cit.; R. W. Clower, *Monetary Theory: Selected Readings*, pp. 7–14.
[14] Cf. Kevin C. Sontheimer, 'A Technological Representation of Money', University of Buffalo Discussion Paper (mimeo), 1970.

always reduce his average holdings of money to any desired level, however small, by so synchronizing his sales and purchases in organized markets that money receipts are almost instantly reflected in money expenditures. But if trading costs are U-shaped functions of average holdings of commodity inventories, it is easy to show that individuals normally will not aim at perfect synchronization of sales and purchases. For, in general, the minimum point of the trading cost function for one commodity will not occur at a value of average inventory holdings that coincides with the value of average inventory holdings at the minimum point of the trading cost function for any other commodity or collection of other commodities. In general, therefore, individuals will find it desirable to avoid perfect synchronization of purchases and sales. This implies the existence of a positive demand for money for purposes of exchange. In effect, money is just one among many trade inventories, and average holdings of money for trading purposes are determined jointly with average holdings of all other commodities.[15]

The factors governing desired holdings of money and other inventories will include, among other things, current holdings of inventories, desired average rates of production and consumption of each commodity, actual and imputed rates of interest, and anticipated rates of change of prices. Current as distinct from desired inventory holdings will be governed by prevailing market conditions that affect realized purchases and sales and realized rates of production and consumption. To formulate an explicit formal model that accurately portrays the dynamics either of individual or market behaviour in a monetary economy is obviously an extremely difficult task—so difficult that it has yet to be carried out for any but special cases.[16] Nevertheless, it seems clear on the basis of existing work that formal analysis of these problems will yield little qualitative information that is not already obtainable from more informal analysis of the sort presented

[15] Cf. R. W. Clower, op. cit. (1970).
[16] The essential problem is to devise models that permit us explicitly to analyse price–quantity behaviour in economic systems where trade takes place at other than equilibrium prices—what are commonly (but, in my opinion, inappropriately) called 'non-tâtonnement models'. Thus far only limited progress has been made in this direction. Cf. Herschel Grossman, 'Theories of Markets Without Recontracting', *Journal of Economic Theory*, Dec. 1969, pp. 476–9; Herschel Grossman, 'A General Disequilibrium Model of Income and Employment', *American Economic Review*, Mar. 1971; and Peter Frevert, 'Disequilibrium in a Macroeconomic Model', in *Papers in Quantitative Economics*, Quirk and Zarley, ed., University of Kansas Press, 1968. Reference should also be made to recent (but as yet unpublished) work by Richard W. Ruppert and Robert Russell ('Intermarket Spillover of Excess Demand and the Stability of Non-tâtonnement Adjustment Processes'), and by John Ledyard ('Growth, Stability, and a Disequilibrium Action Process').

here. In particular, there is no reason to suppose that conclusions from dynamic models of individual inventory-holding behaviour will differ significantly from common sense inferences that can already be drawn from static models. All the same, if monetary theory is ever to provide a reliable guide to policy action, explicit formal models must be developed.

My discussion thus far—like most of the literature on monetary theory—rests on the tacit assumption that money consists of a single commodity like gold or fiat currency. To come to grips with any practical problem, we clearly must be willing to contemplate more realistic situations in which money consists of currency, demand deposits, and trade credit—the last item being especially important since it is used as means of payment in virtually all business transactions. In principle, there are few difficulties in this area. To account for positive holdings of different kinds of money, it is only necessary to recognize that trading costs will depend to some extent on modes of payment, and that trading cost functions associated with one mode of payment normally will not lie uniformly below trading cost functions for other modes. Thus different modes of payment may coexist in a money economy even under stationary conditions. This is a matter of some importance because the proliferation of payment modes in any actual economy typically entails the use of one kind of money as a reserve for others. The pyramiding of monetary instruments would be of little importance in a stationary world, but (as history shows) it can become crucially important in situations of monetary disequilibrium.

III. THE ROLE OF MONEY IN ECONOMIC ACTIVITY

The preceding discussion assigns money a passive rather than active role in the determination of real economic magnitudes, for the great bulk of outstanding stocks of means of payment will consist in any advanced economy of claims whose nominal quantity is endogenously determined by factors over which no individual or government authority can exercise effective short-run control. This is not to say that money is unimportant, either in terms of the long-run effects upon real economic welfare of monetary trading arrangements or in terms of the short-run effects upon real economic magnitudes of autonomous changes in various components of the money stock. However, it does suggest that the task of identifying causal interrelations among real and monetary magnitudes is considerably more complicated than some theories of monetary phenomena might lead us to suppose.

Let us approach this subject by distinguishing two classes of monetary economies: the first, economies in which there exist no non-monetary financial assets; the second, economies in which the bulk of all financial assets consist of claims that are not money. The simplest case of an economy without non-monetary financial assets is one in which money consists either of privately produced nuggets of gold (inside money) or fiat currency notes issued and declared to be legal tender by some central authority (outside money). On either assumption, holdings of money will be governed by conditions of taste and technology that determine individual holdings of commodity inventories. Of course, changes in nominal stocks of money associated with changes in mining technology or with new issues of fiat notes will induce transient adjustments in both real money balances and in commodity inventories. In this simple system, however, the demand for money clearly will be a stable function of a few key variables, so we should not expect money to play an independent role in determining real magnitudes even if the economy is subject to frequent random shocks. The single-asset monetary economy is the appropriate frame of reference for those who regard money as a 'temporary abode of general purchasing power', for in this kind of economy the function of money is purely that of a trade inventory.[17]

The role of money becomes more complex if we admit the existence of two kinds of money commodities, one consisting of, let us say, privately produced gold nuggets, the other of privately issued promises to pay a stated number of gold nuggets on demand. Under stationary conditions of taste and technology, the performance characteristics of this model should be essentially the same as those of a single money-asset model, for in normal circumstances individuals would regard private notes as good substitutes for gold as means of payment. Except in a system where notes were backed 100 per cent by gold, however, random shocks might set off monetary expansions or contractions in which money played a temporarily independent role via changes in the ratio of notes to gold. One can even conceive of inventory cycles in connection with this model, for the existence of commodity inventories together with fractionally-backed issues of private notes opens the door to speculative investment in inventories in periods of monetary expansion and to panic attempts to exchange notes and inventories for gold in periods of monetary contraction.

If we consider a more general model in which privately granted but non-negotiable trade credit routinely serves as money in most exchange transactions, the potential speculative impact of autono-

---

[17] This view, popularized by Milton Friedman, is implied by but does not itself entail a means-of-payment conception of money: cf. Harry Johnson, op. cit., p. 100.

mous or induced changes in negotiable components of the money supply becomes painfully obvious. In ordinary circumstances, there will be a fairly stable monetary pyramid with gold at the apex, gold-backed notes in the middle, and gold- and note-backed trade credit at the bottom. But suppose that an exogenous shock produces an unanticipated increase in stocks of some inventories which, in turn, leads some individuals to reduce new orders. The initial effect may well be to expand trade credit as sales fall and inventories continue to rise; but soon there must be a sharply increased demand for notes and gold to meet the demand of trade creditors, and after this point a monetary contraction of major proportions may well ensue.

Arguments conducted on the basis of plausible rather than demonstrative reasoning do not prove anything, of course, but proof is not my object. On the contrary, my purpose is to emphasize that in any but the simplest single money-asset world, the use of money as a temporary abode of purchasing power in normal circumstances entails its potential use as a semi-permanent form of investment in abnormal circumstances. The economic significance of this conclusion depends on the extent to which changes in the demand for money directly impinge upon current flows of income and expenditure. If holdings of money balances were not closely linked with and sensitively dependent upon holdings of commodity inventories, the direct influence of monetary changes upon production and consumption activity would surely be slight. If modern trends in monetary theory are on the right track, however, the links connecting money holdings with commodity inventories are so close as to guarantee that monetary changes will invariably exert a direct and important influence upon production and consumption flows.

So much for monetary systems without non-monetary financial assets. The more general case of systems in which a major portion of all financial assets consists of non-monetary claims does not admit of any but brief and superficial treatment here. It goes without saying that such systems will be more vulnerable to speculative influences than economies without developed capital markets. Exactly as in simpler systems, changes in the demand for money will influence production and consumption decisions directly via their impact upon holdings of commodity and money inventories. Such changes will also directly affect fixed investment decisions, via their effect upon security markets;[18] for there is no difference in principle between inventories

[18] For a persuasive analysis of this sphere of monetary influence, see Patrick Hendershott and George Horwich, 'The Monetary-Interest Rate Mechanism and its Policy Implications: A Critique of Milton Friedman' (Purdue University mimeo, 1970).

of fixed capital and inventories of working capital and finished goods,[19] and in a money economy all inventory decisions will be affected directly by changes in money flows that alter either the level or composition of the stock of money. Monetary influences will also affect real economic magnitudes via familiar channels—interest rates, wealth effects, and so forth—but not, I suspect, in ways that can be inferred from the existing literature. For the very essence of the role of money in economic activity lies in the fact that it *constrains* rather than *facilitates* market exchange of other commodities in situations of widespread disequilibrium—and contemporary economic theory provides no techniques to analyse such situations.

IV. MONETARY POLICY

The bearing of the preceding discussion on the issue to which this paper is addressed, namely, the present state of the theoretical foundations of monetary policy, may be summed up in a phrase: the foundations don't exist. This being the case, my paper cannot include comments about the constituents of a 'rational' scheme of monetary policy, for surely we cannot deal effectively with such delicate issues except on the basis of a reasonably precise, logically coherent, and empirically acceptable conception not merely of the role of money in economic activity but also of related dynamic interrelations among real and monetary magnitudes. The emergence of such a conception is, I think, clearly foreshadowed in the recent literature; but the promise has yet to be realized. As of the present time, therefore, I have no basis other than 'hunch' and 'feel' for affirmative pronouncements about contemporary policy issues. However, I think some fairly definite remarks of a negative kind are in order—and also some comments about desirable directions for future research.

First, the negative remarks. Contemporary discussion of monetary policy centres upon the work of Milton Friedman, the leading apostle of a school of thought that David Fand has aptly described as 'monetarist'.[20] The growing influence of this school is regarded by some as a triumph of scientific truth over Keynesian dogma, by others as a regrettable retreat into orthodoxy, by yet others as the replacement of one fashion in half truths by another. My position—as reflected in earlier comments—is best described as 'sympathetic' to the last of these possibilities. But let me elaborate.

[19] Cf. Hicks, op. cit., Chapter 3.
[20] David I. Fand, 'A Monetarist Model of the Monetary Process', *Journal of Finance*, May 1970, pp. 275–89. Also see Johnson, op. cit., pp. 84 ff.

The basic assumption of the monetarist school—according to both its leading exponent and its leading supporters—is that there exists a stable demand function for money, money being interpreted for most purposes as currency and commercial bank demand and time deposits.[21] No doubt this is an essential point of departure; a school of thought that denies the assumption is obviously in serious trouble before it begins. But this assumption taken by itself—or even in conjunction with a set of other assumptions that guarantee the existence of monetary equilibria corresponding to arbitrarily given initial conditions—leads absolutely nowhere in the discussion of monetary policy unless it is combined with numerous other assumptions about the structure and dynamic response of the economic system to changes in the stock of money and other controllable policy parameters.[22] If the assumption of a stable demand function for money and related comparative statics propositions constituted the only fixed stars in the monetarist universe, therefore, we might conclude without further ado that the monetarists were hopelessly lost in space.

In truth, monetarist doctrine involves numerous other components; specifically, a large collection of so-called 'empirical hypotheses' about the relation between short-run changes in the stock of money and short-run changes in overall economic activity. Unfortunately, this category of hypotheses is not one that has been catalogued and dealt with by specialists in logic. Presumably these empirical hypotheses could be restated as logical propositions and subjected to conventional tests of consistency to ascertain whether they merit further testing in the light of empirical evidence—a procedure that is surely standard in other areas of empirical science. However that may be, no such procedure has been followed by monetarist writers. Acting on the classic maxim that truth follows more surely from error than from confusion, James Tobin has attempted to put some of the monetarist 'empirical hypotheses' into a form where they can be subjected to conventional tests of logical consistency and factual relevance;[23] but his attempt has been dismissed by Prof. Friedman as 'imprecise, inaccurate and misleading'.[24] I pass no judgment on this exchange, except to remark that the burden of effort in arriving at a precise,

[21] Harry G. Johnson, 'Monetary Theory and Policy', *American Economic Review*, June 1962, p. 351.

[22] Cf. M. L. Burstein, *Economic Theory: Equilibrium and Change* (London and New York: Wiley and Sons, 1968), Chapter 13, esp. pp. 289–90 and pp. 296 ff.

[23] James Tobin, 'Money and Income: Post Hoc Ergo Propter Hoc', *Quarterly Journal of Economics* 84, May 1970, pp. 301–17.

[24] Milton Friedman, 'Comment on Tobin', *Quarterly Journal of Economics* 84, May 1970, p. 327.

accurate and authoritative account of monetarist doctrine has yet to be accepted and borne by any monetarist writer.

I shall not dwell further on a line of argument the implications of which should already be evident. Since the monetarist school has not provided an explicit formal account of the dynamics of monetary adjustment, the uncommitted student of monetary economics can hardly help but regard the bulk of monetarist literature as so much sound and fury, signifying little more than the personal charm, dialectical skill and encyclopedic factual knowledge of its chief apostle, Milton Friedman. The monetarist literature is important—and highly so—for the questions it forces us to ask about observed patterns of behaviour; but it is worth almost nothing as far as answers to these questions, or guidance in seeking answers, is concerned.[25]

So much for negative comments. Since (as indicated earlier) my own grasp of short-run monetary dynamics is at best only slightly more firm than that of the monetarists, I shall not state my own prejudices about monetary policy and related matters. It seems to me that the first duty of academic economists is to confess ignorance about matters on which they are in fact ignorant. To be sure, I may be the only academic student of monetary economics who *is* so ignorant in this area as to feel that he must eschew any but the blandest public statements about policy issues; but I suspect that I have plenty of company. So let me go one step beyond my denial of allegiance to the monetarist camp of policy proposals and declare my lack of allegiance to any other camp, Keynesian or otherwise. I am committed in truth to just one proposition, which is that I know too little about monetary dynamics to commit myself to any systematic scheme of monetary policy, passive or active, that has been or might be proposed at this time.

This is already an over-long and discursive paper, so I shall conclude with a brief comment about directions for future research. The conception of a money economy that I have outlined does not encourage me to regard monetary policy as a sensitive or reliable instrument of economic control at the present time. Nor do I believe that its potential merits, or lack thereof, can be properly assessed on the basis of time-series and cross-section evidence of the sort that is presently available.

[25] This observation is not in any way intended to detract from the scientific importance of Prof. Friedman's work, but rather to put it into perspective and to question its immediate usefulness as a basis for theoretical and empirical research by less talented writers. For a more elaborate appraisal and appreciation of Prof. Friedman's contributions to monetary economics, see my 'Monetary History and Positive Economics', *Journal of Economic History* 24, Sept. 1964, pp. 364–80.

Accordingly, I see little point in ever more elaborate statistical analyses of alternative demand functions for money or in similar studies of full-scale econometric models. However, I think we might learn a good deal about the dynamics of observable processes of monetary adjustment, and about related possibilities for economic control, if we had access to information of the sort that would be provided by a continuous cross-section sample of a representative selection of trans-actors whose asset holdings, sales, purchases, and income and expenditures were recorded in detail on a monthly or quarterly basis. Much of the theoretical and empirical research required to ensure proper design of such a sample, and accurate definition and measurement of relevant sample data, has already been carried out, but with other objectives in mind and without explicit reference to a generally acceptable theory of monetary phenomena. It is in this direction—the elaboration of a scheme of data collection and processing that will permit reliable empirical testing of alternative formal models of monetary adjustment—that I see some hope of future progress in monetary theory and policy and a possible end to the inconclusive debates that have plagued monetary economics for nearly two centuries. In the absence of work along these lines, I see no hope at all.

PART III

MONEY SUPPLY AND DEMAND

9

WHAT TRADITIONAL MONETARY THEORY
REALLY WASN'T

Being something of a jackass even now where monetary questions are concerned, I share Professor Samuelson's misgivings about some currently fashionable interpretations of classical and neoclassical monetary theory.[1] The trouble with jackasses is that their thoughts can't safely be inferred from the expressions on their faces. It is good of Samuelson to give us the inside story of what it was like once to have been a jackass, but he will be the first to appreciate that some of us other jackasses just will not trust our fellows—particularly when they look as if they've just had a change of heart.

Samuelson assures us that he and his friends "back in the bad old days" were not such monetary simpletons as some modern writers would have us believe. For though he admits that his early thoughts were sometimes less than coherent—bordering, indeed, on the schizophrenic—he denies ever having recognized any but one legitimate dichotomy between real and monetary aspects of economic analysis,[2] namely, the familiar *positive dichotomy* (based on zero-degree homogeneity of criterion functions in money prices and nominal money balances)[3] that permits us to assert that the nominal quantity of money ultimately determines nothing but the scale of money prices in a monetary economy.[4]

So far, so good. I accept all of this, and I agree with Samuelson's contention that the positive dichotomy is the only one to which any classical economist from Hume to Pigou could be said to adhere as a matter of theoretical principle.[5] But this is not the only dichotomy to which Professor Samuelson commits himself in the course of his discussion. For having set out relevant conditions for long-run demand-

---

[1] P. A. Samuelson, "What classical and neoclassical monetary theory really was," *Canadian Journal of Economics*, 1 (Feb. 1968), 1–15.

[2] *Ibid.*, 2–5.

[3] *Ibid.*, 4. Also P. A. Samuelson, *Foundations of Economic Analysis* (Cambridge, Mass., 1947), 119.

[4] Cf. R. W. Clower and M. L. Burstein, "On the invariance of the demand for cash and other assets," *Review of Economic Studies*, 28 (Oct. 1960), 32–6.

[5] Samuelson, "What classical and neoclassical monetary theory really was," 3.

for-money equilibrium in an illustrative classical model, he goes on to argue that the positive dichotomy implies as a corollary a second, *normative dichotomy*, between private and social costs of holding real cash balances.[6]

The second dichotomy is not original with Samuelson. It appears first to have been enunciated by Professor Friedman[7] and has since come to play a prominent role in several areas of monetary thought.[8] As far as I am aware, however, Samuelson is the first writer to provide anything resembling a fully reasoned account of the matter. Accordingly, his statement of the normative dichotomy deserves to be quoted at length:

Each man thinks of his cash balance as costing him foregone interest and as buying himself convenience. But for the community as a whole, the total M^* is there and is quite costless to use. Forgetting gold mining and the historical expenditure of resources for the creating of M^*, the existing M^* is, so to speak, a free good from society's viewpoint. Moreover, its *effective* amount can, from the community's viewpoint, be indefinitely augmented by the simple device of having a lower absolute level of *all* money prices.

Evidently we have here an instance of a lack of optimality of laissez-faire: there is a kind of fictitious internal diseconomy from holding more cash balances, as things look to the individual. Yet if all were made to hold larger cash balances, which they turned over more slowly, the resulting lowering of absolute prices would end up making everybody better off. Better off in what sense? In the sense of having a higher U, which comes from having to make fewer trips to the bank, fewer trips to the brokers, smaller printing and other costs of transactions whose only purpose is to provide cash when you have been holding too little cash.

From society's viewpoint, the optimum occurs when people are satiated with cash and have: $\partial U/\partial M = 0$. ... But this will not come about under laissez-faire, with stable prices.[9]

---

[6] *Ibid.*, 7–9.

[7] Milton Friedman, *A Program for Monetary Stability* (New York, 1959), 71–5. Friedman's discussion is foreshadowed in an earlier article by George S. Tolley, "Providing for growth of the money supply," *Journal of Political Economy*, 65 (Dec. 1957), 477.

[8] See, for example, James Tobin, "Towards improving the efficiency of the monetary mechanism," *Review of Economics and Statistics*, 42 (Aug. 1960), 276–9; Clark Warburton, "Prohibition of interest on demand deposits," in *The Federal Reserve System after 50 Years*, vol. 3. Committee on Banking and Currency, U.S. House of Representatives, Hearings (April 1964), 2080–92, reprinted in R. A. Ward, ed., *Monetary Theory and Policy* (Scranton, 1966), 280–303; H. G. Johnson, "Money in a neo-classical one-sector growth model," *Essays in Monetary Economics* (London, 1967), 170; Edmund S. Phelps, "Anticipated inflation and economic warfare," *Journal of Political Economy*, 73 (Feb. 1965), 8–12; Alvin L. Marty, "Gurley and Shaw on money in a theory of finance," *Journal of Political Economy*, 68 (Feb. 1961), 57–8; James Tobin, Alvin Marty, and others, "Issues in monetary research, 1967," *Journal of Political Economy*, 76 (July/Aug. 1968), 833–92.

[9] Samuelson, "What classical and neoclassical monetary theory really was," 9–10.

In effect, the normative dichotomy asserts that real cash balances are in the nature of a social elixir; for the total quantity of such balances directly influences individual indices of euphoria without in any way affecting individual or social production possibilities. On this view, it surely is true that any device that serves to lower money prices will, *ceteris paribus*, increase human happiness at no cost in physical or psychological resources. But is the normative dichotomy valid?

That something is amiss with Samuelson's argument may be seen intuitively by noting that the only vector of money prices that can be counted upon to "satiate people" with real cash balances is the zero vector; i.e., money prices would have to be so low that the purchasing power of a single unit of money was infinite. But what sense could be made in this case of the budget equations of representative men or the profit equations of representative firms? To phrase the issue more concretely, can anyone seriously believe that there exists some "simple device" by which all money prices can be *permanently* reduced without either changing the nominal quantity of money (the positive dichotomy) or altering prevailing technological possibilities? Forcing people to hold larger cash balances (lengthening transaction periods), the device suggested by Samuelson, would not do—for carried to its logical extreme, it would entail a postponement of all trade to the millennium, which would hardly be a "simple" affair in a world where people are mortal.

So much for heuristics. Consider Samuelson's formal model. To paraphrase an earlier Samuelson account of exactly similar models,[10] in every problem of monetary theory certain variables are designated as unknowns, in whose determination we are interested. Their values emerge as a solution of a specified system of relationships imposed upon the unknowns by assumption or hypothesis. To make the analysis meaningful in an operational sense, it is necessary *explicitly* to introduce into the system certain data in the form of parameters which, in changing, cause the values of unknown variables to change. The usefulness of the theory emerges from the fact that we are often able to determine by this procedure the qualitative response of our unknowns to designated changes in one or more parameters.

Does Samuelson's neoclassical monetary model contain any explicit parameter, other than the nominal quantity of money, the value of which could be assumed to be variable at no cost to society? The answer is in the negative. Equilibrium real cash balances are a *constant* in Samuelson's system, for the positive dichotomy implies that equilibrium real cash balances are invariant with respect to changes in the

---

[10] Samuelson, *Foundations of Economic Analysis*, 7.

nominal quantity of money. The logical musculature of the model, as distinct from its verbal fat, does not permit us to discuss changes in equilibrium holdings of real cash balances except in terms of changes in *unspecified* parameters that implicitly underlie the definition of individual utility and production functions. This being so, Samuelson's assertions about people being "better off" for making "fewer trips to the brokers" when they are "made to hold larger cash balances," are analytically vacuous and operationally meaningless.

To be sure, Professor Samuelson's assertions about the blessings of cheap money may be true for some economy (though not, I suspect for any economy in which money is desired solely for its value in exchange). In his model, however, it is not true that the marginal cost of producing real cash balances is zero. Strictly speaking, his model provides no information one way or the other as to what the social cost of varying real cash balances might be at the margin or elsewhere—for no variations can be legitimately contemplated. If Samuelson has views on the subject (and his verbal description of his model suggests that he does), he should express them in terms of an explicit model that the rest of us can examine and evaluate. As matters stand, the conceptual experiments that he asks us to join him in performing are logically inadmissible; hence the conclusions that he asks us to accept are devoid of analytical or empirical meaning. It is almost as if, in an otherwise serious discussion of nonconservative physical systems, we were suddenly asked to contemplate the wonders of perpetual motion—achievable by the "simple device" of eliminating all friction. To speak of removing friction from nonconservative physical systems is a contradiction in terms. Is it not just as much a contradiction to speak of satiating people with real cash balances in a monetary economy?

Let me answer my own query by offering what I should consider a correct statement of the implications of the *whole* of Samuelson's argument, due account being taken not only of his equation systems but also of his cogent background remarks about the reasons why individuals might hold and use money once the advantages of money as compared with barter exchange ". . . had been realized by the adoption of market structures using M."[11]

The immediate victim of Samuelson's background remarks would be the curiously specialized production possibility function set out on p. 9 of his paper; for whatever else Samuelson might say about the nature of the money economy his paper is supposed to portray, he

---

[11] Samuelson, "What classical and neoclassical monetary theory really was," 3, and see 2, 5, 8.

cannot claim in the light of his verbal remarks that the production functions of individuals are independent either of real holdings of commodity inventories or of real holdings of cash. The crucial error in his argument consists in overlooking the fact that money balances cannot be useful in trade unless they release resources for use in other directions. The normative dichotomy arises, in truth, from tacitly supposing that trading activities—unlike the hallowed Walrasian rituals of production and consumption—are carried on *costlessly* under any and all circumstances. But if one really wants to make this assumption, why bother with money? It's just a notational nuisance in a conventional Walrasian model.

Having replaced Samuelson's anachronistic production possibility function with a relation that takes reasonable account of real costs associated with trading processes, my summary of the implications of his argument would run approximately as follows.

In long-run demand-for-money equilibrium, each man thinks of his cash balances as costing him forgone interest and as buying himself resource savings (time, effort, bookkeeping and transport activity, etc.) by permitting him to avoid needlessly frequent small-lot transactions. For the community as a whole, nominal cash balances are free, but real cash balances are as costly to society (and also as beneficial) as they are costly (and beneficial) to individuals. Private rationality requires that holdings of cash be chosen such that the value of resources saved are equal at the margin to the value of goods and services that the same resources would produce in their best alternative use. From society's viewpoint, the effective amount of real cash balances can be altered only by devices that increase the technological efficiency of monetary institutions or by changes in existing parameters of production technology and personal taste.

Evidently we have here a classic instance of the optimality of *laissez-faire*. Each individual thinks of himself as choosing his own cash balance on the basis of selfish maximizing motives. Yet no matter how large or how small may be the nominal quantity of money objects possessed by the community, the real amount of cash is determined ultimately by productivity and thrift—the same real forces as determine inventory holdings in a moneyless barter economy.

I do not question the substantial validity of Professor Samuelson's interpretation of the implicit beliefs of "classical and neoclassical" monetary theorists. Indeed, the only aspect of his interpretation that must in all justice be challenged is that which deals with the normative dichotomy. For though classical and neoclassical writers may be charged with many sins, it would be monstrous to foist upon them this peculiarly modern collector's piece of analytical sophistry.

10

IS THERE AN OPTIMAL MONEY SUPPLY?

The Pareto optimality of competitive equilibrium in a money economy is an interesting question not so much for its own sake as for the light that attempts to answer it have shed upon weaknesses in the foundations of contemporary monetary theory. More specifically, it seems to me that modern discussions of monetary optimality have so far yielded little more than a restatement of standard conclusions of welfare economics; for the conception of money implicit in most of these discussions does not permit us to distinguish analytically between "money" and any other commodity the demand for which depends partly on its usefulness as a store of value. Thus the question of an optimal supply of real money balances effectively has been disposed of as if it were equivalent to the question of an optimal supply of pearls or Old Masters.[1]

I am not suggesting that this procedure has generated false conclusions; on the contrary, my argument is simply that the premises explicitly adduced by previous writers are insufficient to support any definite conclusions about monetary optimality in a world where money commodities play a significant role as exchange intermediaries. In this paper, therefore, I propose to reconsider the entire question of an optimal supply of money, starting with what might be regarded as contemporary wisdom and ending with what I hope may be regarded as wisdom of a slightly higher order.

I. MONETARY OPTIMALITY: THE CONTEMPORARY PARADIGM

Perhaps the clearest statement of prevailing doctrine is provided by Samuelson's incidental remarks on the subject of monetary optimality

[1] The literature on the subject is too extensive to be cited in detail here, but its essential flavor may be gleaned from the following sample: G. S. Tolley, "Providing for Growth of the Money Supply," *Journal of Political Economy*, Vol. 65 (Dec., 1957), pp. 465–85; James Tobin, "Notes on Optimal Monetary Growth," *Journal of Political Economy*, Vol. 76 (July/August, 1968), pp. 833–59; A. L. Marty, "The Optimal Rate of Growth of Money," *Journal of Political Economy*, Vol. 76 (July/August, 1968), pp. 860–73; P. A. Samuelson, "What Classical and Neoclassical Monetary Theory Really Was," *Canadian Journal of Economics*, Vol. 1 (Feb., 1968), pp. 1–15; Milton Friedman, "The Optimum Quantity of Money," *The Optimum Quantity of Money and Other Essays* (Chicago: Aldine, 1969), pp. 14–21.

in a recent paper on classical and neoclassical monetary theory.[2] Samuelson's discussion deals with an economy in which the representative transactor chooses optimal stationary values of consumption and money balances subject to a long-run budget equation in which the cost of holding money balances consists of virtual interest income forgone on alternative earning assets. In this model, equilibrium requires that the marginal utility of money be positive and proportional to the rate of interest. Having set out this result, Samuelson goes on to argue:

Each man thinks of his cash balance as costing him foregone interest and as buying himself convenience. But for the community as a whole, the total (stock of money) is there and is quite costless to use. Forgetting gold mining and the historical expenditure of resources for the creating of (the money stock), the existing (stock) is, so to speak a free good from society's viewpoint. Moreover, its *effective* amount can, from the community's viewpoint, be indefinitely augmented by the simple device of having a lower absolute level of *all* money prices.

Evidently we have here an instance of a lack of optimality of laissez-faire: there is a kind of fictitious internal diseconomy from holding more cash balances, as things look to the individual. Yet if all were made to hold larger cash balances, which they turned over more slowly, the resulting lowering of absolute prices would end up making everybody better off. Better off in what sense? In the sense of having a higher (utility), which comes from having to make fewer trips to the bank, fewer trips to the brokers, smaller printing and other costs of transactions whose only purpose is to provide cash when you have been holding too little cash.

From society's viewpoint, the optimum occurs when people are satiated with cash (so that the marginal utility of cash is zero) . . . . But this will not come about under laissez-faire, with stable prices.[3]

Samuelson's intuitive conception of a monetary economy presupposes that the main function of money is to serve as a medium of exchange; hence, his suggestion that larger holdings of cash balances will be associated with fewer trips to banks and brokers and so with smaller transaction costs per unit of time. But this presupposition is not embedded in Samuelson's formal model; strictly speaking, Samuelson's analysis does not permit us to assert even that money is used in exchange transactions, much less to say that the turnover rate of money will decrease if the effective quantity of money is increased. And if money is not used for transaction purposes, but is held simply as a store of value—the only possibility that is directly suggested by Samuelson's formal model—then any gain accruing to individuals through a rise in real money balances is just as much a social illusion

---

[2] Cited in footnote 1, above.
[3] *Ibid.*, pp. 9–10.

as is the apparent cost to individuals of holding money balances.[4] Society cannot be shown to be "better off" in terms of any of the factors mentioned by Samuelson for the simple reason that these and other possible sources of real transaction costs nowhere enter his formal model.

I have singled out Samuelson's argument not because it is more open to objection than similar arguments advanced by other writers, but rather because no other writer has so carefully set out a formal model before proceeding to discuss the question of monetary optimality. Friedman's recent essay on "The Optimum Quantity of Money,"[5] might have been chosen on similar grounds; but this would not have affected the outcome of our discussion in any significant respect, for Friedman's analysis, like Samuelson's, is vitiated by the absence of any explicit account of the relation between real money balances and real transaction costs.[6]

The same objection applies to all discussions of monetary optimality whose theoretical roots lie in the soil of conventional value theory; for conventional value theory is essentially a device for logical analysis of *virtual trades* in a world where individual economic activities are costlessly coordinated by a central market authority. It has nothing whatever to say about delivery and payment arrangements, about the timing or frequency of market transactions, about search, bargaining, information and other trading costs, or about countless other commonplace features of real-world trading processes.[7] In this respect, value theory is analogous to Newton's theory of a frictionless "ideal fluid"—an intellectually stimulating and conceptually fruitful model the implications of which are seriously at variance with the most elementary facts of experience. Hydrodynamic theory began to bear significant practical fruit only after Newton's model was generalized

---

[4] Compare K. Wicksell, *Lectures on Political Economy* (London: George Routledge and Sons, 1935), Vol. II, pp. 8–9.

[5] Cited in footnote 1, above.

[6] *Ibid.*, pp. 2–3. Like most other writers, Friedman refers verbally to transaction costs of various kinds (e.g., at p. 14 and at pp. 17–18); but his formal model is entirely innocent of such complications.

[7] This point has been made by many writers, but most especially by Sir John Hicks in his *Critical Essays in Monetary Theory* (Oxford: The Clarendon Press, 1967), pp. 6–7. Interesting attempts to fill this gap in conventional theory have recently been made by Armen Alchian, T. R. Saving, Karl Brunner and Allan Meltzer, Joseph Ostroy, Jack Hirshleifer, Jurg Niehans, Preston Miller, and E. Feige and M. Parkin, to mention just those authors whose work I have been privileged to see. As of this time, however, no writer has provided an entirely satisfactory conceptual framework for analyzing the phenomena in question.

around the turn of this century to deal explicitly with non-ideal, vis-
cous fluids—such fluids being the only kind that exist in actual fact.[8]
A similar generalization of value theory is evidently required if we
are ever to establish an acceptable theoretical foundation for explicit
analysis of monetary exchange processes. The problem of monetary
optimality is just one of many issues the solution to which must remain
in doubt in the meantime.

II. THE TECHNOLOGY OF MONETARY EXCHANGE

It is one thing to recognize a problem, another to solve it. Ideally,
transaction and other costs of market exchange should be introduced
into microeconomic analysis via the formulation of an explicit dynamic
model in which holdings of commodity and money inventories at any
given point in time are a function of planned intertemporal patterns
of market purchases and sales. The conceptual and mathematical
difficulties of this procedure are too great, however, for it to be regarded as a practical possibility at this time. A far from ideal, but
currently feasible, alternative is to introduce trading costs into statical
representations of stationary solutions to implicit dynamical models.
The objection to this approach is that it takes for granted what cannot
be proved, namely, the existence and qualitative characteristics of
stationary solutions to dynamical models the precise characteristics of
which are never specified. Since the practical force of this objection
can be gauged only in the light of experience, however, we need not
regard it as fatal.

Proceeding as suggested, let me begin by considering the qualitative
properties of the stationary solution to a dynamical problem the details
of which are reasonably clear, at least to me: namely, the problem of
managing my own finances. As most of my friends know, my expenditures tend always to exhaust my income, and my income, particularly
in recent years, has been regrettably constant. So my holdings of
assets—mostly negative—are, on average, constant over time although
my holdings of money and consumer good inventories fluctuate considerably from day to day and week to week. All things considered,
therefore, my "state" as an economic man is effectively stationary.

Now, the most notable fact about my asset position concerns my
holdings not of currency, demand deposits, bonds or jewels, but rather
my holdings of consumer good inventories. My average inventory of

[8] Cf. G. Birkhoff, *Hydrodynamics* (Princeton: Princeton University Press, 1960), pp.
3–5; L. Prandtl and O. G. Tietjens, *Hydro- and Aeromechanics* (New York: McGraw-Hill,
1934), Vol. I.

money is normally minuscule compared with the dollar value of my holdings of canned goods, milk, soap, cigarettes, bread, coffee, gasoline, shirts, typing paper, razor blades, etc. In holding physical commodity inventories, I obviously incur some storage and deterioration charges as well as costs in terms of forgone interest income. To justify what at first sight might be regarded as irrational behavior on my part, I have only to remark that *not* to hold sizeable inventories of most of the goods I regularly consume would cost me dearly in terms of time and effort spent in frequent trips to market. Rational behavior on my part requires that my average holdings of consumption good inventories be maintained at a level such that the value to me of their imputed marginal yield of leisure and energy is at least as great as the direct marginal cost of holding them.

Unfortunately, my recurrent shopping activities involve certain indirect as well as direct inventory costs; for in order to purchase goods regularly, I have to carry a certain inventory of cash as a passport for entry into the organized market provided by local shops. Since any money I have on hand adds something to the interest cost of my current overdraft, I attempt to keep my average holdings of cash as small as possible. But this does not mean that I shop and pay bills only on pay day—the one procedure that would effectively reduce my average cash balance to zero—for this would force me to carry huge inventories of consumer goods through most of the month, and the costs of doing this would outweigh any real or monetary savings associated with lower cash balances and less frequent trips to market. What I in fact do is to choose the frequency and timing of my shopping trips in the light both of direct costs of holding commodity inventories and related indirect costs of holding money balances.

This personalized description of the factors governing my choice of commodity and money inventories may be clarified by a diagram. Let the trading cost curve $T(q^0)$ in Figure 1 indicate the dollar cost per unit of time of leisure and energy devoted to trade, corresponding to alternative possible dollar values of average holdings of consumption good inventories, Q, and some given flow of consumption expenditure, q^0. The trading cost curve is drawn on the assumption that trading costs depend partly on the frequency of market purchases per unit trade period (for which the ratio q^0/Q is a convenient proxy), partly on the quantity of goods purchased per shopping trip (for which Q is a proxy). Up to a point, therefore, there are economies of scale in holdings of commodity inventories; but the trading cost curve ultimately reaches a minimum and thereafter rises without limit.

Direct waiting costs associated with alternative holdings of commodity inventories are shown in Figure 1 by the curve W_Q, indirect

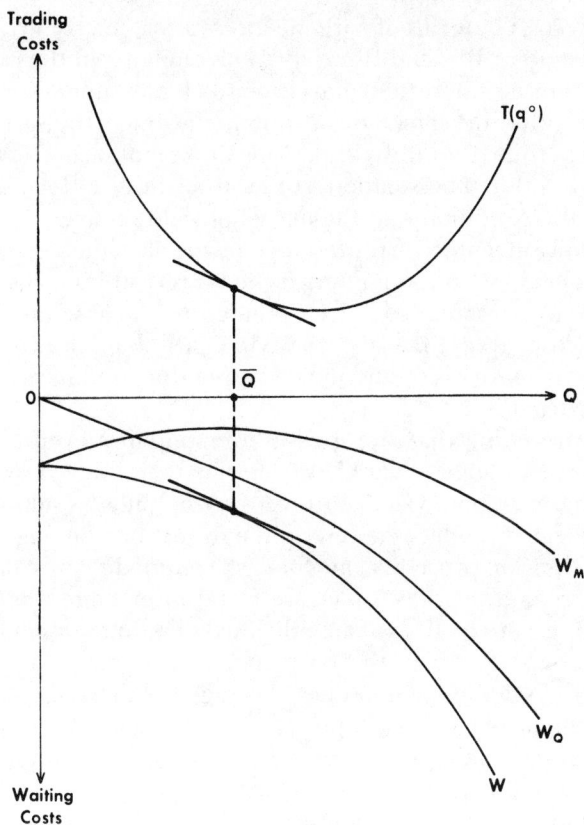

Figure 1

waiting costs by the curve W_M, and total waiting costs (the vertical sum of W_Q and W_M) by the curve W. The amount of indirect waiting costs (interest income foregone) corresponding to any given value of Q depends on the timing and frequency of purchases in relation to the timing and frequency of income receipts, and upon money prices. In general, these costs will decline, up to a point, as purchases and sales become more closely synchronized, but will thereafter rise indefinitely, as suggested by the form of the curve W_M. Direct waiting costs (interest income foregone, plus storage and other charges) are, of course, a strictly increasing function of the dollar value of average inventory holdings as indicated by the curve W_Q. Except in special cases, indirect waiting costs will be relatively small compared with direct waiting costs since money costs little or nothing to store whereas storage and other costs of holding commodity inventories may loom very large in relation to costs in terms of forgone interest income. In general, therefore, the curve W will differ only moderately from the curve W_Q.

The choice of an optimal average stock of commodity inventories (equivalently, the choice of an optimal average transaction period) requires that the individual minimize total marketing costs, $T + W_Q + W_M$. The solution to the problem is defined in the usual way by the condition that the marginal yield on average holdings of commodity inventories (represented by the absolute slope of the trading cost curve T) be equal to marginal direct waiting costs plus marginal indirect waiting costs (represented by the absolute slope of the waiting cost curve W). As the curves in Figure 1 are drawn, the optimal average inventory is $\overline{Q}$, and the corresponding optimal average transaction period is $2Q/q^0$.[9]

The preceding diagram grossly oversimplifies even the statics of monetary exchange. What I have described as a single decision process involving aggregate values of inventory holdings would appear in a disaggregated model as a description of just one among many interrelated decision processes, one for each commodity purchased or sold. Trade being a two-way street, we could infer from a more general model alternative values of an individual's holdings of money balances from knowledge about the frequency and money value of his purchases and sales of commodities. Average holdings of cash as a "temporary abode of purchasing power"[10] would then be determined along with average holdings of commodity inventories by the requirement that cash holdings be minimal relative to any given set of values of production and consumption flows.

The elaboration of a full scale model along the lines suggested poses no problems of principle, but neither is it likely to yield any essentially new information. One can only go so far with statical techniques of analysis—especially when the dynamics remain shrouded in intuition. In any event, we have gone far enough to assert what is important for present purposes, namely, that equilibrium holdings of real money balances are inextricably linked with equilibrium holdings of com-

---

[9] The model outlined here bears an obvious resemblance to the classic inventory models of Baumol and Tobin. The essential difference lies in the addition to the present model of relevant indirect waiting costs—an item that is entirely overlooked in earlier discussions of the problem. The crucial point is simply that every exchange involves at least two commodities; hence, holdings of inventories of one exchangeable commodity (money or goods) entail holdings of inventories of at least one other commodity. On this, see R. W. Clower, *Monetary Theory: Selected Readings* (London: Penguin Books, 1969), pp. 7–14.

[10] The phrase is Friedman's, and aptly characterizes the essential function of money as an exchange intermediary.

modity inventories, and *vice versa*. We may also assert that the link between real money balances and commodity inventories is much too complex to permit us to infer anything either about turnover rates of inventories from information about real cash balances, or about average holdings of real cash balances from information about commodity inventories. More pointedly, it is incorrect to suggest—as numerous writers have done—that real transactions balances can be produced at no cost to society; for, in general, every change in real balances will be associated with changes in socially costly holdings of commodity inventories. Moreover, it is incorrect to suggest that a change in interest rates that makes money balances less costly for individuals to hold will tend to increase equilibrium holdings of real money balances; for it is entirely possible that interest-induced changes in equilibrium holdings and turnover rates of commodity inventories will produce exactly the opposite effect.[11]

III. MONETARY OPTIMALITY: AN ALTERNATIVE VIEW

The central point that emerges from the preceding discussion is that real marketing costs depend in an essential way on turnover rates of commodity inventories and cannot be inferred directly from information about individual or aggregate holdings of real money balances. On this view, the question of an optimal supply of money should be rephrased to read: "Is There an Optimal Supply of Money and Other Trade Inventories?" The answer to this question is provided, at least in principle, by the diagrammatic argument of the preceding section. What is required for Pareto optimality is that the marginal cost of holding commodity and money inventories, as viewed by individuals, should accurately reflect corresponding marginal social costs. Now, this condition will be satisfied only if marginal *indirect* waiting costs associated with holdings of transactions balances correspond to social opportunity costs; for unless this requirement is met, the real rate of return on some commodities held as trade capital will exceed the real rate of return on the same commodities used as capital goods in production. Thus a transfer of commodity inventories from the trading sector to the production sector of the economy, even though it entails an increase in trading costs via increased turnover rates of trade inventories, will yield a marginal increase in aggregate output of goods and services.

This conclusion obviously accords with that reached by Friedman,

[11] For examples of the assertions in question, see any of the papers cited in footnote 1, above.

Samuelson, Tobin, Johnson, Marty, Phelps, Levhari and Patinkin, and other writers who have approached the problem of monetary optimality by a more conventional route.[12] In the present case, however, the conclusion can be justified by reference to identifiable sources of social cost and benefit. In effect, our analysis supplies a needed theoretical rationale for the intuitive ideas that underlie earlier discussions of the monetary optimality problem.

It is an altogether more difficult matter to determine the practical circumstances in which marginal indirect waiting costs will accurately reflect social opportunity costs. Presumably this condition will be satisfied under *laissez-faire* in an economy where transactions balances consist entirely of "inside money," e.g., of privately issued bonds or of privately produced nuggets of gold. And presumably the condition will not be satisfied in an economy where the supply of means of payment is determined by government fiat and consists of commodities that do not bear interest. But the world as we know it contains many kinds of money commodities, some provided by government, some by banks and other business concerns. In recent years, for example, any household transactor that wished to economize on cash could do so fairly effectively by arranging appropriate non-interest bearing lines of credit with department stores, banks, and credit card companies. Such action should, in principle, yield a more optimal allocation of resources within the household sector, but its effect on other sectors of the economy, particularly when we consider administrative and other costs connected with credit means of payment, might well be adverse. Apparently this example involves a problem of second best, but is this not typical of the world in which we live?

Even if it were possible accurately to identify situations in which holdings of commodity and money inventories were Pareto nonoptimal, there would still be serious question whether anything should be done to move the economy in the direction of optimality. For example, suppose it were feasible to pay direct interest subsidies to

---

[12] See the papers cited in footnote 1, above; also H. G. Johnson, "Money in a Neo-Classical One-Sector Growth Model," *Essays in Monetary Economics* (London: Allen and Unwin, 1967), p. 170; E. S. Phelps, "Anticipated Inflation and Economic Warfare," *Journal of Political Economy*, Vol. 73 (Feb., 1965), pp. 8–12; D. Levhari and D. Patinkin, "The Role of Money in a Simple Growth Model," *American Economic Review*, Vol. 58 (Sept., 1968), pp. 713–53. For a contrary opinion on this matter, see R. W. Clower, "What Traditional Monetary Theory Really Wasn't," *Canadian Journal of Economics*, Vol. 2 (May, 1969), pp. 299–302, and B. P. Pesek, "Comment on the Optimal Growth Rate of Money," *Journal of Political Economy*, Vol. 76 (July/August, 1968), pp. 885–92. Mention should also be made of the stimulating but rather equivocal discussion of the problem by S. C. Tsiang, "A Critical Note on the Optimum Supply of Money," *Journal of Money, Credit, and Banking*, Vol. 1 (May, 1969), pp. 266–80.

holders of money balances or, alternatively, suppose it were feasible to induce a steady rate of price deflation by imposing appropriate lump sum taxes on money holdings of individuals. Then, in principle, waiting costs on currency and demand deposits could be reduced to zero, and technical efficiency considerations would seem to favor action to accomplish this result. In practice, however, no program of government intervention is costless. Moreover, since direct waiting costs on holdings of commodity inventories are likely to be vastly greater than indirect waiting costs associated with holdings of transactions balances, it is not at all clear that the complete elimination of indirect waiting costs would have any appreciable effect upon inventory turnover rates or, therefore, on social welfare. In general, mere ability to identify Pareto nonoptimal situations provides no basis whatever for policy prescriptions.

IV. CONCLUSION

Let me end on the note with which I began. The question of monetary optimality, like most questions in welfare economics, is important not so much for its own sake as for the stimulus it has given to monetary theorists to re-examine the foundations and strengthen the superstructure of their subject. As of the present time, the optimality question has provoked more assertion than analysis, more confusion than enlightenment, and more controversy than agreement; but that is just what has long been needed to rescue monetary theory from the arid wastes of Post-Keynesian general equilibrium analysis.[13] Perhaps we shall never have a definitive answer to the optimality problem, but we shall certainly have many attempts at it. And in the process we shall get what is most urgently needed: an improved theoretical understanding of the actual working of the economy in which we live.

[13] Cf. Axel Leijonhufvud, *Keynesian Economics and the Economics of Keynes* (New York: Oxford University Press, 1968), Chapters 1 and 2.

11

ON THE INVARIANCE OF DEMAND FOR CASH AND OTHER ASSETS

If the stock of cash held currently by an individual trader is defined to be the sum of his net receipts in previous periods plus some arbitrary initial balance, and if fiat money is the only asset that traders can carry over from one market period to another, then as Messrs. Archibald and Lipsey have recently demonstrated,[1] the trader's *equilibrium* demand for real cash balances is independent of the general price level and of initial balances and is governed instead by tastes and real income.[2] It is not clear, however, whether this result is valid in a model where money balances may be used to purchase and hold income-earning assets. If an individual can buy and sell bonds, for example, he can presumably effect a *permanent* change in his real income by substituting bonds for cash in his asset portfolio. Under these circumstances, real income is a variable rather than a parameter and the invariance of equilibrium real balances against a change in nominal money stocks or in the general price level would seem to be endangered.

Archibald and Lipsey also show that, for an economy in which money is the only asset, equilibrium relative prices are invariant with respect to changes in the aggregate quantity of money, regardless of the way in which such a change affects the distribution of money stocks among individual traders.[3] But the validity of this result also seems to be questionable in an economy where windfall variations in money stocks are capable of leading to permanent changes in the distribution of real income.

On closer analysis, however, it turns out that neither of these doubts is justified. Provided we adhere to the standard assumption of the

The authors are particularly indebted to Alvin Marty for helpful comment and criticism and also to Messrs. Archibald and Lipsey, Friedman, Hahn, Harwitz, Jaffé, Liviatan, Patinkin and Peters.
[1] G. C. Archibald and R. G. Lipsey, "Monetary and Value Theory: A Critique of Lange and Patinkin," *Review of Economic Studies*, October, 1958, p. 3ff.
[2] Priority for this result appears to belong to C. E. V. Leser. See "The Consumer's Demand for Money," *Econometrica*, April, 1943, pp. 133–4. Mitchell Harwitz called our attention to Leser's demonstration.
[3] Archibald and Lipsey, *op. cit.*, pp. 8–9.

uniqueness of equilibrium states,[4] invariance propositions similar to those enunciated by Archibald and Lipsey continue to hold not only for a bond-and-money economy but also for more general systems. The purpose of the present paper is to elaborate upon this theme and to indicate some of its more immediate implications.

I

Dealing first with notational and terminological preliminaries, suppose that in any given market period (say period t) the typical trader (call him trader "j") receives "...like manna from heaven..." quantities $s_j \equiv (s_{1j}, \ldots, s_{nj})$ of n nondurable commodities which may either be consumed directly or traded during the period at market prices $p(t) \equiv [p_1(t), \ldots, p_n(t)]$ so as to achieve at the close of the period a desired consumption pattern represented by $d_j(t) \equiv [d_{1j}(t), \ldots, d_{nj}(t)]$. Suppose further that the trader holds a quantity $S_{M_j}(t)$ of money and a quantity $S_{B_j}(t)$ of bonds at the outset of period t, but assume that these quantities may be increased or decreased through market trading so as to achieve at the end of the period a desired asset portfolio represented by the variables $D_{M_j}(t)$ and $D_{B_j}(t)$.[5] By hypothesis, bonds are perfectly standardized perpetuities which, in each market period, pay one unit of money to their holder and entail payment of one unit of money by their issuer. The market rate of interest, $r(t)$, is therefore equal to the reciprocal of the price of bonds, and the money value of the trader's bond income in period t is numerically equal to his bond holdings, $S_{B_j}(t)$.

II

Turning now to behavior postulates, we follow Patinkin[6] and suppose that the demand for each commodity and the real demand for bonds (equivalently, bond income) and for cash balances is in every case a function of real income, relative commodity prices, the rate of interest, real bond income and real money balances. The behavior of the jth trader is thus described, in part, by the relations

---

[4] *Ibid.*, p. 18, ftn. 2.

[5] No explicit constraint is imposed on the quantity of bonds issued by a trader in any single period, but the existence of some kind of limit is implicit throughout the subsequent discussion. On this and related matters see Patinkin, *Money, Interest, and Prices* (Row Peterson, Evanston, Ill., 1956), p. 53; Archibald and Lipsey, *op. cit.*, p. 2, ftn. 3.

[6] Patinkin, *op. cit.*, p. 53.

$$d_{ij}(t) = d_{ij}[s_j; \; p(t)/P(t); \; r(t); \; S_{B_j}(t)/P(t); \; S_{M_j}(t)/P(t)] \qquad (i = 1, \ldots, n) \quad (1)$$

$$D_{B_j}(t)/P(t) = D_{B_j}[s_j; \; p(t)/P(t); \; r(t); \; S_{B_j}(t)/P(t); \; S_{M_j}(t)/P(t)] \qquad (2)$$

$$D_{M_j}(t)/P(t) = D_{M_j}[s_j; \; p(t)/P(t); \; r(t); \; S_{B_j}(t)/P(t); \; S_{M_j}(t)/P(t)] \qquad (3)$$

where $P(t) \equiv \Sigma w_i p_i(t)$ represents "the general price level" in market period t and $j = 1, \ldots, m.$[7]

Following Archibald and Lipsey,[8] however, we suppose that the behavior of the stock quantities $S_{B_j}(t)$ and $S_{M_j}(t)$, respectively, is described by the relations[9]

$$S_{B_j}(t) = S_{B_j}(t_0) + \sum_{\theta = t_0}^{\theta = t - 1} [D_{B_j}(\theta) - S_{B_j}(\theta)] \qquad (4)$$

and

$$S_{M_j}(t) = S_{M_j}(t_0) + \sum_{\theta = t_0}^{\theta = t - 1} [D_{M_j}(\theta) - S_{M_j}(\theta)].^{[10]} \qquad (5)$$

Then for any given set of values of the parameters s_j, $p(t)/P(t)$ and $r(t)$, and for arbitrary values of the "initial asset" quantities $S_{B_j}(t_0)$ and $S_{M_j}(t_0)$, the recursive system (1)–(5) provides a total of $n + 4$ equations for any fixed value of j to determine the values of the $n + 4$ unknowns $d_j(t)$, $D_{B_j}(t)$, $D_{M_j}(t)$, $S_{B_j}(t)$ and $S_{M_j}(t)$ for all values of $t \geq t_0$. In particular, requiring that $\triangle S_{B_j}(t) = \triangle S_{M_j}(t) = 0$ and recalling the uniqueness assumption introduced earlier, (1)–(5) yields a determinate statical model comprising $n + 4$ equations to determine the *equilibrium values* $\overline{d}_j$, $\overline{D}_{B_j}$, $\overline{D}_{M_j}$, $\overline{S}_{B_j}$, $\overline{S}_{M_j}$ of the $n + 4$ variables over which the

[7] All trading is assumed to be constrained by Walras' Principle (i.e., expenditure "sinks" are exactly matched by income "sources," and vice versa); hence the condition

$$D_{M_j}(t) \equiv S_{M_j}(t) + [1/r(t)] [S_{B_j}(t) - D_{B_j}(t)] + S_{B_j}(t) - \sum_i p_i(t) [d_{ij}(t) - s_{ij}]$$

is tacitly embedded in the set of equations (1)–(3). Cf. footnote 6, below; also Patinkin, *op. cit.*, pp. 292ff.

[8] Archibald and Lipsey, *op. cit.*, pp. 2ff.

[9] This asserts that an individual trader is always in a position to acquire any desired quantity of an asset during a single market period. This seems reasonable for a fictional system in which prices are established by *tâtonnement*, despite its artificiality as applied to any concrete market situation. Patinkin says nothing on this subject, perhaps because to say anything at all about the determination of current asset balances is to say more than can easily be granted on casual empirical grounds. For this reason, Patinkin's model of a "bond-and-money" economy is more flexible (less restrictive in its assumptions) than ours or, for that matter, the model described by Archibald and Lipsey.

[10] Alternatively, (5) might be written (cf. footnote 3, above):

$$S_{M_j}(t) = S_{M_j}(t_0) + \sum_{\theta = t_0}^{\theta = t - 1} ([1/r(t)] [S_{B_j}(\theta) - D_{B_j}(\theta)] + S_{B_j}(\theta) - \Sigma p_i(\theta) [d_{ij}(\theta) - s_{ij}]).$$

individual trader exercises direct control. Solving to obtain the usual reduced form equations, therefore, we may write the identities

$$\left.\begin{array}{ll} \bar{d}_{ij} \equiv f_{ij}[s_j; \, p(t)/P(t); \, r(t)] & (i = 1, \ldots, n) \\ \overline{D}_{B_j}(t)/P(t) \equiv f_{B_j}[s_j; \, p(t)/P(t); \, r(t)] \\ \overline{D}_{M_j}(t)/P(t) \equiv f_{M_j}[s_j; \, p(t)/P(t); \, r(t)] \\ \overline{S}_{kj}(t)/P(t) \equiv f_{kj}[s_j; \, p(t)/P(t); \, r(t)] & (k = M, B). \end{array}\right\} \quad (S1)$$

The equilibrium values defined by (S1) are obviously independent of "initial assets."[11] More precisely, since the quantities $S_{B_j}(t_0)$ and $S_{M_j}(t_0)$ enter the dynamical system (1)–(5) as arbitrary constants (initial conditions) rather than "structural" parameters, they do not appear in the equations defining a stationary solution of the system. Moreover, since the system (S1) is homogeneous of order zero in the quantities $p_i(t)$, $\overline{D}_{kj}$ and $\overline{S}_{kj}$, the uniqueness assumption implies that the real demand for money and for bond income is independent of the general price level.

The same conclusions may be reached by an alternative route, arguing directly from the properties of the system (1)–(5). Starting from any initial equilibrium state, represented by a set of values of the "real" variables $\bar{d}_{ij}$, $\overline{D}_{kj}/P(t)$, $\overline{S}_{kj}/P(t)$, a once-over change in nominal asset balances or in the general price level involves a momentary relaxation of the dynamical assumptions underlying the system. If the initial "real" equilibrium state is stable, however, the system must ultimately tend to return to its initial "real" position. In this sense, equilibrium real balances are invariant against changes in nominal asset stocks. Notice, however, that it is meaningless to talk about the comparative statics effects of a change in initial asset balances in any *statical* system obtained from (1)–(5); for the only asset quantities that

[11] Following a suggestion by Mr. Hahn, "rational behavior" on the part of an individual trader would seem to require that manna income and real income from bonds be treated as perfect substitutes. If this suggestion is carried through (i.e., if the typical trader is assumed not to discriminate among different values of S_{B_j}/P and $\Sigma_i p_i s_{ij}/P$ so long as the numerical sum of the two items is the same), then it can be shown that the appropriately modified version of (S1)—i.e., a system of equilibrium identities in which the bond variables S_{B_j} and D_{B_j} in (S1) are replaced by the "composite" income variables $S_{yj} \equiv S_{B_j} + \Sigma_i p_i s_{ij}$ and $D_{yj} \equiv D_{B_j} + \Sigma_i p_i s_{ij}$—is independent of the manna variables s_{ij} as well as the initial asset variables $S_{B_j}(t_0)$ and $S_{M_j}(t_0)$. The explicit appearance of the variables s_j in the system (S1) appears to entail the existence of "manna illusion" on the part of the individual trader; but this is merely a possible, *not* a necessary consequence of our model.

can appear in such a system are $\overline{D}_{B_j}$, $\overline{D}_{M_j}$ and $\overline{S}_{kj}$, and these are dependent variables rather than (arbitrary) parameters.[12]

III

Extending the preceding analysis to deal with the determination of commodity prices and the rate of interest, we begin by assuming that the values of the variables $p_i(t)$ and $r(t)$ are chosen via some kind of *tâtonnement* process so as to ensure the simultaneous satisfaction of the set of $n + 1$ "market clearance" conditions

$$\sum_{j=1}^{j=m} [d_{ij}(t) - s_{ij}] = 0 \qquad (i = 1, \ldots, n) \tag{6}$$

$$\sum_{j=1}^{j=m} [D_{B_j}(t) - S_{B_j}(t)] = 0, \tag{7}$$

and simply add to these requirements the relations (1)–(5) set forth in section II, above. The resulting dynamical system, which we will call (S2), contains a total of $m(n + 4)$ relations describing *individual* behavior of which only $m(n + 4) - 2$ can be specified independently from a *market* point of view. More particularly, since the total quantity of bonds held by "creditors" at the beginning of any period is necessarily equal to the total quantity of bonds issued and sold by "debtors" up to the beginning of the same period, the set of equations (4) must satisfy the linear relation

$$\sum_{j=1}^{j=m} S_{M_j} \equiv 0. \tag{8}$$

Similarly, since the aggregate of individual holdings of money balances in any period must equal the total stock of money in the economy, the set of equations (5) must satisfy the linear relation

$$\sum_{j=1}^{j=m} S_{M_j} \equiv S_M \equiv \text{Constant.}[13] \tag{9}$$

Taking the identities (8) and (9) into account along with (1)–(7),

[12] The preceding results can be broadened to apply to a more general "individual experiment" in which individual traders buy and sell physical assets as well as securities and money, and in which the "manna" quantities s_j are themselves functions of relative prices and other "real" variables. On this, see below, footnote 14.

[13] It should be remarked that, by virtue of the constraint (9), the aggregate stock of money, S_M, may be regarded as a "structural parameter" in the dynamical system (S2). The constraint (8), on the other hand, does not fix the value of the aggregate stock of outstanding bonds, $S_B \equiv [1/2]\Sigma_j |S_{B_j}|$.

the dynamical system (S2) is determinate in the usual sense; i.e., it contains a total of $m(n + 4) + n + 1$ independent equations to determine the values of the $m(n + 4) + n + 1$ variables $d_1, \ldots, d_m$; $D_{B_1}, \ldots, D_{B_m}$; $D_{M_1}, \ldots, D_{M_m}$; $S_{B_1}, \ldots, S_{B_m}$; $S_{M_1}, \ldots, S_{M_m}$; p; and r.

Now suppose that the system (S2) has a stable "steady state" solution, $\bar{p}_i, \bar{r}, \bar{d}_{ij}, \bar{D}_{B_j}, \bar{D}_{M_j}, \bar{S}_{B_j}, \bar{S}_{M_j}$, corresponding to any given set of values s_j^0, S_M^0 of the parameters s_j and S_M. Then by direct inspection it can be seen that the set of values $\lambda\bar{p}_i, \bar{r}, \bar{d}_{ij}, \lambda\bar{D}_{B_j}, \lambda\bar{D}_{M_j}, \lambda\bar{S}_{B_j}, \lambda\bar{S}_{M_j}$, is the unique "steady state" solution of the system when s_j retains the value s_j^0, but S_M is assigned the new value λS_m^0 (λ being any positive constant). From this it follows that, in equilibrium, relative commodity prices, the rate of interest, and real asset balances are all invariant with respect to changes in the aggregate stock of money. Alternatively, it may be noted that the statical system obtained from (S2) by setting $\Delta S_{B_j} = \Delta S_{M_j} = 0$ can be solved uniquely to yield reduced form identities from which the aggregate money stock parameter, S_M, is altogether absent; thus

$$
\left.
\begin{aligned}
\bar{p}_i/P &\equiv g_i(s_1, \ldots, s_m) & (i &= 1, \ldots, n) \\
\bar{r} &\equiv g(s_1, \ldots, s_m) & & \\
\bar{d}_{ij} &\equiv h_{ij}(s_1, \ldots, s_m) & (i &= 1, \ldots, n; j = 1, \ldots, m) \\
\bar{D}_{B_j}/P &\equiv h_{B_j}(s_1, \ldots, s_m) & (j &= 1, \ldots, m) \\
\bar{D}_{M_j}/P &\equiv h_{M_j}(s_1, \ldots, s_m) & (j &= 1, \ldots, m) \\
\bar{S}_{B_j}/P &\equiv h_{B_j}(s_1, \ldots, s_m) & (j &= 1, \ldots, m) \\
\bar{S}_{M_j}/P &\equiv h_{M_j}(s_1, \ldots, s_m) & (j &= 1, \ldots, m)
\end{aligned}
\right\} \quad (S3)
$$

These conclusions have to be modified if one considers a model in which the total (nominal) stock of bonds is fixed in advance, that is, in which

$$
S_B \equiv [1/2] \sum_{j=1}^{j=m} |S_{B_j}| \equiv \text{Constant.}
$$

For in this case the ratio between the aggregate stock of bonds and the aggregate stock of money, i.e., S_B/S_M, appears as an explicit parameter in the reduced form equations corresponding to (S3). Even in this instance, however, all "real" quantities are invariant with respect to equiproportionate changes in the aggregate nominal stock of money *and* bonds. This emphasizes what is perhaps the most interesting feature of the dynamical system (S2), namely, that the stock of bonds is "geared" to the stock of money *via a market adjustment mechanism in* such a fashion that changes in the aggregate stock of bonds are, in equilibrium, directly proportional to changes in the stock of money.

Results precisely analogous to the above can be obtained for an economy containing fixed supplies of physical assets (which yield an income in "kind"). Provided no trader suffers from "money illusion," and provided individual traders are permitted to issue new securities and to retire outstanding debts in the light of changing market conditions, the effects of a change in the aggregate stock of money can and will be entirely offset by an equiproportionate rise in money prices and in nominal asset balances.

More generally, if we consider an economy in which all commodities except money are produced, consumed, and held in the form of assets, and if the relevant supply and demand functions of the system depend only on relative prices and other real variables, then it can be shown that the equilibrium demand for commodities, for real bond income, for physical assets, and for real money balances are all invariant against a change in the nominal stock of money. To put the matter another way, *the equilibrium distribution of real wealth and real income in such an economy is determined by "tastes and technique" and is otherwise independent of historical accidents.* This, it appears, is the most general statement of the Archibald–Lipsey "invariance principle."[14]

---

[14] A rigorous demonstration of these and related results would require more space than can be devoted to them here. The interested reader may pursue the matter further by consulting relevant portions of Bushaw and Clower, *Introduction to Mathematical Economics* (Richard D. Irwin, Inc., Homewood, Ill., 1957), and particularly pp. 36, 76, 128–34, 160–63, 166–71; also R. W. Clower, "An Investigation into the Dynamics of Investment," *American Economic Review*, March, 1954, pp. 69–71 and pp. 73–77.

12

SAY'S PRINCIPLE, WHAT IT MEANS
AND DOESN'T MEAN

> The doctrine in question only appears a paradox, because it has usually been so expressed as apparently to contradict . . . well-known facts; which, however, were equally well known to the authors of the doctrine, who, therefore, can only have adopted from inadvertence any form of expression which could to a candid person appear inconsistent with it.
>
> J. S. MILL, SOME UNSETTLED QUESTIONS OF POLITICAL ECONOMY (1844)

Students with some exposure to macroeconomics will recall that the standard verbal statement of "Say's Law" (SL) is "Supply creates its own demand." Students will also recall—at least if they have had the usual indoctrination in these matters—that the rejection of SL was associated with the development of Keynesian macroeconomics. Classical (pre-Keynesian) economists, so it is said, could not explain prolonged unemployment because they believed in SL, but Keynes denied the validity of SL and so was able to lay the foundations for a modern and reasonably adequate theory of income and employment . . . etc.[1]

Like most fairytales, this one contains an element of truth. Anyone who bothers to delve into the matter[2] will discover that textbook discussions of SL are seldom fair to pre-Keynesian writers. This is not surprising. Doubts about the meaning and significance of SL have been perplexing economists more or less continuously for nearly two centuries. The extensive literature since Keynes has done little to resolve these doubts, largely because it has failed to address squarely the main issues in dispute and so has got bogged down in a mire of conceptual and semantic confusions.

To avoid the same mistake, we shall ignore the previous literature for the time being and start by explaining and analyzing a simple but

---

This pedagogical excursion originated in a set of mimeographed "Class Notes on Say's Principle" written by Leijonhufvud and distributed to students at the Economics Institute, University of Colorado, in 1972. The original notes have been extensively rewritten and extended.

[1] For example, McConnell (1972), pp. 203–7.
[2] A good book to start with is Sowell (1972).

fundamental proposition that we shall call "Say's Principle" (SP). This principle, though elementary and outwardly trivial, is crucial for clear understanding of macro-theory. Indeed, there is hardly a single problem in macro-theory (or, for that matter, micro-theory) that can be consistently analyzed without it. The same principle permits us to resolve all issues of substance associated with earlier discussions of SL. It is essential, therefore, that students acquire a clear understanding not only of what SP means and does not mean, but also of what it implies and does not imply.

I. FUNDAMENTALS

In the following paper the term "commodity" will refer to any exchangeable object. Thus the usual macro-model, involving labor services, goods, bonds and money, has four commodities. Similarly, we shall use the term "transactor" (or individual) to refer to any economic agent or decision-making unit.[3] For reasons that will become clear later, we shall deal directly with just one type of economic activity, namely exchange. Occasional references to consumption, production and other non-trade activities are introduced only by way of illustration.

To lend direction to the argument, we begin by associating SP with a brief verbal statement that is easy to remember—not, however, with the phrase "Supply creates its own demand." A mnemonic much to be preferred is: *the net value of an individual's planned trades is identically zero.* (Notice, for reasons to be made clear later, we do not say net market value.) This is a restriction that we impose on the commodity trades that transactors are permitted to contemplate within the conceptual framework of economic theory, trades that we shall later refer to as theoretically admissible. It is not an assertion about the income and expenditure plans of flesh-and-blood humans (the world is full of thieves and philanthropists as well as people who can't calculate the cost of their weekly groceries). Neither is it an assertion that applies to all commodity transfers that occur in the real world (the acquisition of cash by a pickpocket is a case in point). What the restriction does and does not entail, however, is better indicated by argument than example.

Starting from familiar ground, consider one of the first exercises

---

[3] We will not bother to distinguish among households, business firms, financial intermediaries, government agencies and so on.

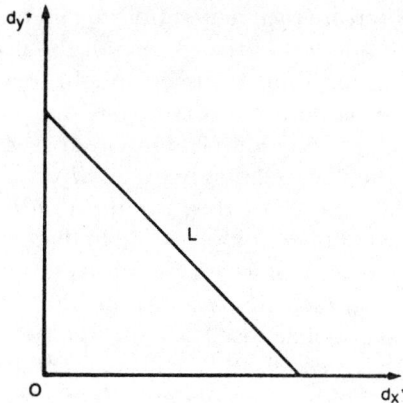

Figure 1

encountered in microeconomics, namely, the household decision problem of determining how a given amount of money, $s_{m,0}$, will be allocated to purchase quantities d_x and d_y of two commodities that are available at given money prices p_x and p_y. In this problem, the set of all possible budgets may be associated with the set of all points $d* = (d_x^*, d_y^*)$ in the non-negative (northeast) quadrant of the diagram shown in Figure 1. However, if the head of the household is presumed to be honest—or merely risk-averse—the set of all theoretically admissible trades of money for commodities will consist of points that lie on a single budget line (shown as L in Figure 1). This line is defined by the equation:

$$p_x d_x^* + p_y d_y^* - s_{m,0} = 0, \tag{1}$$

where (by hypothesis) p_x, p_y and $s_{m,0}$ are given decision parameters (i.e., constants, from the point of view of the individual). Points to the northeast of L represent budgets that have a value greater than $s_{m,0}$ dollars, while points to the southwest represent budgets that have a value less than $s_{m,0}$ dollars. Only those points that lie on the budget line represent budgets that have a value of precisely $s_{m,0}$ dollars. Let us denote budgets that satisfy equation (1) by $d = (d_x, d_y)$. The set of budgets d is, of course, a subset of the set of all possible budgets $d*$. By definition it is literally true that

$$p_x d_x + p_y d_y - s_{m,0} \equiv 0; \tag{2}$$

that is to say, all theoretically admissible budgets d identically satisfy equation (1).[4] This zero-net-value identity, i.e., identity (2), is an exact rendition of SP as it appears in the context of the present discussion.

At first sight, the preceding argument might seem to suggest that SP is implied by the assumption that household purchases are constrained by the budget equation (1). On closer inspection, however, it will be seen that the true relation between SP and the budget equation is precisely the reverse of this, for the validity of SP is tacitly presupposed in our initial definition of the budget equation. Thus SP appears in this instance as an independent assumption rather than a derived conclusion. In fact, this instance illustrates the general rule rather than the exceptional case; i.e., the restriction on individual trading behavior that we call SP is a fundamental postulate of economic theory that holds quite independently of other behavior assumptions.

The full significance of the last observation will become clear later. Meanwhile, the following comments may be helpful:

The budget equation (and so the budget line) is a special case of a class of behavioral restrictions that occur over and over again in economic analysis, restrictions that follow from a completely general proposition that we shall call *Say's Principle*. This proposition asserts, broadly speaking, that trade is a two-way street; i.e., individuals can expect to acquire commodities from other individuals only by giving commodities (or money) of equal market value in exchange. Say's Principle might seem almost too obvious to be worth stating, but it is as well to take nothing for granted at this point. It should be remarked, for example, that Say's Principle (and the budget equation) refers not to quantities actually purchased or to prices actually paid, but rather to expected purchase prices and planned quantities purchased. It is evident that if one pays, say, $10 for all groceries that he *actually* acquires in a supermarket, the total value of the separate items purchased must add up to $10—or else the supermarket checkout clerk has made a mistake. But it is neither obvious nor always true that a shopper who *plans* to spend $10 on groceries in a supermarket also plans to walk out of the store with a collection of goods that is valued at just $10; the shopper may be a shoplifter as well as a customer! In

[4] It may help clarify the distinction between d and d^*, and the related distinction between the conditional equation (1) and the identical equation (2), if we consider a simple analog. Suppose that an algebraist is assigned the problem of choosing one value of the variable x^* that satisfies the equation $x^{*2} = 9$. Clearly, most values of x^* that might be considered won't do. However, two values of x^*, namely, $x^* = 3$ and $x^* = -3$, do satisfy the equation. The set of theoretically admissible solutions to the original problem thus consists of two numbers. The original problem, which involves choosing some element x^* of the set of all real numbers, is thus transformed into the more restricted problem of choosing some element x of the set of just two real numbers, $|3, -3|$. Since the latter set is defined in such a way that all of its elements satisfy the conditional equation $x^{*2} = 9$, it follows trivially that any element x of the set $|3, -3|$ satisfies the same equation *identically*; i.e., $x^2 \equiv 9$. The algebraist, like the household, still has a choice to make, but the choice is narrowed down considerably by the requirement that $x^2 \equiv 9$ as compared with the weaker requirement that $x^{*2} = 9$.

effect, Say's Principle constitutes an implicit definition of the concept of a transactor as distinguished from the concept of a thief or a philanthropist. Thus it restricts our vision as economists to just one aspect of individual behavior, for it excludes (by assumption) facets of behavior which, although they involve the acquisition and disposal of commodities—and so are of economic interest in some sense—fall outside the purview of formal economic analysis.[5]

II. EXTENSIONS

In keeping with the logical primacy of SP, let us now reverse direction and consider the consequences of applying SP to situations that are more general (and less obviously contrived) than the problem of household choice outlined in the previous section. Let us start by considering a simple generalization of the household choice model in which we permit some of the money available for expenditure to be retained by the household for future disposal. Applying SP to this case, we may suppose that the set of theoretically admissible budgets, $d = (d_x, d_y, d_m)$, is defined by the zero-net-value identity:

$$p_x d_x + p_y d_y + (d_m - s_{m,0}) \equiv 0, \tag{3}$$

where d_m denotes the quantity of money that the household plans to hold for future disposal (other variables are defined just as before).

Another easy extension of our model is accomplished by admitting the possibility that the household may be a supplier of non-money commodities as well as a supplier of money. In this case, application of SP yields the zero-net-value identity:

$$p_x(d_x - s_{x,0}) + p_y(d_y - s_{y,0}) + (d_m - s_{m,0}) \equiv 0,^6 \tag{4}$$

where the symbols $s_{x,0}$ and $s_{y,0}$, like the symbol $s_{m,0}$, represent decision parameters and denote (non-negative stocks of non-money commodities currently available for possible sale (the values of $s_{x,0}$ and $s_{y,0}$ may be zero, of course, for one or both commodities).

Yet another extension of our model is obtained by supposing that the individual is a potential trader of a large but finite number of commodities. Using numerical subscripts, $1, 2, \ldots, m$ to distinguish

---

[5] Quoted from Clower and Due (1972), pp. 64–65.

[6] More accurately, SP yields the set of budgets defined by identity (4) if, as is conventional, we assume that each of the non-money commodities (x) and (y) can be traded directly for each other as well as for money. We shall not elaborate on this theme here; for additional details see Clower (1967) and Veendorp (1970). However, in general, a single constraint such as identity (4) can be used to define the set of admissible budgets only in a world where individuals consider themselves able to trade any given collection of commodities directly for any other collection in a *single* exchange transaction.

different commodities, and treating the m-th commodity as money, we obtain:

$$p_1(d_1 - s_{1,0}) + p_2(d_2 - s_{2,0}) + \ldots \qquad (5)$$
$$+ p_{m-1}(d_{m-1} - s_{m-1,0}) + (d_m - s_{m,0}) \equiv 0,$$

as the zero-net-value identity implied by SP. Notice that this condition —like analogous relations set out earlier—holds for all values of the price variables, p_i, and not just for one or a few specially chosen price lists. Further notice that the validity of identity (5) does not depend in any way on the assumption that the symbols $s_{i,0}$ represent (given) decision parameters rather than (unknown) decision variables whose values have to be determined by the individual decision maker. This being so, it is superfluous to work with gross demands and gross supplies when we are considering transactors as commodity traders, for only net demands and net supplies are relevant in this case. Accordingly, to simplify notation let us define the individual's excess demand (ED) for the i-th commodity by the relation:

$$x_i = d_i - s_i \quad (i = 1, \ldots, m). \qquad (6)$$

In general, x_i may be positive, zero or negative. In the last case, the individual would appear as a potential seller rather than buyer (or non-trader) of the i-th commodity, in which event we might call x_i the individual's excess supply (ES) of the i-th commodity. Using the notation of equation (6), identity (5) now takes the simpler but logically equivalent form:

$$p_1 x_1 + p_2 x_2 + \cdots + p_{m-1} x_{m-1} + x_m \equiv 0.^{7} \qquad (7)$$

As a final generalization consider a large (but finite) collection of transactors; we distinguish among quantities associated with different transactors by adding a second numerical subscript, $1, 2, \ldots, k$ to relevant variables (e.g., the variable x_{ij} denotes the j-th transactor's ED for the i-th commodity). For simplicity, suppose that all transactors face the same money prices; this uniform price assumption is so conventional in general equilibrium theory that its presence is sometimes not even recognized.[8] We also assume (as usual) that the trading be-

---

[7] The money price of a unit of money is necessarily unity, i.e., $p_m \equiv 1$; so identity (7) is equivalent to the more symmetrical identity:

$$p_1 x_1 + p_2 x_2 + \ldots + p_{m-1} x_{m-1} + p_m x_m \equiv 0 \qquad (7')$$

[8] For future reference, we observe here that the assumption involves a drastic oversimplification; it means we ignore differences in price for the same good between different localities, bid–ask spreads for the same good in the same locality, discrepancies in prices charged for different sellers, etc. These omissions represent serious abstractions from reality. However, they do not affect the logic of our argument (which would merely become more complicated if the assumption of uniform prices were relaxed).

Table 1. *Matrix of admissible trades*

Transactors (I_j)	Commodities (C_i)				Money C_m	Net value
	C_1	C_2		C_{m-1}		
I_1	$p_1x_{1.1}$	$+ p_2x_{2.1} +$	$\cdots\cdots$	$+ p_{m-1}x_{m-1.1}$	$+ x_{m.1}$	$\equiv 0$
I_2	$p_1x_{1.2}$	$+ p_2x_{2.2} +$	$\cdots\cdots$	$+ p_{m-1}x_{m-1.2}$	$+ x_{m.2}$	$\equiv 0$
.						
.						
.						
I_k	$p_1x_{1.k}$	$+ p_2x_{2.k} +$	$\cdots\cdots$	$+ p_{m-1}x_{m-1.k}$	$+ x_{m.k}$	$\equiv 0$
Aggregate excess demands	p_1X_1	$+ p_2X_2 +$	$\cdots\cdots$	$+ p_{m-1}X_{m-1}$	$+ X_m$	$\equiv 0$

havior of each and every transactor is constrained in accordance with SP. On these assumptions, we obtain not one, but rather a set of K zero-net-value identities to characterize the set of admissible net trades that transactors as a group are permitted to contemplate. These relations are displayed in matrix form in Table 1.

Each row in Table 1 shows the money value of the corresponding transactor's EDs—valued at some arbitrary set of money prices (the same set for all transactors). In accordance with SP, the sum of these money values is identically zero (right-hand column). Of course, some of the individual terms in each sum may also be zero, indicating that the transactor in question neither plans to buy nor sell units of those commodities. In particular, if the i-th commodity is assumed to be an imaginary object, or a commodity that has no concrete counterpart (e.g., the English monetary unit called the "guinea"), then $x_{ij} \equiv 0$ for all transactors since, by its very definition, such a commodity cannot seriously be contemplated as an object of trade by any transactor.[9]

The first k terms in each of the first M columns of Table 1 indicate which transactors are net suppliers and which are net demanders of the corresponding commodity. We shall refer to the sum of the individual EDs in each column as the aggregate ED for the corresponding commodity. In symbols:

[9] The relevance of this outwardly trivial observation will become clear below.

$$\sum_{j=1}^{j=k} x_{ij} \equiv X_i, \quad (i=1,\ldots,m) \tag{8}$$

On the assumption that a common price is relevant for valuing all individual EDs, we may then write the money value of aggregate ED for the i-th commodity as:

$$\sum_{j=1}^{j=k} p_i x_{ij} \equiv p_i \sum_{j=1}^{j=k} x_{ij} \equiv p_i X_i, \quad (i=1,\ldots,m) \tag{9}$$

Because the money value of individual EDs may be negative as well as positive or zero, the magnitude and sign of $p_i X_i$ may be positive, negative or zero. However, since the (row) sum of the money values of any single transactor's EDs is identically zero, and since the sum of K zeroes is zero, it follows that the money value of all individual EDs summed over all transactors and all commodities, is identically zero.[10] Even though we can place no restrictions on the size or sign of any of the first M terms in the bottom row of Table 1 we may assert unequivocally that the last term is zero; i.e., the money value of the sum of all aggregate EDs is identically equal to zero.[11] In symbols,

$$\sum_{i=1}^{i=m} p_i X_i \equiv 0, \quad (i=1,\ldots,m) \tag{10}$$

This proposition effectively summarizes the whole of the preceding argument. In the final analysis it asserts much the same concept as the simple individual version of SP defined earlier; however, it applies to a group of transactors rather than a single individual. Where we specially wish to emphasize that we are referring to the group identity (10), we shall identify it henceforth as the aggregative version of SP (where the sense of our argument is not in doubt, however, we shall omit qualifying phrases and speak simply of SP).

[10] Notice that this proposition is valid even if the prices used to value individual EDs are not the same for different transactors:

$$\sum_{j=1}^{j=k} \sum_{i=1}^{i=m} p_{ij} x_{ij} \equiv 0, (i=1,\ldots,m) \text{ and } (j=1,\ldots,k) \tag{9'}$$

where p_{ij} represents the money price of the i-th commodity as seen by the j-th transactor. Hence, the proposition holds even more strongly if prices are uniform over all transactors (i.e., if $p_{ij}=p_i$ for all values of j).

[11] For the record we can find no hints of any such aggregative proposition in J. B. Say's economic writings. In our view, however, it would be historically accurate to credit J. B. Say with the weaker (but still fairly powerful) proposition (9') where the sum of all individual notional EDs, valued at money prices as seen by individual transactors, is identically zero. This, or some similar disaggregative version of SP, is, we believe, what most pre-Keynesian writers had in mind when referring to "Say's Law of Markets."

Three features of the aggregative version of SP merit special emphasis before we proceed:

1. *The proposition is valid for any (uniform) set of prices and for every theoretically admissible set of aggregate EDs;*
2. *No general statement can be made about the sum of the money values of any proper subset of the aggregate EDs*; i.e., if one or more of the terms $p_i X_i$ is excluded from the summation in identity (10), we can place no restrictions whatever on the sign or magnitude of the sum of the remaining terms;
3. The aggregate ED for each commodity in identity (10) is defined by identity (8) as the sum over all transactors of *planned* (notional, intended, desired) purchases or sales of the same commodity. *If aggregate EDs were defined in terms of anything other than planned quantities, we should have no assurance that the aggregative version of SP would still hold.*

III. STANDARD THEMES AND DOCTRINES

We are now in a position to discuss certain interpretations of SP that appear frequently in the economic literature.

A. Old Familiar Phrases

1. "A general glut of commodities is impossible." This sounds archaic—which is natural, since it is a version of SP that was much in vogue among early nineteenth century economists. Glut means ES (negative ED). If general glut is interpreted to mean notional ES prevailing for all commodities simultaneously, then such a situation is flatly inconsistent with SP in any of its variants and, in that sense, the statement is true.
2. "Supply creates its own demand." This is perhaps the most ambiguous statement that students of economics are ever asked to ponder. Consider, for example, the following alternatives:
   i.   "Supply of a commodity at some price gives rise to an equal demand for the same commodity at that price." This version is, of course, false. But it illustrates one possible interpretation of a special case of the version of SL that the Classical economists are often accused of believing (see Section C, below).
   ii. "No one plans to supply anything of value without also planning some use for the proceeds from the sale, which may

include simply planning to hold money until a later decison is made to purchase other commodities." This statement is correct and sensible.

iii. "Confronted with given prices, each transactor must plan to supply commodities of sufficient value to finance all his planned net demands." This statement is also correct.

iv. "If prices are given, each transactor's planned sales will create the means to finance his planned purchase." This statement resembles (ii) but it is quite different—false rather than true. Suppose that aggregate ES exists for all commodities that the transactor plans to sell; it is then likely that actual sales will be less than planned (perhaps nil). Hence, planned receipts will not serve to finance planned purchases. SP refers only to purchase and sale intentions; it asserts absolutely nothing about the possibility of their realization.

B. General Equilibrium

An economic system may be said to be in equilibrium when the values of all variables that are considered relevant for describing its observable behavior are equal over time to the values of a corresponding set of theoretical variables that define the virtual (notional) behavior of the system along a postulated equilibrium path. This very general concept is consistent with the existence of non-stationary equilibrium paths. In elementary accounts of general equilibrium theory, however, equilibrium paths are typically defined in terms of constancy over time of the values of a set of relative prices, $\overline{P} = (p_1, p_2, \ldots, p_m)$, where one commodity, say the m-th, serves as a unit of account or *numéraire* so that $\overline{p}_m = 1$. This simple definition of economic equilibrium is arrived at by conceptualizing the economic system as a collection of named, but otherwise nondescript, transactors whose trading activities are centrally coordinated by some kind of "trading authority" that acts as a bargaining agent and commodity distribution center for all transactors. At the beginning of any given bargaining period (implicitly defined as a time interval of sufficient length for everything we wish to talk about to occur), each transactor formulates a definite trading plan on the basis of a set of provisional prices, P_0, which are announced by the trading authority. These plans are communicated to the trading authority, who first checks each plan to see that it satisfies SP (individual version), and then sums all plans to arrive at a set of provisional aggregate EDs, $X_0 = (X_{1,0}, \ldots, X_{m,0})$. If X_0 includes some elements that are non-zero (by SP—the aggregate version—at least *two* elements must be non-zero in this case), the trading authority knows that individual plans are not mutually consistent at the price vector P_0 (i.e., not all planned net trades can be executed as scheduled). It then selects and announces a new set of provisional prices, P_1, and requests the assembled mob of transactors to formulate new plans. This process continues until some stage, say the t-th, when the trading authority manages to announce a price vector P_t at which each and every aggregate ED is exactly equal to zero: i.e., $X_{i,t} = 0$ $(i = 1, \ldots, m)$. In this case, all individual trades can be executed as planned (through the collection and distribution facilities conveniently—and costlessly—provided by the authority), and the prices, P_t, are called equilibrium prices for the current trading period. In the absence of changes in technology, preferences, or other data that might influence individual trading plans, the same prices should yield equilibrium in all subsequent periods.

Such, in brief, is the story that underlies the condition $P = \overline{P} = $ constant, as a comprehensive criterion for equilibrium in elementary general equilibrium theory. According to this story, constancy of prices over time implies corresponding constancy of trading plans. But neither of these conditions can prevail unless, in every period, $X_i = 0$ for all commodities. Hence the condition $P = \overline{P} = $ constant is logically equivalent to the economically more informative requirement:

$$X_i = 0 \quad (i = 1, \ldots, m). \tag{11}$$

We emphasize that this simple requirement is in no sense sufficient to characterize general equilibrium except in very simple models; however, it is usually (but not always) a necessary condition and, for the purposes of the present argument, it may be regarded as both necessary and sufficient. In what follows, therefore, we shall refer to equation (11) as the general equilibrium condition.

Whether or not we wish to regard equation (11) as the only condition for general equilibrium (as in fact we do here), we might treat it as a universally valid, necessary condition for what might be called full coordination of economic activities, that is, situations in which, for each and every commodity, purchase and sale intentions are consistent in the aggregate. In a world without a central trading authority, knowing that equation (11) is fulfilled does not assure us that all trading plans can in fact be executed. It is conceivable (just barely) that each and every transactor could actually carry out each of his intended purchases and sales and not end up in a situation where all the sellers known to him are out of stock and all the buyers he contacts are unwilling to buy. As a practical matter, however, even this weak requirement that all aggregate EDs be zero is unlikely ever to be realized in any real-world situation; hence, the probability that all transactors should ever simultaneously achieve full execution of their individual trading plans may be set at zero.

Having run through essential preliminaries, we turn now to the relation between SP and the concept of general equilibrium. Without being too formal let us suppose that we have to deal with an economy in which there exists one and only one price vector, $\bar{P}$, for which the general equilibrium condition equation (11) is satisfied.[12] We know that SP is satisfied in the present model for *all* price vectors P; the rules imposed by the trading authority positively guarantee this. But not all price vectors are consistent with general equilibrium; indeed, under our present assumptions only one such vector exists. Hence we conclude: the satisfaction of SP implies nothing whatever about the satisfaction of the general equilibrium condition; neither has general equilibrium any bearing on SP. If the general equilibrium condition is satisfied, it is obvious that:

$$\sum_{i=1}^{i=m} X_i \equiv 0,$$

but this fatuous proposition should never be confused with Say's Principle.[13]

Suppose that the general equilibrium condition is not satisfied, so that aggregate ED for at least two commodities is non-zero. In this case, the economy may be said to be in a state of disequilibrium. It is impossible for all trades to be executed as planned, so prices and trading plans must be revised. Some of the commodities in aggregate ES may be labor services. It follows that SP is entirely consistent with the existence of large-scale unemployment.

SP is also consistent with indefinite persistence of unemployment on a large scale, for it involves no assumptions and yields no implications about the dynamic adjustment behavior of the economic system. Imagine observing the system in a state of serious disequilibrium. Knowing that SP holds true for the system will *not* permit us to predict whether or not this disequilibrium will tend automatically to disappear

[12] For any specified state of resource endowments, production technology, property and contract laws, and consumer tastes, there exists a unique price vector $\bar{P}$ for which $X_i = 0$ for all commodities.

[13] Even great economists sometimes nod: "... Say's Law is valid only in a state of perfect equilibrium ..." Schumpeter (1954), p. 619.

with the passage of time. (Hence, SP is totally irrelevant to any ideological discussion and in particular to discussion of the pros and cons
of so-called *laissez-faire*). For example, SP would still hold in a system
where *every* commodity was subject to effectively enforced price control. (Shortages and surpluses would be felt everywhere, but aggregate
EDs would still have a total zero money value.)

That a general glut is impossible is not an empty statement. SP
refutes, for example, the recurrent, fearful popular notion that pro-
ductivity-increasing innovations (automation, nuclear power, or whatever) will create or increase aggregate ESs for some commodities
without affecting the aggregate EDs for the others. But the reassur-
ance that this knowledge entails is very limited. It is utter nonsense,
for example, to maintain (as some students, unfortunately, have a
tendency to do) that, although the Principle is consistent with each
and every aggregate ED being non-zero and large, it still asserts that
the economy will be in overall equilibrium in that total demand and
total supply are equal in money value. It is nonsense because the
statement completely empties the term equilibrium of all meaning.
This particular piece of nonsense is not always so easy to spot. Quite
a few otherwise reputable economists have put in print the proposition
that Classical economists were unable to provide a meaningful and
useful theory of large-scale unemployment because they believed in
Say's Law. This is simply inane: SP, by itself, could not possibly pose
a mental block to the development of unemployment theory. On the
contrary, correct and systematic application of it is necessary for the
construction of a consistent theory of any disequilibrium (or equilibrium) phenomenon.

Needless to say, it does not follow that all, or even most, Classical
economists fully understood what the Principle means and does not
mean. A doctrinal investigation might well show, for example, that
some notable writers muddled the conceptual distinctions between SP
and propositions relating to the existence and stability of general
equilibrium. We do not lack, after all, latter-day examples of the
confounding of these separate issues.[14] The existence problem concerns the question whether a price vector exists such that, if it were

---

[14] "However, the satisfaction of *all* the stability conditions ... is not implied in Say's
Law. Say's Law implies only that enough of the stability conditions of the system hold,
to assure the existence of a stable equilibrium for two broad classes of commodities,
namely, the class of products and the class of factors and direct services." Cf. O. Lange
(1942), p. 59. A proposition that states that the money values of some or all aggregate
EDs sum to a certain number implies nothing about the fulfillment of any stability
condition. Moreover, the notion of equilibrium for broad classes of commodities is just
as empty and misleading as that of overall equilibrium which we have just criticized.

to be obtained, aggregate ED for each commodity would be zero. SP alone will not allow one to deduce an answer one way or another to this question. The stability problem concerns the question whether it can be deduced that prices will adjust so as to reduce the absolute magnitude of aggregate EDs until, eventually, all aggregate EDs are zero (presuming such an equilibrium solution exists). SP contains no laws of motion of prices, nor is it even helpful in deducing what these laws might be. A fairly large set of assumptions, completely independent of the Principle, must be made in order to obtain answers to stability questions.

Many pre-Keynesian writers, who simply believed in the existence of general equilibrium, assumed "flexible prices"; they also assumed or argued that flexible prices would tend to move in such a manner as to reduce aggregate EDs to zero. Some of them may have been unable to conceive of persistent mass unemployment as a realistic possibility; however, it was clearly these sundry beliefs and assumptions—*not* SP—that constituted mental blocks for them.

C. National Income Analysis

In macroeconomics texts, SP (aggregative version) is sometimes said to imply that aggregate demand always equals aggregate supply. If one's definitions of aggregate demand and aggregate supply are, respectively, the summed money value of all commodities in aggregate ED and the summed money value of all commodities in aggregate ES, then, naturally, this is what SP means. (It is not an implication of the Principle, but simply a restatement.) However, the accepted, conventional definitions of aggregate demand and aggregate supply are quite different. The coinage of both terms is associated with the development of Keynesian macroeconomics, and it is the usage within that body of doctrine that must be decisive. In macroeconomics, aggregate demand is defined as the summed value of the demands for all final goods and services; similarly, aggregate supply is defined as the summed value of supplies of all final goods and services.

Final goods and services are a subset of all currently produced commodities. (Current production of intermediate goods and services is excluded.) Current output is, in turn, a subset of all commodities in the system that excludes not just money but also all existing assets and many inputs as well. Suppose, then, that of the commodities in Table 1, those indexed 4 through 17 are designated as final goods and services. It is immediately apparent that the sum of the values of the demands for these goods (aggregate demand) cannot be asserted to equal the sum of the values of the supplies of the same goods. To assert this we should have to know—in addition to SP—that the sum of the values of the EDs for goods 1 through 3, and 18 through m, is zero, and the latter condition, of course, will not in general be fulfilled. This example suffices to disprove the general validity of the proposition that SP implies equality between aggregate demand and aggregate supply.

There is another point to be made in this connection. In national income analysis, the term aggregate demand has come to mean the total value of actual spending—not *planned spending*—on final goods and services. If actual prices differ from equilibrium prices, actual spending will almost certainly differ from planned purchases (since not all plans can be carried out). SP, to repeat, is a proposition about trading *plans* and carries with it no direct implications about the realization of plans. On this account, therefore, the assertion that SP implies equality between aggregate demand and supply is seen to be the product of muddled thinking.[15]

D. General Deflation

Of all the innumerable disequilibria that are consistent with SP, one subset is particularly worth singling out because of the potential practical seriousness of the conditions defining it: namely, disequilibria in which the sum of the values of EDs for all currently produced commodities is negative and equal in value to the positive ED for money. This means, on balance, that the entire business sector is under general deflationary pressure.[16] The typical industry will be laying off workers. If there are some industries hiring, they won't hire enough; unemployment will be widespread.

If the real money supply (i.e., the stock of money in relation to the general price level) could be increased in this situation, prevailing deflationary pressures could be relieved—though that alone would not necessarily permit the economy to snap into general equilibrium. The supply of money in real terms might be increased in two ways: 1) by letting excess supplies drive prices down so that the general price level is reduced in relation to an unchanged stock of nominal money balances; 2) by increasing the nominal money stock at pre-

---

[15] Another version of the same muddle consists of the assertion that SP implies coincidence at every point between the aggregate demand function and the 45° line in standard "Keynesian cross" diagrams.

[16] General deflationary pressure means here a situation in which ESs cannot be eliminated by merely changing relative prices.

vailing prices. Alternative 1 is the automatic solution; but if prices and wages are rigid downward, this way out is simply not open to us. Even if prices and wages are not rigid, the process envisaged in this solution may be a long-drawn-out affair that entails heavy costs in terms of resource unemployment and human misery and which, therefore, might well be regarded as unacceptable. Alternative 2, the interventionist solution, might seem more promising than 1 as a procedure for accomplishing the same results more quickly and at less social cost. But its use raises other issues. To whom is "the engine of inflation" to be entrusted? What limits to that party's discretionary use of the throttle would it be advisable to impose?

The Classical economists were not unaware of this class of disequilibria or of their seriousness. John Stuart Mill, for example, diagnosed general depressions of trade in precisely these terms. It is also true, however, that many British Classical economists tended to discuss the problem as if the automatic alternative 1 offered the only way out. Some of them did not regard the nominal money supply as a policy instrument that the Bank of England of the time could control. Others were of the view that the central bank had or could be endowed with the power to control the money stock, but believed very strongly that the central bank on the whole ought to let balance-of-payments deficits and surpluses determine variations over time in the monetary base and, hence, in the money stock.[17]

Reliance on the automatic solution, in this view, is argued to be the lesser of two evils. Naive *laissez-faire* notions do not figure at all in the theory of economic policy of the British Classical school. Nor was Classical thinking on this subject in any way inhibited by prevailing views about "Say's Law of Markets." SP is entirely consistent with confirmed disbelief in the possibility of general gluts and, simultaneously, with clear recognition of the actuality of frequent and prolonged bouts of general deflation. John Stuart Mill's *Principles*, the "Bible of Economics" during the later Classical period, is the perfect illustration.

E. Lange's Laws: A Restatement and Criticism

The aggregative version of SP, as we have defined it earlier, is formally equivalent to a proposition that is known more familiarly in the lit-

---

[17] From the standpoint of domestic stabilization policy, this is a self-denying ordinance—the monetary authorities cannot at one and the same time be bound by such a rule and retain discretion to intervene in domestic economic affairs whenever they deem it advisable.

erature as Walras' Law, a label that was first attached to it by Oscar
Lange (1942). Two names for the same concept is, in general, a luxury
that economics can well do without. But we have good reasons for
making an exception in the present case. The central portions of
Lange's argument are concerned with conceptual experiments that
involve just two models, namely:

(i) A model of a barter economy with $m-1$ commodities, all of which
     are either currently produced final goods and services or currently
     supplied factor services. Commodities not classified in this manner
     cannot be traded at all. In particular, nothing called money is
     included in the set of tradable commodities, which means that the
     system is "equivalent to a barter economy."

(ii) A model of a money economy that is identical with the first in all
     respects except that an m-th commodity called money is added to
     the set of tradable commodities—functioning as "medium of ex-
     change as well as *numéraire*. . . . "[18]

Since money does not exist in the first economy, it cannot be traded.
However, it still can be regarded by us as a unit of account (*numéraire*)
for expressing prices, so we may continue to speak of the money value
of aggregate EDs even when referring to the barter system.[19]

The proposition that the sum of the money values of all EDs in
system (i) is identically zero is called Say's Law by Lange.[20] The proposition that the sum of the money values of all EDs in system (ii) is
identically zero Lange then called Walras' Law. Since the two propositions are identical, the reader may well wonder why Lange assigns
them different names. The answer to this apparent mystery is that
Lange, unlike us, starts by considering only a so-called "money economy" (system (ii)). He defines Walras' Law in relation to this kind of
system, and then asks, in effect: In what circumstances will the total
money value of ED for all commodities exclusive of money be zero?
Not very surprisingly, he discovers that his condition will be satisfied
if and only if the ED for money is zero, a state of affairs that he calls
"monetary equilibrium." He then defines SL *not* as a proposition that
holds only for situations of monetary equilibrium, but rather as a
proposition that together with Walras' Law, holds identically for all

[18] Lange (1942), p. 64; p. 49.
[19] Individuals in system (i) would be concerned, of course, only with *ratios* of such
money prices, i.e., with rates of exchange between pairs of tradable commodities.
[20] Lange simply assumes that the proposition is true for the system described, but
the proposition could be shown to hold as a consequence of standard assumptions
underlying the definition of the demand and supply functions that Lange introduced
at the outset of his analysis.

possible states of system (ii). These two stipulations effectively make system (ii) indistinguishable from system (i).

From this point onward Lange's argument is all downhill. In order to elaborate the implications of what he calls "Say's Law," he first asks: What conclusions follow if we suppose that aggregate EDs in a money economy such as (ii) simultaneously satisfy *both* Walras' Law and SL? The words in which the ensuing discussion are couched strongly suggest that the simultaneous assumption of Walras' Law and SL leads one to economically nonsensical results. Thus, he argues that money prices are indeterminate (obviously, since only ratios of money prices are relevant in system (i)). Lange argues further that people will never desire to change their money balances (obviously, since money in system (i) is like romantic love—you take what you can get, but it's not for sale!). He goes on to observe that money in such a system is merely a worthless medium of exchange and standard of value. (Here the nonsense is Lange's, for whatever else money may be in system (i), it can't be a medium of exchange, worthless or otherwise). Clearly, if one focuses attention not on the words Lange uses but rather on the properties of the system he is talking about (namely, system (i) rather than system (ii)) all of his results appear to be either entirely sensible or to involve confusion or errors of logic on his part. An example of the latter is his assertion that ". . . under Say's Law an excess supply of primary factors and direct services *always* implies an excess demand of equal amount for products, and vice versa. This tends directly to restore equilibrium." As we have emphasized in earlier remarks, SP has no bearing whatever on the dynamic adjustment properties of any economic system.

Using the terms as he defines them, Lange concludes that Walras' Law is true in general and that SL is true for barter but not for money economies. Since Lange's distinction between the two types of economies is purely verbal, not analytical, this conclusion is fatuous. In Lange's article (and in the present paper) the word "money" serves only to name one commodity, specifically, that commodity (it might be any of them) that serves as a unit of account for expressing prices. At no stage in Lange's formal analysis is money endowed with any other special properties as compared with other commodities.[21]

Attributing a belief in SL (in his sense) to Classical economists, Lange also argues that pre-Keynesian theories of employment, interest and money are (a) logically false, and (b) economically nonsensical

---

[21] This may be seen most easily by noticing that if what Lange calls money were a liquid asset that came in bottles marked "100 proof Scotch Whisky" rather than pieces of paper labelled "In God We Trust," no one would notice it.

because they rest on the assumption that SL is valid for a monetary economy. In this part of his argument, Lange is guilty not only of repeated sins of verbal sophistry but also of gross historical inaccuracy. As argued earlier, the statement that the summed values of aggregate EDs over a subset of tradable commodities is identically zero involves a most elementary error.[22]

So what remains of Lange's analysis when all is said and done? Our answer is, quite bluntly: nothing of value. Nonetheless, Lange's terminological innovations—including, in particular, the entirely superfluous term Walras' Law—somehow have taken root in macroeconomics; and his associated criticisms of Classical economics are now part of the mythology of the subject.

F. Say's Principle and Walras' Law

As we remarked at the outset of the preceding section, what we have called the aggregative version of SP is formally equivalent to what Lange called Walras' Law. Formally equivalent they certainly are, but economically equivalent they sometimes are not. Two observations will suffice to make clear the sense and validity of this distinction.

1. Walras' Law is sometimes described as asserting that, if prices are such that all markets for non-money commodities satisfy the general equilibrium condition (i.e., if $X_i = 0$ for $i = 1, 2, \ldots, m-1$), then the money market must also be in equilibrium (i.e., $X_m = 0$ also);[23] or, more succinctly, that if supply equals demand on $m-1$ markets then the same equality must also hold on the m-th.[24]

Now, our definition of SP (aggregative version) involves the concept of aggregate demand in an essential way, but it does not in any way depend upon nor refer to the concept of a market. Our avoidance of any reference to the word market was quite deliberate. The term market, as used in ordinary discourse, carries with it a host of intuitive associations that have no counterpart in standard accounts of individual decision-making behavior. In common parlance, a market is (among other things) a place where one pays (receives) money to (from) another person in exchange for some commodity at some date in time. To establish a theoretical analog to this conception, we should have to specify the logistics of commodity trade in fine detail—fine

---

[22] As far as we know, no major Classical economist has ever been shown to commit this error outright; but even if such a sinner could be found by hunting around among lesser figures, we (the authors) should follow Mill's gracious example and attribute the blunder to inadvertence.

[23] Patinkin (1965), p. 25.

[24] Arrow and Hahn (1971), p. 4.

enough detail, indeed, to permit us to assert within the framework of formal theory precisely when and where each transactor trades what commodities with whom and in exchange for which other commodities. No such specification is even attempted in existing accounts of macro- or microeconomic theory.[25] Thus, to speak of markets for labor services, goods, bonds, money, etc., in connection with conventional theoretical models is, strictly speaking, meaningless. It is entirely sensible to speak of aggregate ED for these commodities but to link aggregate EDs with markets is to invite needless confusion and misunderstanding.[26]

To insist on this terminological distinction between aggregate ED for a commodity and market ED (for the same commodity) may seem overly fastidious. And it is, in fact, not necessary in a discussion that does not go beyond SP. In more general contexts, however, the distinction is far from pointless. When one moves on to the task of constructing a theory that describes how the economic system adjusts when in disequilibrium, it is traditional to use the term "market excess demand" to denote the relevant forces governing price adjustment. It is a distinct and potentially dangerous jump in logic, however, to take it for granted that these forces are always measured by aggregate EDs (which is the custom in the existing literature). For example, in models where market ED cannot be obtained by aggregating over individual planned net demands and supplies, we have no assurance whatsoever that the sum of measured market EDs, valued at the prevailing market prices, is equal to zero or any other number (though SP, in the generalized form given by equation (9), above, holds as usual for the aggregate of individual planned EDs).

2. Most statements of Walras' Law in the existing literature, unlike our statement of SP, tacitly presuppose that the trading plans of individual transactors satisfy one or another of the optimality conditions (i.e., maximize some criterion function) in addition to relevant behavior constraints. This is certainly true for the statements of Lange, Patinkin, Debreu and Arrow and Hahn, all of whom assume that individual ED functions (or correspondences) are defined independently of Walras' Law. This corresponds to the point of view adopted in the first section of this paper, where we first illustrated the nature

[25] An instructive example of just such a careful specification is provided by Ostroy (1973).

[26] A common example of such confusion arises in macroeconomic theory in the mere listing of four markets, one for each distinct commodity. Since exchange necessarily involves at least two commodities, the very phrase "market for commodity Z" presupposes that we know what commodity or commodities Z is traded for or else it must be regarded as a contradiction in terms.

of SP. It differs sharply, however, from the view adopted later. While we have no logical objection to the approach of other writers, we should remark that such a procedure makes SP appear much more limited in application than it actually is. SP is also significantly diminished as a theoretical proposition by suggesting incorrectly that it is valid only if all individuals in the economic system are behaving optimally.

REFERENCES

K. Arrow and F. H. Hahn, *General Competitive Analysis* (San Francisco: Holden-Day, 1971).

R. W. Clower, "The Microfoundations of Monetary Theory," *Western Economic Journal*, 6 (December 1967), 1–8.

R. W. Clower and J. F. Due, *Microeconomics* (Homewood, Ill.: Irwin, 1972).

O. Lange, "Say's Law: A Restatement and Criticism," in O. Lange et al. (eds.), *Studies in Mathematical Economics and Econometrics* (Chicago: University of Chicago Press, 1942).

C. R. McConnell, *Economics* (New York: McGraw-Hill, 1972).

J. S. Mill, *Principles of Political Economy*, 7th ed. (London: Longmans, Green, Reader and Dyer, 1871).

J. M. Ostroy, "The Informational Efficiency of Monetary Exchange," *American Economic Review*, 63 (September 1973), 597–610.

D. Patinkin, *Money, Interest, and Prices*, 2nd ed. (New York: Harper & Row, 1965).

J. Schumpeter, *History of Economic Analysis* (New York: Oxford University Press, 1954).

T. Sowell, *Say's Law* (Princeton, N.J.: Princeton University Press, 1972).

E. C. H. Veendorp, "General Equilibrium Theory for a Barter Economy," *Western Economic Journal*, 7 (March 1970), 1–23.

13

THE TRANSACTIONS THEORY OF THE DEMAND
FOR MONEY: A RECONSIDERATION

Most of what passes for contemporary wisdom about the transactions demand for money derives directly from the classic but transparently rudimentary inventory-theoretic model of Baumol (1952) and Tobin (1956). Our purpose in this paper is to outline and explore the implications of a more general class of models in which individual economic agents freely choose not only the frequency of both sales and purchases but also the time phasing of transactions.[1] Our first and most significant findings are that demands for trade inventories, that is, trade-related holdings of both goods and money, are in general discontinuous functions of the relative frequency of sales and purchases, and that commonly accepted comparative-statics propositions about the demand for money are of dubious validity except in cases that are too specialized to be of serious practical interest. Our analysis also sheds fresh and occasionally unexpected light on a variety of other issues: for example, the conditions in which individual traders will choose to hold money in positive amounts, the nature of potential gains from paying competitive interest on money, the economics of hyperinflation, the effects upon individual demands for money of the availability of trade credit and bonds, and the inadequacy of received price theory for analyzing even the most elementary aspects of interpersonal exchange in economies characterized by individual diversities in the frequency and time phasing of sale and purchase transactions.

We are indebted to Joel S. Fried, R. A. Jones, J. M. Ostroy, Mack Ott, and John Riley for suggestions and critical comments on earlier versions of the paper. We have also benefited from reading the results of investigations on a closely related problem as reported in a privately circulated memorandum from D. W. Bushaw (see n. 2 below).

[1] The Baumol–Tobin model has been extended in various directions; see especially Clower (1970), Johnson (1970), Feige and Parkin (1971), Perlman (1971), Fried (1973), Grossman and Policano (1975), Barro and Santomero (1976), and Policano (1977). In every instance, as also in the original Baumol–Tobin model, formal analysis has been confined to special cases in which individual traders choose a trading frequency for just one commodity, and in which the time-phasing problem is ignored. Some of these papers (e.g., Feige and Parkin 1971) deal nominally with trading frequencies for more than one commodity, but in each such case trading frequencies of all goods are assumed to satisfy integer constraints so that each frequency is an exact multiple or divisor of every other.

166

I. THE BASIC MODEL

Our first task is to characterize the stationary-equilibrium behavior of a representative trader in an idealized exchange economy where goods can be traded in organized markets only in exchange for units of a pure stock commodity called "money."[2] In keeping with familiar doctrine, we suppose that on each purchase and sale the trader incurs a set-up cost that is independent of the quantity traded. As a consequence, the trader will choose to execute trades only at discrete points rather than continuously in time and so may be expected to hold positive stocks of goods or money (or both) between successive sale and purchase dates. The holding of trade inventories is presumed to impose other costs on the trader, reflecting forgone consumption opportunities and the use of resources to maintain storage facilities. Thus to maximize long-run real income the trader must strike a balance between frequent transactions with low holding but high trading costs and infrequent transactions with low trading but high holding costs. We now proceed to formalize these general ideas.

A. Fundamental Assumptions

We begin by considering an individual trader who produces and sells units of just one stock-flow good (S) and who purchases and consumes units of just one other stock-flow good (D). To avoid superfluous notation, we assume that the money prices of both goods are equal to unity, and we use generic symbols S, D, and M, respectively, to denote measurable quantities of (S), (D), and the money commodity (M). For similar reasons (also to avoid dealing with feedbacks of trading and holding costs upon the trader's stationary-state level of consumption) we treat all costs as subjective (forgone leisure or consumption) or as charges that are incurred "outside" the model. We further suppose that the trader's rate of production of (S) is predetermined at a constant level of y units per unit of time, and that the trader holds no precautionary stocks of goods or money—that is to say, a purchase is made only when the trader's stock of (D) has just been exhausted, and a sale is made only when the trader wishes to dispose of the whole of his accumulated stock of (S). Finally, as con-

---

[2] A nonstationary version of the problem analyzed here was studied by D. W. Bushaw and five other mathematicians during a summer institute in applied mathematics at Washington State University in 1972. The difficulty of the problem is reflected in the paucity of unambiguous results obtained by this group (which included some leading specialists in dynamical polysystems). One of us has made some progress on a simpler problem involving only two goods (see Howitt 1977).

ditions for stationary equilibrium we require that the trader consume
(D) at the constant rate y, sell (S) in lots of constant size S at uniform
time intervals of length S/y, and purchase (D) in lots of constant size
D at uniform time intervals of length D/y.

We suppose initially that at date zero a purchase and sale occur
simultaneously. On this and earlier assumptions, the time paths of
the trader's holdings of (S) and (D) are given by the familiar sawtooth
patterns of Figure 1. Average holdings of (S) and (D) are $\overline{S} \equiv S/2$ and
$\overline{D} \equiv D/2$. Since the trader receives S units of money on each sale date
and gives up D units of money on each purchase date, the time path
of money holdings is represented by the irregular step function of
Figure 1. This path begins just prior to date zero, with an amount of
money M_0 that is just sufficient to prevent the path ever from becoming negative.

For our purposes, the most important feature of the path of money
holdings is its average value, $\overline{M}$. This value obviously is defined unambiguously by the choice variables S and D, a fact that we may express
formally by writing $\overline{M} = F(S, D)$. Indeed, it can be shown that the
function F—hereafter referred to as the finance function—may be
written explicitly as

$$\overline{M} = F(S, D) = \overline{S} + \overline{D} - G(S, D), \tag{1}$$

where $G(S, D)$—hereafter referred to as the divisor function—is equal
to the greatest common divisor of S and D if S/D is rational and
otherwise is equal to zero.[3]

The graph of the finance function (1) corresponding to any given
(constant) value of S is illustrated in Figure 2.[4] Its most notable characteristic is that for any given value of S the finance function contains
a jump discontinuity at every value of D for which S/D is rational.
These discontinuities have a straightforward economic interpretation.
The trader can economize on money balances most effectively by so
coordinating purchases and sales that sales often or always occur simultaneously with purchases, in which case S and D will have a com-

---

[3] For a discussion of some elementary properties of the divisor function, see Niven
and Zuckerman (1972, pp. 4–6). The interested reader will find it easy to verify with
specific numeric examples that the required value of M_0 equals $D - G(S, D)$. Thus the
total value of all inventories just before date zero is $S + M_0 = S + D - G(S, D)$. But,
this total value is constant over time because of our stationarity assumption; so it must
equal $\overline{M} + \overline{S} + \overline{D}$. Formula (1) follows immediately. General proofs of these formulas
can be found in Clower and Howitt (1976). These proofs necessarily involve the use
of number theory—a branch of mathematics unfamiliar to most economists.

[4] Since $G(S, D)$ is homogeneous of degree one in S and D, the absolute magnitude
of S is of no significance.

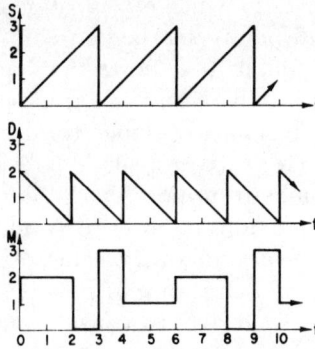

Figure 1. Time paths of inventories in the special case: $S = 3$, $D = 2$, $y = 1$, $m = 0$, $M_0 = 1$

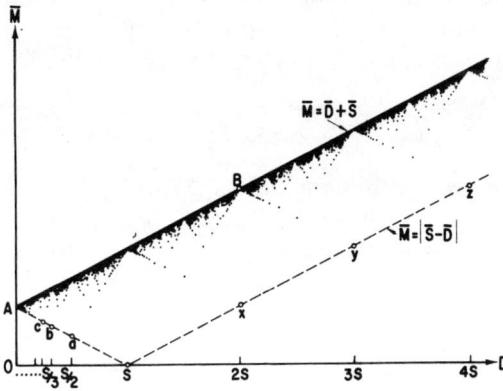

Figure 2. The finance function

mon divisor that differs significantly from zero. If, instead, most or all sales are poorly coordinated with purchases, most purchases will have to be financed with money carried over from previous sales, and S and D will have a common divisor that is close to or equal to zero. For example, suppose that $S = D$; then $G(S, D) = S$, and the trader can avoid entirely the holding of money. But if D is reduced by a very small amount, then $G(S, D)$ will fall very close to zero and the trader's money balances will rise discontinuously because the first several purchases after date zero will occur just before the corresponding sales.

The lower boundary of the finance function (points x, y, ..., and a, b, ...) is attained when D is an exact multiple or divisor of S, in which case $\overline{M} = |\overline{S} - \overline{D}|$. The upper boundary (the extended line AB) is attained when S/D is irrational, in which case $\overline{M} = \overline{S} + \overline{D}$. All other cases (i.e., all cases in which S/D is rational but neither S/D nor D/S is an integer) yield points that lie between these two extremes.

So far we have assumed that the trader has no reason to avoid making simultaneous purchase and sale transactions. In some situations this assumption may be acceptable, for example, in cases where sales and purchases take place at a single location. But in many circumstances it is plausible to suppose that traders purposely separate sale and purchase transactions in order to avoid bunching costs—that is, costs of rapid communication or travel between different locations, costs associated with rapid clearance of payments, and so forth. Formally we can allow for such costs by considering the time phasing as well as the frequencies of purchases and sales. Specifically, suppose that a sale occurs at date zero but that the first purchase does not occur until date $m > 0$. Since the choice of an origin to our time scale is arbitrary, we may also suppose that m equals the minimum distance between any contiguous sale and purchase. Obviously m will be constrained by the choice of S and D. More precisely, it can be shown that

$$m \le G(S,D)/2y. \tag{2}$$

As before, the time paths of holdings (S) and (D) are represented by the sawtooth patterns shown in Figure 1, except that the time path for (D) is everywhere displaced to the right by the amount m. The value of $\overline{M}$ in this case is given by

$$\overline{M} = F(S, D) + ym, \tag{3}$$

which of course reduces to (1) if at some date a sale and purchase occur simultaneously so that $m = 0$.

B. Solution of the Model

Stated formally, the trader's decision problem is to choose S, D, and M so as to minimize the sum of trade-related costs:

$$C = \rho(\overline{D} + \overline{S} + \overline{M}) + \beta\overline{S} + \alpha\overline{D} + \gamma\overline{M} + ay/D + by/S + f(S, D, m). \tag{4}$$

The first term represents waiting costs, where ρ is the trader's rate of time discount and, by virtue of our stationarity assumption, $\overline{D} + \overline{S} + \overline{M}$ is the total value of inventory holdings at each point in time. The next three terms represent storage costs, where storage-cost coefficients α, β, and γ are expressed as rates per unit time per unit commodity. The next two terms represent set-up costs per unit time, where a and b are the set-up costs per transaction, and where y/S and

y/D are the frequencies of sale and purchase. The last term represents bunching costs per unit time. The exact form of the bunching-cost function $f(S, D, m)$ is left unspecified, except for the obvious requirement that it be decreasing with respect to m. Analysis of specific examples makes it clear that the bunching-cost function will generally exhibit the same kind of jump discontinuities as the finance function (see Clower and Howitt 1976). We refer to the sum of waiting and storage costs as holding costs and to the sum of set-up and bunching costs as trading costs.

The specification of the cost function (4) is extremely simple and conventional in form, but it generalizes earlier work in four significant respects. First, we allow the trader to choose the frequency of sales as well as purchases. The usual procedure in the past has been to regard the frequency of sales (the income period) as predetermined.[5] Second, we impose no a priori restrictions on the relative trading frequency, S/D. The standard approach in earlier work with similar models has been to suppose that S/D can take on only integer values (see Grossman and Policano 1975). Third, we allow the trader to choose the time phasing of purchases and sales, an issue that has been ignored by previous writers, all of whom assumed, implicitly or explicitly, that $m = 0$.[6] Fourth and finally, we permit the previously ignored phenomenon of bunching costs to influence the trader's decision.

None of these generalizations is radical; indeed, each is suggested naturally by previous work or by the internal logic of our model. Yet in combination these generalizations yield a model of the timing of transactions with implications that differ fundamentally from those of any model considered in the existing literature.

To simplify the analysis of the trader's decision problem, suppose initially that there are no bunching costs, that is, that $f(S, D, m) \equiv 0$. In this case it is clear from (3) and (4) that the trader will choose $m = 0$, because that choice will permit holding costs associated directly with money to be minimized. The trader's decision problem then reduces to

$$\underset{\{S,D\}}{\text{minimize}} \ (2\rho + \alpha + \gamma)D/2 + (2\rho + \beta + \gamma)S/2 - (\rho + \gamma)G(S, D)$$
$$+ \ ay/D + by/S. \tag{5}$$

Because the divisor function $G(S, D)$ is discontinuous, standard calculus techniques cannot be used directly to establish the existence or

[5] See Baumol (1952), Feige and Parkin (1971), and Perlman (1971). Barro and Santomero (1976) deal with the determination of the income period.
[6] See any of the references cited in n. 1 above.

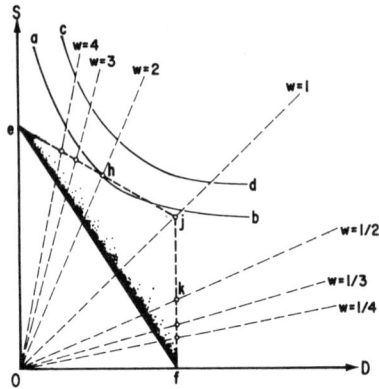

Figure 3. The first-stage decision problem

properties of solutions to (5). This problem can be effectively circumvented here, however, by working with graphical methods. Let the curves *ab*, *cd*, etc. in Figure 3 represent iso-trading-cost (*ITC*) loci corresponding to alternative constant values of trading costs. These loci are continuous, downward sloping, and convex to the origin; and "higher" loci (larger values of S and D) correspond to lower values of total trading cost. Let the points on or within the triangle *efj* represent an arbitrarily chosen iso-holding-cost (*IHC*) set corresponding to some given value of holding costs. The points at which D is an exact multiple or divisor of S lie on the upper boundary of the *IHC* set, indicated by the lines *ej* and *jf*, the slopes of which are, respectively, $(\gamma - \alpha)/(2\rho + \beta + \gamma)$ and $(2\rho + \alpha + \gamma)/(\gamma - \beta)$. The points at which S/D is irrational lie on the lower boundary of the *IHC* set, indicated by the line *ef*, the slope of which is $-(2\rho + \alpha + \gamma)/(2\rho + \beta + \gamma)$. All other points lie strictly inside the triangle *efj*. Because the finance function is discontinuous, the *IHC* set consists entirely of isolated points except along its lower boundary (for a proof, see Clower and Howitt 1976).

Using this diagram, we can illustrate the solution to (5) in two stages. A necessary condition for any solution is that trading costs be minimal for any given level of holding costs. Thus in searching for a solution we may restrict attention to points such as *h* in Figure 3 that lie on the highest possible *ITC* curve that intersects the given *IHC* set. If bunching costs are identically zero (as we are presently assuming), then trading costs and holding costs will both be homogeneous functions of the variables S and D; hence the set of all points that minimize trading costs for given levels of holding costs will lie on a common ray through the origin. The slope of this ray, $w = S/D$, is therefore equal to the relative trading frequency of the solution to (5). Thus the first stage in solving (5) is to determine the optimal relative trading frequency, $\hat{w}$. Having determined $\hat{w}$ we may treat the equation $\hat{w} = S/D$ as a constraint and use it to rewrite (5) as:

$$\underset{|D|}{\text{minimize}} \ [(2\rho + \gamma)(1 + \hat{w}) + \alpha + \beta\hat{w} - 2(\rho + \gamma)G(\hat{w}, 1)]D/2$$
$$+ (a + b/\hat{w})y/D. \quad (6)$$

The solution to (5) can then be derived as:

$$\hat{D} = \sqrt{\frac{2y(a + b/\hat{w})}{\alpha + \beta\hat{w} + (2\rho + \gamma)(1 + \hat{w}) - 2(\rho + \gamma)G(\hat{w}, 1)}}, \quad (7)$$

$$\hat{S} = \hat{w}\hat{D}, \quad (8)$$

and

$$\hat{\bar{M}} = \hat{S}/2 + \hat{D}/2 - G(\hat{S}, \hat{D}). \quad (9)$$

Regrettably, these formulas do not permit us to calculate numerical solution values for $\hat{D}$, $\hat{S}$, and $\hat{\bar{M}}$ corresponding to given values of the parameters y, a, b, α, β, γ, and ρ. The difficulty lies in the first-stage problem—the determination of $\hat{w}$. Of course, in any particular problem we could attempt to find a numerical value for $\hat{w}$ by trial and error, but except in contrived special cases such a procedure is unlikely to yield anything but frustration.

A more promising approach is to establish limits on admissible solution values of $\hat{w}$ by imposing artful and (strictly speaking) invalid restrictions on the finance function (1). Suppose, for example, that we follow earlier literature and approximate the finance function by fitting straight lines through the lower boundary (i.e., the points satisfying integer constraints). This is equivalent to approximating the upper boundary of the *IHC* set in Figure 3 by the straight lines *ej* and *jf*. Following the same two-stage procedure as before yields the solutions:

$$(\hat{S}, \hat{D}) = \begin{cases} [\sqrt{2by/(2\rho + \beta + \gamma)}, \sqrt{2ay/(\alpha - \gamma)}], & \text{if this makes} \\ \qquad\qquad\qquad \hat{S} > \hat{D} > 0; \\ [\sqrt{2by/(\beta - \gamma)}, \sqrt{2ay/(2\rho + \alpha + \gamma)}], & \text{if this makes} \quad (10) \\ \qquad\qquad\qquad \hat{D} > \hat{S} > 0; \\ [\sqrt{2(a + b)y/(2\rho + \alpha + \beta)}, \sqrt{2(a + b)y/(2\rho + \alpha + \beta)}] \end{cases}$$

otherwise;

and $$\overline{\hat{M}} \;=\; |\,(\hat{S}|2) - (\hat{D}|2)\,|. \tag{11}$$

As may be easily verified, the value of $\hat{w}$ (or $\hat{w}^{-1}$, if $\hat{w} < 1$) determined by these equations approximates its "true" value in the general solution to (5) to the nearest integer. In virtually every case this approximation will lead quickly (two trials) to an exact numerical solution, for because of the discontinuities it is clear from Figure 3 that the "true" solution to (5) usually will correspond to a point on the upper boundary of some *IHC* set, and all such points define integer values of w or $1/w$. But the rule suggested by this line of reasoning is not universal, because examples can be constructed in which neither $\hat{w}$ nor $1/\hat{w}$ is an integer.[7]

If we now relax the assumption that bunching costs are negligible, the decision problem becomes more complicated, but the same general principles apply. Generally speaking the *ITC* curves will consist of sets of isolated points, similar to the *IHC* sets, because of the discontinuities in the bunching-cost function. This produces an even greater presumption that the solution to the trader's problem will satisfy an integer constraint. However, the two-stage procedure described above no longer applies, for there is no reason to think that the bunching-cost function will possess the required homogeneity properties.[8] Another obvious implication of the assumption of positive bunching costs is that the trader will be more likely to choose positive average money holdings, for to avoid holding any money at all, the trader must not only choose $S = D$ but must also choose a corner solution, $m = 0$ (see Section IIB).

II. IMPLICATIONS AND EXTENSIONS

In subsequent pages we discuss some implications and extensions of our basic model. Our analysis is in no sense exhaustive; its purpose is not so much to elucidate logical properties of our basic model (though we do this) as to illustrate the wide range of economic insights—critical as well as constructive—that may be gained by adding even modest elements of generality to earlier and more spe-

[7] Suppose that $y = 1$, $a = 5/11$, $b = 1$, $\rho = .01$, $\alpha = \beta = .2$, $\gamma = 0$. Pick the *IHC* set with holding cost equal to 1.0. Then the *ITC* curve with trading cost equal to (3.36)/11 touches two adjacent points on the upper boundary of the given *IHC* set for which $w = 1$ and $w = 2$; but the same *ITC* curve passes to the left of the point with $w = 3/2$ in the given *IHC* set, so $\hat{w}$ must lie strictly between 1 and 2.

[8] The example of Clower and Howitt (1976) produces a nonhomogeneous trading-cost function.

cialized inventory-theoretic models of the transactions demand for money.

A. Comparative Statics: General Observations

It cannot be emphasized too strongly that the discontinuities in our basic model arise not from strained assumptions about the discreteness of time or the atomistic character of commodity and money units, but rather from the fact that trades involve stocks rather than flows so that small changes in the relative timing of transactions can produce large jumps in average finance requirements and in average bunching costs. These jumps would be less obvious if our model dealt with nonstationary processes so that between-trade time intervals were not necessarily uniform. As a matter of logic, however, jumps analogous to those implied by our model must occur in any ongoing economy where trades take place at discrete points rather than continuously in time. Appearances to the contrary notwithstanding, therefore, the comparative-statics implications of our model are of more than purely academic interest.

The most important comparative-statics conclusion to be drawn from our model is negative, namely, the consequences of parameter changes upon equilibrium values of S, D, and $\overline{M}$ are generally ambiguous. The source of these ambiguities lies mainly in the different effects of parameter changes upon relative and absolute transactions frequencies. As is clear from earlier graphical analysis (Figure 3), small changes in parameters may leave the relative frequency $\hat{w} = \hat{S}/\hat{D}$ unchanged because one or both of the touching frontiers of the IHC and ITC sets consist of isolated points. In such cases the only effect will be to change the absolute frequencies $y/\hat{D}$ and $y/\hat{S}$, which are determined in the second-stage maximization problem. It is worth remarking that the standard assumption of regarding the absolute frequency of sales (the income period) as predetermined hides this sometimes crucial distinction by making a change in the absolute frequency of purchases equivalent to a change in the frequency of purchases relative to sales.

To illustrate the preceding remarks, let us consider a change in γ, the storage-cost coefficient on money holdings. If we employed the usual approximation giving rise to the square-root formulas (10) above, we would infer that when $S > D$ an increase in γ would lead to an increase in $\hat{D}$. If the change in γ did not affect the relative frequency $\hat{w}$, however, we would infer from the "correct" formula (7) that $\hat{D}$ would decrease. To get the result implied by the usual approximation, we should require the rise in γ to produce (i) a large enough increase in D (decline in w) in the first-stage decision problem to offset (ii) the decrease in D at the second stage. The standard formulas (10) presuppose that the relative effect (i) always dominates the absolute effect (ii), but this cannot always be so because sometimes a change in γ will produce no change in $\hat{w}$.

In simpler models involving integer constraints on S/D or its reciprocal, individual demand functions will exhibit discontinuous steps, but the smoothing properties of aggregation may be invoked to argue that the aggregate demand function is smooth and behaves qualitatively as indicated by the usual square-root formula (see Barro 1976). The present model shows that this is generally not valid. For example, when γ increases, some traders will increase $\hat{D}$ and others will decrease $\hat{D}$; the aggregate effect will depend crucially upon the form of the distribution of traders between the two categories. The form of the distribution is not so crucial in simpler models because they do not allow for the possibility of traders moving in different directions, just for some not moving at all.

This is not to say that comparative-static results cannot be derived from the present approach. On the contrary, the approach allows us to isolate those results that are robust enough to survive some degree of generality. For example, Samuelson's well-known technique (1947, pp. 46–52) for manipulating inequalities associated with an extremum allows us to conclude that an increase in either of the trading-cost coefficients a or b will lead to an increase in average holding of the associated commodity $\overline{D}$ or $\overline{S}$; that an increase in any of the storage-cost coefficients, α, β, or γ, will lead to a decrease in average holdings of $\overline{D}$, $\overline{S}$, or $\overline{M}$; and that an increase in the rate of time preference (interest rate), ρ, will lead to a decrease in the total money value of inventories, $\overline{D} + \overline{S} + \overline{M}$. Note, however, that when ρ increases, any single inventory holding may increase rather than decrease.

One other familiar result that holds in the general case (provided that $m = 0$) is that the income-elasticity of demand for each of the inventories has a value of one-half. This follows from the modified square-root formulas (7)–(9) and from the fact that, because of the homogeneity of trading costs and holding costs in y, S, and D, a change in y will not affect the value of $\hat{w}$ determined in the first-stage decision problem.

B. Positive Money Holdings

Though a trader might be willing to hold positive money balances simply to avoid bunching costs, it appears that such balances would not be held for any other reason unless money were less costly to hold than the most frequently traded good. Otherwise, the trader would choose $\hat{S} = \hat{D}$ and would hold no money at all, for there would be no advantage to holding money rather than goods as a store of purchasing power or consumption. This may be seen most easily from our analysis by supposing that the solution point illustrated in Figure 3 yields a value of $\hat{w}$ greater than unity. Then this point must lie to the left of the ray with $w = 1$. But if $\gamma \geq \alpha$, the line ej will be horizontal or even upward sloping, which implies that total marketing costs could be reduced by moving the solution to point j, where $w = 1$.

These considerations have some bearing on the familiar question, Why do people choose to hold money when all other assets have a higher net return?[9] Our answer is that they will not—at least not in a stationary state without bunching costs. More generally, it appears that the usefulness of money as a means of payment is limited by its costliness to store, which may help to explain why representative monies have tended to displace commodity monies and commodity-backed monies in modern times.

The same considerations also shed light on the holding of money balances during hyperinflation. The coefficient γ in our model may be interpreted as the sum of physical storage costs plus the expected rate of inflation. The model then implies that when inflation reaches some critical point people will hold no money at all, except for brief intervals between transactions which become shorter as the expected rate of inflation increases. This prediction of our model accords well with behavior observed during actual hyperinflations. During even the most severe hyperinflations, however, people appear to be extremely reluctant to forgo trade in organized markets that require them to use conventional media of exchange (see Cagan 1956). That is to say, money continues to circulate with finite velocity even when it is the most costly of all goods to store. This observation, combined with our theoretical analysis, casts serious doubt on the conventional assumption that bunching costs may be ignored. The evidence suggests, on the contrary, that bunching costs are substantial at least for "nearly simultaneous" sale and purchase transactions.[10]

C. Competitive Interest on Money

It has been shown by many authors that social optimality requires the payment of competitive interest on money (see Samuelson 1968;

---

[9] For historical accounts of this question, see Gilbert (1953) and Patinkin (1965).

[10] The failure of previous models to take into account bunching costs may also explain their failure to account for the absolute magnitude of the typical household's money holdings, which these models all tend to underestimate. See Barro and Fischer (1976).

Friedman 1969; Feige and Parkin 1971). Optimality also requires that the money commodity be as inexpensive as possible to produce (see Gramm 1974). Generally speaking, it is taken for granted that the money commodity is almost costless to store relative to the cost of storing a typical nonmoney commodity of equal money value.

We can analyze the effect of paying interest on money by interpreting the coefficient γ as the money storage cost coefficient minus the rate of return paid on money. Suppose that it is possible to find a money commodity that is literally costless to store. Then the optimal situation is to have $\gamma = -\rho$, in which case the trader's decision problem may be written as:

$$\underset{(D,\ S,\ m)}{\text{minimize}}\ (\alpha + \rho)\ (D/2) + (\beta + \rho)\ (S/2) + a(y/D) + b(y/S)$$
$$+ f(S, D, m) \tag{12}$$

subject to (2).

If bunching costs are nonzero, then (2) becomes binding, and

$$\hat{m} = G(\hat{S}, \hat{D})/2y. \tag{13}$$

In this case the formulas for $\hat{D}$ and $\hat{S}$ depend upon the exact nature of the bunching-cost function.

If bunching costs are identically zero, standard calculus techniques can be used to derive the optimal solution:

$$\hat{D} = \sqrt{2ay/(\alpha + \rho)}, \qquad \hat{S} = \sqrt{2by/(\beta + \rho)}. \tag{14}$$

This solution is the one that would be obtained if the trader ignored the interaction of trading frequencies and minimized total holding and trading costs of each nonmoney good separately. Thus the gain from the payment of competitive interest on money (if $f[S, D, m] = 0$) derives from the freedom such a policy gives the trader to choose trading frequencies independently, without regard to cash constraints.

For reasons indicated earlier, it is hard to say what the qualitative effects of such interest payments might be on specific variables. In particular, our example in Section IIA shows that a reduction in γ will have an ambiguous effect on $\hat{D}$ even if we know a priori that $\hat{S} > \hat{D}$. However, two conclusions hold under quite general circumstances. The first is that a reduction in γ will increase $\overline{M}$ (see Section IIA). The second result is that if $f(S, D, m) = 0$, then total trading costs must fall. This follows from the fact that, as may be verified from (4) and (7)–(9), the optimal solution $(\hat{S}, \hat{D})$ always has the property that total trading costs equal holding costs. Since the sum of these costs must fall when γ falls, both component elements of cost must also fall. Of course, it follows that either $\hat{S}$ or $\hat{D}$ must rise (otherwise trading costs could not fall); but in specific examples it is possible also for either $\hat{S}$ or $\hat{D}$ (but not both) to fall.

D. Bond Holdings

The transactions theory traditionally has treated the demand for money as arising from the problem of finding the least costly combination of money and bond holdings with which to bridge time gaps between purchases and sales. The present paper shows how the same approach can be used to address the more fundamental problem of determining the size of the gaps to be bridged. The observation that few people actually engage in temporary bond transactions between monthly pay checks, rather than refuting the transactions approach, as has been frequently asserted, demonstrates the need to focus attention on this more fundamental problem. Nevertheless, since some agents (particularly large firms) are known to engage in frequent bond transactions, it is worth investigating the consequences of extending the present model to allow the trader to hold bonds as well as money as a temporary abode of purchasing power.

To this end, let us suppose that the trader is able to buy or sell bonds at a fixed price, plus or minus a brokerage fee on each transaction. To ensure the existence of a stationary solution, suppose also that the bond rate of interest, i, is no greater than the trader's rate of time discount, ρ. Then it can be shown that the trader will choose to buy bonds at every sale date of (S) following which enough money would otherwise be held for so long that its opportunity cost in the form of bond interest would more than offset the double brokerage fee associated with buying and selling the bonds, and will sell bonds at every purchase date of (D) at which money balances would otherwise run out. If bunching costs are incurred on bond transactions (and to suppose otherwise would be incongruous in a model where it is assumed that such costs are incurred for simultaneous goods transactions), there is an incentive to delay scheduled bond purchases and to advance scheduled bond sales up to the point where the marginal reduction in bunching costs on bonds is just offset by the marginal loss of interest income.

Let $\overline{B}$ denote the average holding of bonds. As in (3) above the average holding of financial assets is given by:

$$\overline{M} + \overline{B} = F(S, D) + ym. \qquad (15)$$

In many circumstances, especially if bond-related bunching costs are significant, the trader will choose $\overline{B} = 0$, which is consistent with empiricial evidence concerning the behavior of most households. Even if $\bar{B} > 0$, none of the findings reported earlier will be significantly affected by this fact. In particular, the trader's decision problem will be relatively insensitive to small changes in parameters because of discontinuities in the finance function and in the bunching-cost function. As in earlier discussions, therefore, we cannot expect to obtain unambiguous comparative-statics results on the basis of a priori considerations. A case in point is the effect of a change in the bond interest rate, i, on average holdings of money balances, $\bar{M}$. One would expect the sign of this partial derivative to be negative (see Grossman and Policano 1975, p. 1110), but that need not be so. If i increases, this might have no effect on relative transactions frequencies. But by using Samuelson's technique of manipulating inequalities, it is easily seen that $\bar{B}$ must increase. If we assume that $m = 0$ before and after the change, then $\bar{D}$, $\bar{S}$, and $\bar{M}$ must all increase in the same proportion as $\bar{B}$.

If the introduction of bond holdings does not make earlier comparative-statics results less ambiguous, neither does it force us to revise earlier conclusions that were unambiguous. For example, it can be shown that the income elasticity of all inventory demands is equal to one-half (if bunching costs may be ignored). Moreover, a necessary condition for positive money holdings in the absence of bunching costs on goods is, again, that the storage-cost coefficient on money balances be less than the corresponding coefficient on the most frequently traded of the two nonfinancial commodities.[11] Finally, the payment of competitive interest on money that is costless to store would still eliminate the discontinuity in the *IHC* sets. In this situation no bonds would ever be held because to do so would be to incur needless trading costs; so the behavior of the trader would be precisely as described in the preceding section.

E. Trade Credit

The introduction of temporary bond holdings into our model does not significantly alter any of our earlier findings. More interesting results follow, however, if we extend our analysis to include a different kind of money substitute. Specifically, suppose that the trader has access to trade credit or bank overdraft facilities that permit the de-

---

[11] One minor change in our results is that the sufficient conditions for positive money holdings are stronger than earlier. The trader may now choose $\bar{M} = 0$ even if $S \neq D$, provided that (i) bunching costs are all zero and (ii) a bond transaction accompanies every commodity transaction.

ferral of cash payment for goods through the nonnegotiable option at each purchase date of incurring a debt (to the seller of goods in one case, to a banker in the other) up to a predetermined limit, L. Suppose also that interest is charged on used credit at the rate s. Let $\overline{C}$ denote the average amount of unused credit and let $L - \overline{C}$ represent the average amount of used credit. As in (3) and (15) above, the sum of the trader's holdings of net financial assets is given by:

$$\overline{M} + L - \overline{C} = F(S, D) + ym. \tag{16}$$

As long as $s \leq \rho$, it will be optimal for the trader to arrange for as much financing as possible to be done by credit. If L satisfies

$$L \geq D + S - 2G(S, D) + ym, \tag{17}$$

then holdings of money may be avoided altogether, for trade credit can be used to finance all of the trader's purchases without exceeding the credit limit (17), provided that all sales of (S) are accompanied by a running down of debt rather than an accumulation of money balances.

On these assumptions the trader's total holding cost will be given by:

$$\rho(\overline{D} + \overline{S} + \overline{M} + \overline{C}) + \alpha\overline{D} + \beta\overline{S} + \gamma\overline{M} + s(L - \overline{C}). \tag{18}$$

The term $\rho\overline{C}$ is included in waiting costs because not to use possible credit lines involves the trader in the same abstention cost as for other commodities. In the case where (17) holds, of course, we have $\overline{M} = 0$. If, in addition, we have $s = \rho$, the holding-cost function (18) reduces to:

$$(\rho + \alpha)\overline{D} + (\rho + \beta)\overline{S} + sL, \tag{19}$$

which is, except for the irrelevant constant term sL, identical to the function implied by our earlier discussion of the payment of competitive interest on money. In other words, competitive trade credit and bank overdraft arrangements provide two alternative routes to monetary optimality equivalent in effect to paying competitive interest on money. This result helps to rationalize—at least on an individual level—the presence in all advanced economies of a wide and (apparently) still expanding array of specialized credit facilities.

F. The Coordination of Individual Trading Activities

Though much of our analysis of individual trading behavior appears to have significant import also for market behavior, we shall limit our discussion of such matters here to a few general observations. To go beyond this would be ill advised, for the existing literature does not contain a satisfactory theoretical account of the overall working of an economy in which the resource costs of trading activity depend in an essential way on the frequency of exchange transactions. (For further elaboration, see Heller 1972.) In the absence of such a theory there is reason to believe that premature generalization of results derived from individual experiments will deal either superficially or not at all with what appears to be a fundamental externality (see Hahn 1973, pp. 229–34, 241; Perlman 1973; Russell 1974).

This externality arises from the fact that, in an economy with set-up costs of trading, individuals will trade only at isolated points in time; hence the set of transaction dates that are feasible for one trader cannot in general be specified independently of choices made by other traders. As Perlman (1971, p. 235) has put it, there exists in such an economy not only a problem of double coincidence of wants but also a problem of double coincidence of timing.

The timing-externality problem cannot be avoided by supposing (à la Debreu–Arrow) that all trades are the result of prearranged contractual obligations that specify exactly the dates at which trades are to be executed, for this procedure begs the question of how traders coordinate the timing of contract negotiations. The neo-Walrasian "auctioneer" is not an answer to but rather an evasion of this question. The only plausible and logically satisfactory solution is to posit the existence of specialist traders who, unlike the primary traders of the present paper, agree to do business continuously at dates chosen by the primary traders with whom they deal.[12]

Such specialist traders—shopkeepers, wholesalers, brokers, agents, marketing managers of manufacturing concerns—play a central role in every developed economy. Their usefulness arises from their willingness in normal circumstances to quote buying or selling prices (or both) at which they are ready to trade in large quantities at dates that suit their customers. By so doing they not only solve the double-coincidence-of-timing problem but also allow primary traders to plan and execute trades in accordance with budget constraints that do not require contingent allowance for possible nonprice rationing.[13] In practice, therefore, specialist traders act as visible fingers for Smith's invisible hand. Our argument suggests that a special class of market

[12] This type of market arrangement is described in more detail by Howitt (1974), Clower (1975), and Clower and Leijonhufvud (1975).

[13] This logical difficulty in specifying the standard budget constraint is discussed by Clower (1965); the existence of specialist traders permits primary traders to make "notional" plans "effective" except in abnormal situations, where stocks of inventories held by specialists are temporarily exhausted or grossly in surplus.

organizers and operators should be assumed to play a similar role in formal economic theory.

REFERENCES

Barro, Robert J. "Integral Constraints and Aggregation in an Inventory Model of Money Demand." *J. Finance* 31 (March 1976): 77–88.

Barro, Robert J., and Fischer, S. "Recent Developments in Monetary Theory." *J. Monetary Econ.* 2 (April 1976): 133–67.

Barro, Robert J., and Santomero, A. M. "Output and Employment in a Macro Model with Discrete Transaction Costs." *J. Monetary Econ.* 2 (July 1976): 297–310.

Baumol, William J. "The Transactions Demand for Cash: An Inventory Theoretic Approach." *Q.J.E.* 66 (November 1952): 545–56.

Cagan, P. "The Monetary Dynamics of Hyperinflation." In *Studies in the Quantity Theory of Money*, edited by M. Friedman. Chicago: Univ. Chicago Press, 1956.

Clower, Robert W. "The Keynesian Counterrevolution: A Theoretical Appraisal." In *The Theory of Interest Rates*, edited by Frank H. Hahn and Frank P. R. Brechling. New York: St. Martin's, 1965.

———. "Is There an Optimal Money Supply?" *J. Finance* 25, no. 2 (May 1970): 425–33.

———. "Reflections on the Keynesian Perplex." *Zeitschrift für Nationalökonomie* 35 (July 1975): 1–24.

Clower, Robert W., and Howitt, Peter W. "Money, Credit, and the Timing of Transactions." Discussion Paper no. 72, Dept. Econ., Univ. California, Los Angeles, 1976.

Clower, Robert W., and Leijonhufvud, Axel. "The Coordination of Economic Activities: A Keynesian Perspective." *American Econ. Rev. Papers and Proc.* 65 (May 1975): 182–88.

Feige, Edgar L., and Parkin, Michael. "The Optimal Quantity of Money, Bonds, Commodity Inventories, and Capital." *A.E.R.* 61, no. 3 (June 1971): 335–49.

Fried, Joel S. "Money, Exchange and Growth." *Western Econ. J.* 11 (September 1973): 285–301.

Friedman, Milton. "The Optimum Quantity of Money." In *The Optimum Quantity of Money and Other Essays*, by M. Friedman. Chicago: Aldine, 1969.

Gilbert, John C. "The Demand for Money: The Development of an Economic Concept." *J.P.E.* 61, no. 2 (April 1953): 144–59.

Gramm, William P. "Laissez-Faire and the Optimum Quantity of Money." *Econ. Inquiry* 12 (March 1974): 125–32.

Grossman, Herschel I., and Policano, Andrew J. "Money Balances, Commodity Inventories, and Inflationary Expectations." *J.P.E.* 83, no. 6 (December 1975): 1093–112.

Hahn, Frank H. "Foundations of Monetary Theory." In *Essays in Modern Economics*, edited by Michael Parkin. London: Longmans, 1973.

Heller, Walter P. "Transactions with Set-up Costs." *J. Econ. Theory* 4, no. 3 (1972): 465–78.

Howitt, Peter W. "Stability and the Quantity Theory." *J.P.E.* 82, no. 1 (January/February 1974): 133–51.

———. "Intertemporal Utility Maximization and the Timing of Transactions." *A.E.R.* 67, no. 2 (March 1977): 156–65.

Johnson, Harry G. "Is There an Optimal Money Supply?" *J. Finance* 25, no. 2 (May 1970): 435–42.

Niven, Ivan M., and Zuckerman, Herbert S. *An Introduction to the Theory of Numbers.* 3rd ed. New York: Wiley, 1972.

Patinkin, Don. "An Indirect Utility Approach on the Theory of Money, Assets, and Savings." In *The Theory of Interest Rates*, edited by Frank H. Hahn and Frank P. R. Brechling. New York: St. Martin's, 1965.

Perlman, Morris. "The Roles of Money in an Economy and the Optimum Quantity of Money." *Economica*, n.s. 38 (August 1971): 233–52.

———. "The Roles of Money in an Economy and the Optimum Quantity of Money: Reply." *Economica*, n.s. 40 (November 1973): 432–41.

Policano, Andrew. "An Inventory-Theoretic Model of Trade Credit Transactions." *Econ. Inquiry* 15 (April 1977): 166–82.

Russell, Thomas. "Feige and Parkin on the Optimal Quantity of Money." *A.E.R.* 64 (December 1974): 1074–76.

Samuelson, Paul A. *The Foundations of Economic Analysis.* Cambridge, Mass.: Harvard Univ. Press. 1947.

———. "What Classical and Neoclassical Monetary Theory Really Was." *Canadian J. Econ.* 1 (February 1968): 1–15.

Tobin, James. "The Interest Elasticity of Transactions Demand for Cash." *Rev. Econ. and Statis.* 38 (August 1956): 241–47.

PART IV

GENERAL PROCESS ANALYSIS

14

REFLECTIONS ON THE KEYNESIAN PERPLEX

The Jury had each formed a different view
(Long before the indictment was read),
And they all spoke at once, so that none of them knew
One word that the others had said.
LEWIS CARROLL, "THE HUNTING OF THE SNARK"

Critical commentaries on the present state of the arts in economic theory have been appearing with increasing regularity in the professional literature during the past few years.[1] Of course, different writers have voiced very different grounds for discontent. One finds modern theory logically pretentious; another deplores its lack of conceptual unity; another faults it for ideological bias; another for lack of social relevance; another for empirical aridity; another for philosophical shallowness; and so on ... and on, and on. Indeed, the only ascertainable element of unity in the cacaphony of complaint is the conviction apparently shared by all writers that the presently lamentable state of economic theory is not attributable to the intractability of the problems addressed by economists. On first reflection, then, one is tempted to ascribe contemporary discontents to the regrettable but notorious proclivity of economists mutually to disparage each others' pursuits.[2] Second thoughts, however, suggest that the true source of dissatisfaction lies deeper.

Popular opinion and television news commentators to the contrary notwithstanding, professional economists are no more prone to idle disputation over the fundamentals of their discipline than are their counterparts in other fields. To be sure, economics has never lacked for critics since Adam Smith elevated it to the status of a separate

An earlier version of this paper was presented at a meeting of the Austrian Economics Association on March 19, 1974, at which time the author was Visiting Professor at the Institute of Advanced Studies, Vienna.

[1] A full list of contributions to this literature would fill several pages. Here it must suffice to mention only some of the more notable items, namely Hicks (1967 and 1974), Arrow (1967), Hahn (1970 and 1973), Leontief (1971), Shubik (1970), Robinson (1974), Kaldor (1972), Davidson (1972), Kornai (1971), Leijonhufvud (1973), Ostroy (1973), Becker (1974), Johnson (1974).

[2] Cf. Edgeworth (1925), Vol. 1, p. 11 and Vol. 2, p. 285; Leijonhufvud (1973*), pp. 327–328.

discipline in 1776. All the same, the first concerted attack on prevailing orthodoxy by an acknowledged leader *from within* the economics profession was that mounted by J. M. Keynes in the 1930's—the so-called Keynesian Revolution. As is now generally acknowledged, the Keynesian Revolution was abortive.[3] Its intended target was the foundations of received doctrine.[4] Its main impact, however, has been not upon the foundations but rather upon the superstructure of economic theory.[5] Thus, what now appears to some as the outbreak of a novel strain of intellectual disorder is, in truth, nothing more than a renewal in unfamiliar guise of the same malaise that Keynes sought unsuccessfully to diagnose and treat some forty years ago.[6]

Such, in brief, is my explanation of the presently unsettled and uncertain state of economic theory. My purpose in the pages that follow is to elaborate upon this theme. Much of the discussion is correspondingly retrospective in orientation. In the concluding sections of the paper, however, I shall go beyond the question, "How did we get where we are?" and attempt to deal constructively with the currently more important question: "Where do we go from here?"

I. KEYNES AND THE NEO-CLASSICS

The intellectual authority of neoclassical economics and, more specifically, of Marshall and his school had ceased to have significant pragmatic justification long before Keynes came on the scene. The rapid pace of European and American industrialization and urbanization in the century preceding World War I and, accompanying that, the growing role of governmental intervention in social and economic affairs had, by 1920, created a world in which the equilibrium and stability presuppositions of established economic theory—the essential basis for traditional indifference to questions about short-run adjustment processes—were palpably anachronistic. Professional awareness of the growing discrepancy between presumption and reality is most clearly apparent in the business cycle literature of the era, but is reflected also in the burgeoning literature of institutional economics,[7]

---

[3] The reasons are fully documented in Leijonhufvud's influential writings (Leijonhufvud, 1967, 1968, 1969, 1973).

[4] See the Preface to Keynes (1936); also Keynes (*Collected Writings*), Vol. 13, pp. 485–487.

[5] See the observations by Leontief (1947), p. 240; also Clower (1965) and Leijonhufvud (1967).

[6] Cf. Leijonhufvud (1973), pp. 28–29.

[7] In the U.S., one thinks mainly of the work of Veblen and Commons in this connection. In Europe, the same kind of work would be called "historical" or "sociological" economics.

in Knight's classic *Risk, Uncertainty and Profit* (1921), in the famous *Economic Journal* debate of the 1920's on economic progress and increasing returns,[8] in the growing literature critical of pure competition,[9] and, perhaps most significantly, in the scientifically escapist literature of welfare economics inaugurated by Pigou (when one can find nothing new to say about *what is*, one's fancy easily turns to *what ought to be*).[10] In plain truth, neoclassical economics furnished no tools to analyze the overall working of an ongoing economic system;[11] at best, it furnished methods to investigate the behavior of particular markets *within* an ongoing system that could itself be regarded as self-adjusting and strongly stable.

So the stage was set for Keynes' *General Theory* well before its appearance in 1936.[12] More accurately, the stage was set not for Keynes and *his* message, but rather for the rapid decline of Marshall and his school and a long-overdue redirection of economic analysis along lines suggested sixty years earlier by Leon Walras. The history of the Keynesian Revolution—more particularly, the reasons why it effectively fizzled out—can be fully appreciated, therefore, only by viewing it as an episode within a broader and ultimately more influential series of doctrinal developments which, for reasons that will soon become evident, I shall refer to as the *neo-Walrasian Revolution*.

It is customary (and, I think, correct) to regard the *General Theory* as an attempt to construct a theoretical model that would serve to rationalize Keynes' deeply felt conviction that modern capitalist economies tend to adjust *slowly and imperfectly* towards a state in which all productive resources are fully employed.[13] One might also regard the *General Theory*—and many have so regarded it—as an attack not merely upon the implicit stability presuppositions but also upon the explicit behavioral assumptions of Marshallian *partial process analysis*;[14] but to so regard it would, I believe, be an egregious error. Keynes' intention surely was not to deny the essential validity of Marshall's conception of the economic process. Keynes must rather have intended to offer the world an analytically manageable aggregative version of the kind

[8] For references, see Kaldor (1972).

[9] See Samuelson (1972), pp. 18–51.

[10] Cf. Johnson (1974), p. 5.

[11] Cf. Keynes (1936), p. 260.

[12] See Winch (1969) for more elaborate documentation of this theme.

[13] The alternative interpretation, to the effect that Keynes sought to deny the existence of *any* forces making for adjustment towards a state of full employment, finds no support in documents published in Keynes (*Collected Writings*), Vols. XIII and XIV. On this, see Patinkin (1975).

[14] I owe the term "process analysis" to my colleague Leijonhufvud. The term is more accurately descriptive of Marshall's method than the more familiar term, "equilibrium analysis."

of *general process analysis* that Marshall himself might have formulated had he ever felt a need explicitly to model the working of the economic system as a whole.

Of course, Marshall never did feel any such need. On the contrary, he went out of his way to deny the practical usefulness of such models in the then existing state of economic science. Marshall's thinly disguised contempt for the work of his distinguished contemporary, Walras, provides evidence enough of his attitude in that regard.[15] Apart from a few scattered remarks in the text and appendices of the *Principles*, Marshall furnished no clues about his own conception of general process analysis. That Marshall had pondered the problem cannot be doubted. That he rejected Walras' formalistic approach to the problem cannot be doubted either.[16] Of all this, Keynes must surely have been aware. We may be quite certain, therefore, that Keynes did *not* view the analysis of the *General Theory* as "Variations on a theme of Walras."[17]

II. HICKS AND THE NEO-WALRASIANS

How is it possible, then, to maintain that developments set in motion by the publication of the *General Theory* can be fully appreciated only by viewing them as part and parcel of a neo-Walrasian revival? To

[15] This observation is based on correspondence between Walras and Marshall reproduced in Jaffé (1965). See also the references to Walras cited in the index to Marshall (1920).

[16] Marshall (1920), pp. 850–852.

[17] A letter from Keynes dated December 9, 1934 (to be published by Hicks in a forthcoming volume of essays in honor of Georgescu-Roegen), is of interest in this connection. It says in part:

"There is one small point which perhaps I may be able to clear up ... You enquire whether or not Walras was supposing that exchanges actually take place at the prices originally proposed when these prices are not equilibrium prices. The footnote which you quote [Keynes refers to p. 345 of Hicks (1934)] convinces me that he assuredly supposed that they did not take place except at the equilibrium prices. For that is the actual method by which the opening price is fixed on the Paris Bourse even today. His footnote suggests that he was aware that the Agents de Change used this method and he regarded that as the ideal system of exchange to which others were approximations. ... On page 364 I should readily agree that you prove that Walras' theory of capital is no more open to objection than the usual theory and, indeed, that it is much the same thing. All the same, I shall hope to convince you some day that Walras' theory and all the others along those lines are little better than nonsense!"

Of course, how Keynes *viewed* his book is one thing, what he *wrote* in it is another. On a literal reading of the *General Theory*, it is hard to avoid the impression that the central core of the analysis is just a carelessly executed version of a few-commodity Walrasian model. Thus there is merit in Grossman's contention (Grossman, 1972) that Keynes was a "Keynesian" in the modern sense of that term.

answer this question, we must think ourselves back, as it were, to the intellectual milieu into which the *General Theory* was projected.

In the mid-1930's, general equilibrium theory was for most economists merely a label for a collection of propositions about the mutual interdependence of economic activities the precise details of which were not worth knowing. The theory then had none of the authority it has since acquired; indeed, it was commonly regarded as little more than an academic exercise in the counting of equations and unknowns even by the elite few who knew something of its details.[18] As for the mass of economists, to them it made as little sense to question the existence of the price system as to question the existence of the universe; why bother to "prove" what was already obvious to anyone with eyes to see? To the rule of ignorance or indifference, however, there were numerous exceptions (especially outside Cambridge, England), and the most notable of these—particularly as concerns the history of the Keynesian Revolution—was J. R. (now Sir John) Hicks.

Hicks began his university career as a mathematics scholar, but turned to economics at the end of his first year at Oxford.[19] Perhaps because he never enjoyed the "advantages" of a formal training in economics (his tutor at Balliol College was a military historian!), Hicks approached the study of economic phenomena with a freedom from preconceived ideas and a freshness of outlook that distinguished him sharply from most of his contemporaries. Moreover, he had special gifts as a linguist and powerful mathematical ability. Encouraged to read Pareto's work on general equilibrium theory by a London School of Economics colleague in the late 1920's, he later turned his attention to Walras and other continental writers and, shortly after, began work on *Value and Capital* (published in 1939), the book that was to become the starting point for virtually all subsequent developments of neo-Walrasian general equilibrium theory.

In common with other leading contributors to the early neo-Walrasian literature, Hicks began with what seems in retrospect a grossly exaggerated notion of the conceptual purview of general equilibrium theory; *everything* of significant economic interest was—or seemed to be—suitable grist for the neo-Walrasian mill.[20] So it is not surprising that Hicks, in his 1936 review of the *General Theory* for the *Economic Journal*,[21] should have interpreted Keynes' work not as a generaliza-

---

[18] Cf. Hicks (1939), p. 60.

[19] Biographical information is drawn from various sources including personal conversations with Sir John, but comes mainly from Hicks' Nobel Lecture (1973*).

[20] Cf. Samuelson (1947), p. 8.

[21] Hicks (1936), p. 246.

tion of Marshallian partial process analysis but rather as a special case of the neo-Walrasian theory that he was then himself engaged in writing out. The review was not a great success.[22] Some of the Keynesian wine simply did not go well in Walrasian bottles. Keynes himself was particularly annoyed by Hicks' suggestion that the distinction between liquidity-preference and loanable-funds theories of the rate of interest could be reduced to an arbitrary choice between two analytically equivalent ways of writing down the excess demand equations of a general equilibrium system. But Hicks, satisfied with the essential "rightness" of his vision, continued thinking along the same lines and later produced a disguised neo-Walrasian version of the Keynes model that not only met with Keynes' quick approval[23] but also established the conceptual framework for virtually all subsequent theoretical contributions to so-called Keynesian Economics. I refer, of course, to Hicks' celebrated paper, "Mr. Keynes and the Classics,"[24] the publication of which marked the beginning of what I have elsewhere called the Keynesian Counter-Revolution.[25]

No doubt the neo-Walrasian Revolution might have proceeded along much the same lines that it later followed even without the additional impetus that Hicks imparted to it by explicitly linking his lucid and scholarly account of general equilibrium theory with the rather unscholarly but vastly exciting and "socially relevant" analysis of Keynes' *General Theory*. In my opinion, however, the neo-Walrasian revival of interest in general equilibrium theory might well have foundered at an early stage on the same reef of professional indifference that sank the original Walrasian ship except that on this occasion the navigators of the vessel could claim that a prime object of their voyage was to sound and chart the newly discovered Keynesian seas.[26] But that is pure conjecture. In actual fact, the links that Hicks forged to connect Keynes' ideas with neo-Walrasian theory were avidly grasped and held on to by the profession at large, and were not seriously questioned thereafter until Hicks himself raised doubts about their solidity in a review of Don Patinkin's *Money, Interest and Prices* in 1957.[27] As a consequence, what is now called "Keynesian Economics" owes as much or more to the author of *Value and Capital* and "Mr. Keynes and the

[22] Cf. Hicks (1973), pp. 8–9, and Hicks (1974), pp. 6–7.
[23] See Hicks (1973), pp. 9–10.
[24] This appeared originally in *Econometrica*, April 1937, but is conveniently reproduced in Hicks (1967), pp. 126–142.
[25] Clower (1965).
[26] See Hicks (1939), pp. 4–5.
[27] Hicks (1957), p. 278. See also Hicks (1974), p. 7.

Classics" as to the author of the *General Theory of Employment, Interest and Money!*

III. KEYNES AND THE KEYNESIANS

To appreciate the full irony of Hicks' transmogrification of Keynes' analysis, we must look more closely at the conceptual experiments that implicitly underlie the Keynesian and neo-Walrasian theories, for only in this way can we distinguish clearly between *what the two theories appear to say* and *what they are actually talking about.*

As emphasized above—and as is now generally recognized[28]—Keynes' basic conception of the organization and working of the economic system was Marshallian rather than Walrasian.[29] In the Marshallian scheme of thought (as in earlier Classical doctrine) the central task of economic science is to provide an intellectually satisfying account of the coordination of economic activities in an ongoing economic system comprised of business firms and households whose informational links with one another are provided by markets in which dealers of various kinds—visible counterparts of Adam Smith's "invisible hand"—stand ready continuously to trade goods for money or money for goods on terms that each trader varies independently in response to forces that impinge directly upon his own working stocks of money and commodity inventories.[30]

On this view, the details of individual behavior are too complex to admit of literal modelling, and are of dubious interest in any case since the focus of theoretical analysis is not upon the isolated actions of particular primary agents (households, firms, etc.) but rather upon the average or representative behavior of groups of primary agents as perceived by dealers in different markets. Discussion of standard microtheoretical problems of household and business behavior—by Marshall as well as Keynes—tends accordingly to be vague and, by contemporary standards, unsatisfactory.[31] In Marshallian analysis,

[28] Useful discussions of this aspect of Keynes' work may be found in Davidson (1972), Patinkin (1975), and Leijonhufvud (1974).

[29] The sharp distinction between Marshall and Walras implied by the terms "Marshallian" and "Walrasian" cannot be justified by reference to their respective writings. The terms provide convenient labels, however, for two fairly distinct doctrinal perspectives that have played a prominent role in post-Keynesian writings. Cf. Friedman (1953), pp. 89–92; Clower and Due (1972), pp. 22–25.

[30] Cf. Clower and Due (1972), Chaps. 2 and 3; Marshall (1919), Book 2, Chaps. 5–8; Whitaker (1974).

[31] Cf. Samuelson (1972), pp. 22–24.

economic agents are conceived to be not so much rational as reasonable. Individuals fumble and grope rather than optimize.[32] They are presumed to know little and care less about efficiency except as competition forces them to attend to it. The coordination of economic activities is carried out *within* particular markets by traders (manufacturers and bankers as well as wholesalers, brokers, and retailers) who either do the task effectively or drift into bankruptcy. As for the coordination of activities *among* markets, since that is not anyone's specific concern it may or may not be done well.

The contrast between the Marshallian conception of economic activity and that underlying the neo-Walrasian literature could hardly be more stark. Neo-Walrasian analysis has no use for the bumbling oafs that populate a Marshallian world. Instead of markets organized to suit the requirements of disparate groups of specialized traders, neo-Walrasian analysis works with just one grand trading center where, thanks to the freely provided services of a *deus ex machina* called "the auctioneer," multilateral trades of anything for everything else are potentially open to every economic agent on terms of exchange that are known in advance of any actual trade. The only visible players on the economic stage are primary production and consumption units. The action revolves around alternative conceptual experiments that usually end happily with a scene in which, following many trials and tribulations, the auctioneer (who does his acting off stage) announces to the players that he (or she, or it) has finally managed to discover a set of exchange rates that ensures the collective compatibility of individual production, consumption and trading plans.[33] The curtain then falls, leaving the audience to wonder how, when (and, indeed, if) scheduled trades are subsequently executed.[34]

On this view, the rationality of economic agents may be taken for granted, for price information is not only complete but also costless to obtain, and quantity information is irrelevant to anyone but the auctioneer. Optimality and efficiency of individual plans are guaranteed (more accurately, defined) by conventional maximization postulates in conjunction with appropriate subsidiary assumptions about technology and preferences. As for the coordination of economic activities, that is not so much a question to be investigated as a proposition to be proved. That the economic system "works" may be taken for granted, for how could it fail to work when every relevant aspect

---

[32] For further elaboration on this theme, see Leijonhufvud (1975).

[33] Cf. Newman (1965), pp. 84–86; Howitt (1973*), pp. 489–496.

[34] On this, see especially Veendorp (1970), pp. 3–5, and Ostroy and Starr (1974), pp. 1093–1094.

of individual behavior is costlessly monitored and controlled by a central coordinator?[35]

At first sight, the Marshallian and neo-Walrasian schemes of thought appear to be utterly incompatible. In truth, they *are* incompatible except in the very special case where attention is restricted to Marshallian states of long-run equilibrium. In this special case, as Schumpeter brilliantly demonstrated more that a half-century ago,[36] general equilibrium analysis can be considered to provide an accurate *partial* description of selected aspects of an ongoing economic system. Flow demands equal flow supplies. Commodity and money inventories fluctuate, but *average* values are stationary over any extended interval of time. Prices of particular commodities are the same for all transactors; and though money changes hands with every exchange transaction, trade proceeds much as if goods were being traded directly for goods without the intervention of money. But this special case is of no use for analyzing short-run disequilibrium adjustment processes; it is useful only for distinguishing between states of the economy that satisfy given criteria for long-run equilibrium and states of the economy that do not. To argue that neo-Walrasian theory has any bearing on the observable behavior of an economy actually in motion, we should have to regard it as providing a *complete* description of *actual* behavior rather than a *partial* description of *virtual* behavior—and that we surely cannot do. Strictly interpreted, neo-Walrasian theory is descriptive only of a fairytale world of notional economic activities that bears not the slightest resemblance to any economy of record, past, present, or future. It is science fiction, pure and simple—clever and elegant science fiction, no doubt, but science fiction all the same.

IV. THE PRESENT PERPLEX

Granted that the conceptual background of Keynes' work is wholly Marshallian, how is it that Hicks, Samuelson, Lange, Modigliani, Metzler, Patinkin, and most other early interpreters of "the economics of J. M. Keynes" could not only overlook the inherent irrelevance of neo-Walrasian modes of thought to the questions raised by Keynes, but could also affirm, at least tacitly, the validity of a precisely contrary view? The answer is, I think, straightforward: the logical and empirical implications—and so also the conceptual limitations—of neo-Walrasian theory were simply not clear to anyone until after the neo-Walrasian Revolution had pretty well run its course. In the interim,

[35] Cf. Clower and Leijonhufvud (1975).
[36] Schumpeter (1934), Chapter 1.

it was only natural for economists generally to proceed on the presumption that general equilibrium theory had no inherent limitations. After all, even quite specialized economic models generally admit of a variety of alternative interpretations; that is to say, it is usually possible to add new variables and behavior relations without having completely to reconstruct the logical foundations of the original model. In mathematics, axiom systems that possess analogous properties are said to be *noncategorical*.[37] That any even moderately "general" economic model should be anything but *noncategorical*, therefore, would hardly occur naturally to any but a very perverse mind. That the elaborate neo-Walrasian model set out in Hicks' *Value and Capital* might fail to satisfy this condition would have seemed correspondingly incredible to any sensible person at the outset of the neo-Walrasian Revolution.

It is an open question, indeed, whether the restrictive character of neo-Walrasian theory would be clearly recognized even today had not the development of the neo-Walrasian Revolution followed a particular course. Economics is difficult enough without borrowing additional trouble by constantly questioning its conceptual foundations. In this instance, however, there was no need to borrow trouble; trouble came knocking at the door as a direct consequence of an early division of the neo-Walrasian literature into two relatively distinct branches, both emanating from intellectual roots planted by J. R. Hicks.

The first branch—which starts from Hicks' *Value and Capital*—includes work by such writers as Samuelson, Hurwicz, Arrow, Debreu, McKenzie, Scarf, Hahn, and Negishi.[38] It is concerned with the purely logical task of establishing sufficient conditions for the notional "existence and stability"[39] of competitive equilibria in formal systems satisfying the usual assumptions of neo-Walrasian theory including, specifically, the assumptions of (i) no disequilibrium trading and (ii) no explicit treatment of money.[40] That this line of research had at most a peripheral bearing on any real-world problem was, I think, taken for granted by all who contributed to it, if not by all who read it.[41] The second branch—which starts from Hicks' "Mr. Keynes and

---

[37] See Kershner and Wilcox (1950), pp. 230–231.

[38] For references, see Negishi (1962), pp. 666–669; also Newman (1965), pp. 124–125.

[39] As Newman has observed (1965, p. 106), the term "convergence" would be more appropriate than the term "stability" in this context. For a colorful but highly instructive account of the process, see Burstein (1968), pp. 201–202.

[40] See Debreu (1959), p. 28; Hahn (1973), pp. 15–16; Veendorp (1970), and references cited there.

[41] Cf. Hahn (1973), pp. 3–6.

the Classics"—is familiarly associated with such names as Lange, Samuelson, Hansen, Modigliani, Tobin, Metzler, Eisner, and Patinkin.[42] It deals with the relatively practical task of constructing analytically manageable aggregative models of a monetary economy that will serve not only for purposes of doctrinal exegesis but also as useful guides to applied research and to the formulation of desirable government policies of economic coordination and control. That this line of research had a direct and immediate bearing on real-world problems was, I think, never seriously doubted by anyone who contributed to it, though certainly some who read it (most notably, Milton Friedman) had very serious doubts indeed.[43]

The two branches of literature converged in the middle 1950's— and produced a collision of ideas that shattered earlier illusions about the "generality" of neo-Walrasian general equilibrium theory.[44] The subject matter content and potential empirical significance of the second branch of literature seemed evident. It purported explicitly to deal with an economy that bore at least a family resemblance to economies of record. The subject matter content and significance of the first branch was by no means transparent, but one thing was clear: *the mathematical structure of the models appearing in it was identical with that of models appearing in the second branch.* The conclusion was then inescapable: *either* (i) the assumptions underlying the first and more formal branch of literature were unduly restrictive *or* (ii) serious second thoughts were in order concerning the empirical and doctrinal relevance of the second line of inquiry.

I need not trace the details of the reconsideration that followed from this conclusion.[45] The outcome of the investigation is adequately reflected in the final chapter of Arrow and Hahn's recent and authoritative *General Competitive Analysis* where it becomes evident that the existing body of neo-Walrasian theory rests upon assumptions that preclude its use for explicit analysis of either disequilibrium trading processes or monetary exchange.[46] Contrary to earlier presumptions, the theory does not admit of a variety of essentially different interpretations. It is categorical rather than noncategorical—closed to extension in certain crucial directions including, specifically, those directions that would permit explicit formal analysis of Keynesian short-run adjustment processes. But these are precisely the kind of

[42] For references, see Clower (1969), pp. 344–346.
[43] Cf. Johnson (1961 and 1971); Friedman (1953), pp. 277–300.
[44] See especially Hicks (1957), Clower (1965), Hahn (1965), Barro and Grossman (1971), Leijonhufvud (1969).
[45] See Leijonhufvud (1969), Hines (1971), Weintraub (1974).
[46] Arrow and Hahn (1972), pp. 366–369.

processes about which economists must be able to speak with scientific authority if their science is to be anything more than a body of idle speculation and a breeding ground for charlatans and quacks. Hence, the present perplex in economic theory; for if neo-Walrasian theory is bankrupt—as, for practical purposes, it most surely is—then where do we go from here?

V. RECONSTRUCTING THE FOUNDATIONS

The crucial flaw in neo-Walrasian theory, as revealed especially by recent work of Ostroy,[47] lies in its silence concerning the logistics of exchange—the absence of an explicit account of the execution as distinct from the scheduling of commodity trades. This flaw is an indirect consequence of the standard neo-Walrasian assumption that trading plans (and actions, if any) are mediated by some kind of central coordinator; for though this assumption does not logically preclude further discussion of the logistics of exchange,[48] it effectively sweeps the problem under the rug and so encourages its continued neglect. Accordingly, it appears that a sensible first step towards the formulation of an acceptable theory of an ongoing economy is to dispense with the assumption of a central coordinator and to suppose instead that trade among individual economic agents is a strictly "do it yourself" affair.[49] This procedure is bound to be a hard pill for some to swallow. Without a central coordinator, hitherto harmonious intellectual reveries about smoothly interlocking individual economic activities become waking nightmares. *Who trades what, for which, with whom, where, and when?* At first sight, these questions may well seem to pose insoluble conundrums; but if that were so, how could the same questions be answered in real life, as they most assuredly are?

As Ostroy and Starr (1974, pp. 1097–1098) have shown, a formal solution to these conundrums may be obtained by supposing that some individual agents hold sufficiently large stocks of commodity inventories to permit them to act as exchange intermediaries. This is, of course, the procedure implicitly followed by Marshall in his account of the role of middlemen as links between producer and consumer (Marshall, 1919, pp. 278–280). But it is one thing to be assured that the conundrums at issue can be resolved in principle, another to persuade ourselves that the solution indicated will emerge as a matter

[47] Ostroy (1973). Also see Veendorp (1970), Kaldor (1972, p. 1248), and Ostroy and Starr (1974).
[48] Cf. Clower and Leijonhufvud (1975).
[49] Cf. Walker (1970), Ostroy (1973).

of course in an economy where trade is initially organized on a "do it yourself" basis. Specifically, can it be shown that, in such an economy, "natural economic forces" will induce some individual agents to accumulate commodity inventories and to act as middlemen in trades involving other economic agents?

A full answer to this question would require far more space than is available here. Briefly and somewhat loosely, the answer is that middlemen traders will emerge *only if* (but not necessarily *if*) search and other costs associated with trade between individuals are not only positive but also independent (at least in part) of the amounts of commodities traded.[50] Provided that certain other intuitively plausible conditions are met (in particular, that subjective rates of time preference are relatively low for some individuals), it can then be shown that otherwise unexploitable gains from trade can be realized if some individuals accumulate stocks of tradeable commodities and proceed to act as exchange intermediaries.[51] It is a short step from this conclusion to the conjecture that some agents will decide to play just such a role, but a formal proof of this conjecture has yet to be found. As of the present time, therefore, the proposition that a class of middlemen traders will emerge naturally out of a situation in which trade is initially carried out on a strictly individual basis must be regarded as simply a plausible conjecture.[52]

For the sake of argument, suppose that the conjecture is true, i.e., suppose that natural economic forces gradually cause an economy without organized facilities for trade to evolve into a "middleman economy" with such facilities. Even so, it does not follow that the organization of trading activity in such an economy will be recognizably "monetary" in character.[53] The development of such highly specialized forms of market organization cannot be accounted for without introducing additional (and very strong) assumptions about technol-

[50] See Clower (1969), pp. 7–14; Hirshleifer (1973), pp. 138–139; Ostroy and Starr (1974), pp. 1110–1111.

[51] An ingenious formal proof is provided by Chuchman (1974). The reasoning underlying Chuchman's argument is a natural continuation of earlier work in search and information theory by Stigler (1961), Hicks (1967), Alchian (1969) and others. See also the recent paper by Lee (1974).

[52] Personally, I doubt if a general proof of the conjecture is possible. If necessary conditions can be provided for a broad enough class of special cases, however, these may serve collectively as an effective substitute. In the latter connection, papers by Reiter (1959 and 1959*), Foley (1970), Hahn (1971), Karni (1973), Mortensen (1973), Kurz and Wilson (1974), and Jones (1975) merit special notice.

[53] On the definition of a "monetary" economy, see Clower (1967 and 1969) and Benassy (1975). Chapter 2 of Flannery and Jaffee (1973) is also of interest in this connection.

ogy, preferences, and the physical characteristics of different commodities.[54] At first sight, this result may seem to pose some very awkward problems. For analytical purposes, however, explicit recognition of monetary considerations is a matter of convenience rather than necessity. In all essential respects, the performance characteristics of an economy in which goods are traded directly for goods through facilities provided by inventory-holding middlemen are qualitatively indistinguishable from those of a strictly monetary economy. That conventional economic wisdom has for so long encouraged us to cling to a contrary belief is attributable, I suspect, to its consistent refusal to deal explicitly with *any* kind of ongoing economic system, monetary or otherwise. In the discussion that follows, I shall proceed generally on the assumption that we have to deal with a world of organized barter. Since monetary exchange is, in any case, merely a special kind of organized barter, this procedure should cause no problems.

A full account of the characteristics of a middleman economy or, more generally, of what I shall refer to henceforth as *neo-Marshallian* theory, is out of the question here. To focus upon any particular formal model would be a mistake in any event, for that would divert attention from the foundations of neo-Marshallian theory, which are fundamental, to its superstructure, which is incidental. As for the foundations, the following sketch, though desperately incomplete, hopefully will serve as a working guide not only to the basic structure but also to the potential empirical implications of neo-Marshallian models considered as a class.

For simplicity of exposition, I shall proceed on the assumption that the typical middleman or "shopkeeper"[55] holds inventories of, and operates a market for, *every* commodity traded in the economy. It might seem more plausible to imagine instead that each shopkeeper deals only with certain *subsets* of commodities; but that procedure (which, in the limit, includes the special case of monetary exchange) would merely complicate the form of the subsequent argument without altering its substance, so we lose nothing by leaving intuition to languish at this point.

Given the arrangements just stipulated, let us further imagine that each shopkeeper decides independently the *terms* on which he stands ready to trade various commodity pairs,[56] while each trader (some of whom will be shopkeepers acting in another capacity) decides inde-

[54] Cf. Brunner and Meltzer (1971); Clower and Leijonhufvud (1975).

[55] This terminology is suggested by Howitt (1974), p. 135.

[56] The word "terms" refers not only to rates of exchange between commodity pairs, but also to trading (rationing) rules, delivery arrangements, etc. Cf. Howitt (1974).

pendently what *quantities* to trade with various shopkeepers. Thus, the economy is *decentralized* in the strictest sense of that term. Supposing that individual traders and shopkeepers seek always to exploit potential gains from trade, however, strong forces making for order will be constantly at work within the system. Specifically, since individual traders have an incentive to search out and trade with those shopkeepers that currently offer relatively favorable terms of trade, rates of exchange set by different shopkeepers will tend towards equality over time. Shopkeepers that are slow to fall into line will be drained of stocks of some commodities, swamped with stocks of others, and so forced eventually either to conform or to close up shop. For analogous reasons, brokerage and other trading fees charged by different shopkeepers will tend towards equality over time at levels that permit representative shopkeepers to earn no more than a normal rate of return on their average holdings of commodity inventories (trade capital).

Explicit modelling of this kind of economy is not a simple matter. It seems natural, and involves no loss of essential generality, to suppose that rates of exchange of all shopkeepers will be expressed in terms of a common unit of account, the unit being a standard quantity of one of the commodities traded in the system. We might then suppose that the prices of all other commodities (i.e., rates of exchange with the standard commodity) will be varied by each shopkeeper in response to his own conception of the adequacy of his existing stocks in relation to present and prospective sales. This would lead us to describe price behavior not in terms of familiar first-order difference or differential equations involving *flow* excess demands but rather in terms of second or higher order equations involving distributed lag functions of past purchases and sales, i.e., *stocks* as well as *flows*. However, since each shopkeeper would be free to establish his own set of price-adjustment procedures, and since these procedures would depend upon costs of holding inventories, costs incurred in adjusting prices, expectations of future market conditions, and so forth, price behavior might follow very different patterns even in outwardly similar markets. Much simplification would be possible if, following Marshall, we could assume that prices set by different shopkeepers tended almost instantaneously to equality, for then we might view the economy as if it contained just one great market; but that procedure would entail a type of implicit theorizing that is best avoided.[57]

This very cursory account of the problem of modelling shopkeeper

[57] An alternative if somewhat artificial procedure is to postulate explicitly that a central "trading warehouse" is established by "social compact"; see Clower and Leijonhufvud (1975).

behavior provides no more than a glimpse of the tip of an iceberg of analytical complications, but hopefully it will serve to indicate the general milieu within which individual traders in a neo-Marshallian world must be presumed to formulate their plans.

Dealing next with the behavior of individual traders, we may suppose that their choice alternatives are defined, in general, in terms of a matrix of price vectors, one vector for each shopkeeper in the system. Each trader must then decide not only with which shopkeepers to trade but also the *timing* of trips to different shops; for the existence of positive transaction costs (a basic presumption underlying the existence of shops) implies that individual traders as well as shopkeepers will hold positive commodity inventories, which implies, in turn, that trades will occur at discrete points rather than continuously in time. To suppose that these considerations might be dealt with explicitly in a *manageable* formal model would, I suggest, be grossly to underestimate the complexity of the problem.[58] As high-energy physicists have had to settle for quantum-theoretic descriptions of subatomic phenomena, so economists probably must settle (at least provisionally) for some kind of surrogate, statistical description of transactor behavior in an ongoing exchange economy.[59]

Granted that individual traders independently decide when and what to trade with specific shopkeepers, commodity stocks held by different shopkeepers will vary randomly with time, for traders in a shopkeeper world are similar in important respects to particles in Brownian motion. Since shopkeepers could never know for sure whether perceived trends in activity were transitory or permanent, we should not expect changes in prices, much less accompanying changes in the distribution of trades and traders among shopkeepers, to reflect *prevailing* economic conditions at all accurately. On the contrary, we should expect current conditions to influence overall economic activity only after what Professor Friedman, in another context, has described as "long and variable lags." For example, prices of some commodities might be rising even when flow excess supplies of the same commodities were positive and stocks were increasing. In a similar vein, shopkeepers might at times (and possibly for long intervals) refuse to trade certain commodities because their present stocks were either exhausted or grossly in surplus. If such system malfunctions

---

[58] Cf. Howitt and Clower (1974), p. 4.

[59] This need not and should not involve any relaxation of established standards of theoretical discourse. If neo-Marshallian process analysis is to be of any permanent value, it must ultimately be expressed in precise and mathematically rigorous terms in keeping with the fruitful tradition established by Hicks, Arrow, Debreu and other leading contributors to the neo-Walrasian literature. Cf. Hahn (1973), p. 241.

were common or, alternatively, if system malfunctions were normally uncommon but exogenous shocks were frequent and occasionally large, then the inability of shopkeepers to maintain effective control of inventories through price adjustments alone might cause some of them to stop operating altogether. This possibility conjures up sobering visions of an otherwise stable homeostatic economic system experiencing recurrent coordination failures because system communication channels are interrupted or become "noisy" when the system departs too far from its "equilibrium" motion.[60] The set of possible variations on this theme is effectively unbounded.

VI. CONCLUSION

Although the implications of a neo-Marshallian view of economic phenomena are moderately radical in some respects, they are thoroughly conservative in others. Some of the more conservative implications merit mention by way of conclusion, for they provide some assurance that the route of escape from the Keynesian Perplex suggested in this paper does not lead us down a tunnel into Bedlam.

First, the whole of established microtheory may be fitted neatly into neo-Marshallian analysis by regarding the former as a schematic characterization of certain necessary conditions for stationary equilibrium. Of course, on this interpretation, it is fallacious to argue that standard theories of individual or market behavior can serve directly as a conceptual basis for models that describe the dynamics of disequilibrium motion; in particular, it would be wrong to regard established microtheory as a suitable foundation for macrotheory, for the central if not sole object of macrotheory is to enhance our understanding of short-run disequilibrium adjustment processes.[61]

Second, the whole of Marshallian economics as well as that part of Keynesian thought that Leijonhufvud has labelled "The Economics of Keynes"[62] can be regarded as explicit special cases of neo-Marshallian analysis. Viewed in this perspective, the author of the *General Theory* will not, I suspect, appear to deserve as much credit for clear thinking as his distinguished mentor; but neither Keynes nor Marshall can be accused (as some have accused them) of constitutional ineptness as economic theorists. As is sufficiently indicated above, precise formal modelling of neo-Marshallian systems is not a straightforward matter, even for persons of genius.

[60] Cf. Leijonhufvud (1973), pp. 32 ff., where possibilities of the kind referred to here are described as "corridor" phenomena.
[61] Leijonhufvud (1968).
[62] Cf. Leijonhufvud (1974).

Third, and finally, neo-Marshallian theory may be easily specialized to deal explicitly with monetary exchange. Perhaps the simplest way to accomplish this is to suppose that each shopkeeper restricts his dealings to just *two* commodities, one of them a commodity called "money" that is traded by *all* shopkeepers in the economy. The properties of such systems have been extensively explored by Peter Howitt in a series of papers,[63] early drafts of which crucially influenced my own thinking about neo-Marshallian models in general. Here it will suffice to say that the analytical implications of Howitt's work are essentially those of the nonmonetary models that are the main concern of the present paper.

It appears that to obtain essentially new kinds of results we must recognize the existence of credit instruments (formal and informal loan contracts) as potential objects of trade. This procedure opens the door to a variety of complications—financial intermediation, endogenous expansion and contraction of means of payment, speculative purchase and sale of futures contracts—which cannot be fitted into neo-Walrasian theory without doing violence either to logic or common sense, but which have a natural place in neo-Marshallian theory (any class of contracts that can be traded at a profit is obviously an "object" of potential interest to profit-seeking middlemen). Clearly, it is just such complications that lie at the heart of Keynes' economics.[64] Just as clearly, that is the direction in which economic theory must go if we are ever to complete the Keynesian Revolution.

REFERENCES

A. Alchian: "Information Costs, Pricing, and Resource Unemployment," *Western Economic Journal (Economic Inquiry)*, June 1969, 7, pp. 109–128.

K. J. Arrow: "Samuelson Collected," *Journal of Political Economy*, October 1967, 75, pp. 730–737.

K. J. Arrow and F. H. Hahn: *General Competitive Analysis*, San Francisco, Holden-Day, 1972.

R. J. Barro and H. I. Grossman: "A General Disequilibrium Model of Income and Employment," *American Economic Review*, March 1971, 61, pp. 82–93.

G. S. Becker: "A Theory of Social Interactions," *Journal of Political Economy*, November/December 1974, 82, pp. 1063–1093.

J. Benassy: "Disequilibrium Exchange in Barter and Monetary Economies," *Economic Inquiry*, June 1975, 13, pp. 131–156.

---

[63] Howitt (1973); also see Howitt (1974).

[64] This has always been a central theme in Hicks' writings, particularly since his "great awakening" in 1957. It has also figured prominently in the work of Paul Davidson and Hyman Minsky (see, especially, Davidson [1972] and Minsky [1972]).

K. Brunner and A. Meltzer: "The Uses of Money: Money in the Theory of an Exchange Economy," *American Economic Review*, December 1971, 61, pp. 784–805.

M. L. Burstein: *Economic Theory: Equilibrium and Change*, London, Wiley, 1968.

G. Chuchman: "A Model of the Evolution of Exchange Processes," University of Western Ontario, Money Workshop, November 1974.

R. W. Clower: "The Keynesian Counterrevolution," in *The Theory of Interest Rates*, F. P. R. Brechling and F. H. Hahn (eds.), London, Macmillan, 1965, 6, pp. 103–125. Reprinted in slightly revised form in Clower (1969), pp. 270–297, and as chapter 3 of this volume.

R. W. Clower: "A Reconsideration of the Microfoundations of Monetary Theory," *Western Economic Journal* (*Economic Inquiry*), December 1967, 6, pp. 1–9. Reprinted in Clower (1969), pp. 202–211, and as chapter 16 of this volume.

R. W. Clower: *Monetary Theory: Selected Readings*, London, Penguin Books, 1969.

R. W. Clower and J. Due: *Microeconomics*, Homewood, Richard D. Irwin, 1972.

R. W. Clower and A. Leijonhufvud: "The Coordination of Economic Activities," *American Economic Review*, May 1975, 65, pp. 182–188.

P. J. Davidson: *Money and the Real World*, London, Macmillan, 1972.

P. J. Davidson: "Money and the Real World," *Economic Journal*, March 1972, 82, pp. 101–115.

G. Debreu: *Theory of Value*, Cowles Foundation Monograph No. 17, New York, 1959.

F. Y. Edgeworth: *Papers Relating to Political Economy*, 3 vols., London, Macmillan, 1925.

M. J. Flannery and D. M. Jaffee: *The Economic Implications of an Electronic Monetary Transfer System*, Lexington, D. C. Heath, 1973.

D. K. Foley: "Economic Equilibrium with Costly Marketing," *Journal of Economic Theory*, 1970, 2, pp. 276–291.

M. Friedman: *Essays in Positive Economics*, Chicago, University of Chicago Press, 1953.

H. I. Grossman: "Was Keynes a 'Keynesian'?" *Journal of Economic Literature*, March 1972, 10, pp. 26–30.

F. H. Hahn: "On Some Problems of Proving the Existence of an Equilibrium in a Monetary Economy," *The Theory of Interest Rates*, F. P. R. Brechling and F. H. Hahn (eds.), London, Macmillan, 1965, pp. 126–135. Reprinted in Clower (1969), pp. 191–201.

F. H. Hahn: "Some Adjustment Problems," *Econometrica*, January 1970, 38, pp. 1–17.

F. H. Hahn: "Equilibrium with Transactions Costs," *Econometrica*, May 1971, 39, pp. 417–439.

F. H. Hahn: "On the Notion of Equilibrium in Economics," An Inaugural Lecture, Cambridge, 1973.

F. H. Hahn: "Foundations of Monetary Theory," *Essays on Modern Economics*, M. Parkin (ed.), London, Longmans, 1973*, pp. 230–242.

J. R. Hicks: "Léon Walras," *Econometrica*, October 1934, 2, pp. 338–348.

J. R. Hicks: "Mr. Keynes' Theory of Employment," *Economic Journal*, June 1936, 46, pp. 238–253.

J. R. Hicks: *Value and Capital*, Oxford, Clarendon Press, 1939 (2nd ed., 1946).

J. R. Hicks: "A Rehabilitation of 'Classical' Economics?" *Economic Journal*, June 1957, 67, pp. 278–289.

J. R. Hicks: *Critical Essays in Monetary Theory*, Oxford, Clarendon Press, 1967.

J. R. Hicks: "Recollections and Documents," *Economica*, February 1973, 40, pp. 2–11.

J. R. Hicks: "The Mainsprings of Economic Growth," Nobel Memorial Lecture, The Nobel Foundation, 1973*.

J. R. Hicks: *The Crisis in Keynesian Economics*, Oxford, Clarendon Press, 1974.

A. G. Hines: *On the Reappraisal of Keynesian Economics*, London, Martin Robertson, 1971.

J. Hirschleifer: "Exchange Theory," *Western Economic Journal* (*Economic Inquiry*), June 1973, 10, pp. 129–146.

P. W. Howitt: *Studies in the Theory of Monetary Dynamics*, Doctoral Dissertation, Northwestern University, 1973.

P. W. Howitt: "Walras and Monetary Theory," *Western Economic Journal* (*Economic Inquiry*), December 1973*, 11, pp. 487–499.

P. W. Howitt: "Stability and the Quantity Theory," *Journal of Political Economy*, January/February 1974, 82, pp. 133–140.

P. W. Howitt and R. W. Clower: "The Optimal Timing of Transactions," Economics Department, University of Western Ontario Discussion Paper, May 1974 (mimeo, 33 pp.).

W. Jaffé (ed.): *Correspondence of Léon Walras and Related Papers*, 3 vols., Amsterdam, North Holland, 1965.

H. G. Johnson: "The General Theory after Twenty-five Years," *American Economic Review*, May 1961, 51, pp. 1–17.

H. G. Johnson: "The Keynesian Revolution and the Monetarist Counterrevolution," *American Economic Review*, May 1971, 61, pp. 1–14.

H. G. Johnson: "Major Issues in Monetary Economics," *Oxford Economic Papers*, July 1974, 26, pp. 212–225.

H. G. Johnson: "The Current and Prospective State of Economics," *Australian Economic Papers*, June 1974*, pp. 1–27.

R. Jones: "The Origin and Development of Media of Exchange," *Journal of Political Economy*, August 1976, Pt. I, 84, pp. 757–775.

N. Kaldor: "The Irrelevance of Equilibrium Economics," *Economic Journal*, December, 1972, 82, pp. 1237–1252.

E. Karni: "Transactions Cost and the Demand for Media of Exchange," Western Economic Journal (*Economic Inquiry*), March 1973, 11, pp. 71–80.

R. B. Kershner and L. R. Wilcox: *The Anatomy of Mathematics*, New York, Ronald Press, 1950.

J. M. Keynes: *Collected Writings of John Maynard Keynes*, London, Macmillan, for the Royal Economic Society, 25 vols., various dates.

J. M. Keynes: *The General Theory of Employment, Interest and Money*, New York, Harcourt, Brace and Co., 1936.

J. M. Keynes: "Poverty in Plenty: Is the Economic System Self-Adjusting? *Collected Writings*,13, pp. 485–491.

F. H. Knight: *Risk, Uncertainty and Profit* (1921). Reprint, New York, Augustus M. Kelley, 1964.

J. Kornai: *Anti-Equilibrium*, Amsterdam, North Holland, 1971.

M. Kurz and R. Wilson: "On the Structure of Trade," *Economic Inquiry*, December 1974, 12, pp. 493–516.

C. H. Lee: "Information Costs and Markets," *Economic Inquiry*, December 1974, 12, pp. 460–475.

A. Leijonhufvud: "Keynes and the Keynesians," *American Economic Review*, May 1967, 57, pp. 401–410.

A. Leijonhufvud: *On Keynesian Economics and the Economies of Keynes*, New York, Oxford University Press, 1968.

A. Leijonhufvud: "Keynes and the Classics," International Economic Association Occasional Paper No. 30, London, 1969.

A. Leijonhufvud: "Effective Demand Failures," *Swedish Journal of Economics*, 1973, 73, pp. 27–48.

A. Leijonhufvud: "Life Among the Econ," *Western Economic Journal* (*Economic Inquiry*) 1973*, 11, pp. 327–337.

A. Leijonhufvud: "The Varieties of Price Theory: What Microfoundations for Macrotheory?" Department of Economics, UCLA, Discussion Paper No. 44, January 1974, 53 pp.

A. Leijonhuvfud: "Maximization and Marshall," Marshall Lectures, Michaelmas Term, Cambridge University, 1974.

W. W. Leontief: "Theoretical Assumptions and Nonobservable Facts," *American Economic Review*, March 1971, 61, pp. 1–7.

W. W. Leontief: "Postulates: Keynes' *General Theory* and the Classicists," *The New Economics: Keynes' Influence on Theory and Public Policy*, S. E. Harris (ed.), New York, Alfred A. Knopf, pp. 232–242.

A. Marshall: *Industry and Trade*, London, Macmillan, 1919.

A. Marshall: *Principles of Economics*, 8th ed., London, Macmillan, 1920.

H. Minsky: "An Exposition of a Keynesian Theory of Investment," *Mathematical Methods in Investment and Finance*, Szego and Shell (eds.), Amsterdam, North Holland, 1972, pp. 207–233.

D. T. Mortensen: "Search Equilibrium in a Simple Multi-Market Economy," Center for Mathematical Studies in Economics and Management Science Discussion Paper No. 54, October 1973 (mimeo, 48 pp.).

T. Negishi: "The Stability of a Competitive Economy," *Econometrica*, October 1962, 30, pp. 635–669.

P. K. Newman: *Theory of Exchange*, Englewood Cliffs, Prentice-Hall, 1965.

J. M. Ostroy: "The Informational Efficiency of Monetary Exchange," *American Economic Review*, September 1973, 63, pp. 597–610.

J. M. Ostroy and R. M. Starr: "Money and the Decentralization of Exchange," *Econometrica*, November 1974, 42, pp. 1093–1113.

D. Patinkin: *Money, Interest, and Prices*, Evanston, Row, Peterson, 1956 (2nd ed., New York, Harper & Row, 1965).

D. Patinkin: "The Collected Writings of John Maynard Keynes: From the *Tract* to the *General Theory*," *Economic Journal*, June 1975, 85, pp. 249–271.

S. Reiter: "Market Price Formation," Abstract in *Econometrica*, April 1959, 27, pp. 313–314.

S. Reiter: "A Market Adjustment Mechanism," Institute for Quantitative Research, School of Industrial Management, Purdue University, 1959 (mimeo, 26 pp.).

J. Robinson: "The Second Crisis of Economic Theory," *American Economic Review*, May 1974, 64, pp. 1–10.

J. Robinson: "What Has Become of the Keynesian Revolution?" *Challenge*, January/February 1974*, pp. 6–11.

P. A. Samuelson: *Foundations of Economic Analysis*, Cambridge, Harvard University Press, 1947.

P. A. Samuelson: *Collected Scientific Papers*, Vol. 3, R. C. Merton (ed.), Cambridge, MIT Press, 1972.

J. Schumpeter: *The Theory of Economic Development*, Cambridge, Harvard University Press, 1934.

M. Shubik: "A Curmudgeon's Guide to Microeconomics," *Journal of Economic Literature*, June 1970, 8, pp. 405–434.

G. J. Stigler: "The Economics of Information," *Journal of Political Economy*, June 1961, 69, pp. 213–225.

E. C. H. Veendorp: "General Equilibrium Theory for a Barter Economy," *Western Economic Journal* (*Economic Inquiry*), March 1970, 8, pp. 1–23.

D. A. Walker: "Léon Walras in the Light of his Correspondence and Related Papers," *Journal of Political Economy*, July/August 1970, 78, pp. 685–701.

E. R. Weintraub: "Arrow and Hahn's General Competitive Analysis: A Perspective," *Economic Inquiry*, March 1974, 12, pp. 105–113.

J. Whitaker: "The Marshallian System in 1881: Distribution and Growth," *Economic Journal*, March 1974, 84, pp. 1–17.

D. Winch: *Economics and Policy: A Historical Study*, London, Hodder and Stoughton, 1969.

15

THE COORDINATION OF ECONOMIC ACTIVITIES:
A KEYNESIAN PERSPECTIVE

Almost four decades have elapsed since the publication of Keynes's *General Theory of Employment, Interest and Money*. In the interim we have learned, or at least we have been told, a great deal about "what Keynes said"—and also about "what Keynes meant," "what Keynes *really* meant," and, most recently, "what Keynes really meant, *really*." Still the debate continues. If past experience is any guide, indeed, numerous questions about Keynes's theory—including some of considerable intellectual and historical interest—will never be settled. Rather than add further tidbits to what looks suspiciously like an infinite regress, therefore, we propose to address ourselves on this occasion to the other aspect of the Keynesian debate that is mentioned in the title of this session: the model, or rather family of models, that economists have developed in response to the stimulus of Keynes's great work— "IS–LM, and all that."

What does "A Critical Look at the Keynesian Model" reveal? It seems to us that what it reveals most clearly is that *the Keynesian model produces useful and sensible conclusions only in such measure as the user of the model is a good economist.* After all, the basic textbook model imposes next to no constraints on what may be argued from it; worse yet, it is open to *ad hoc* modification and common sense extension in numerous directions at the whim of its user. As a consequence, virtually any bundle of policy measures may be advocated in "Keynesian" language and, in recent years, almost all policy discussions have been couched in just such terms. To state the case succinctly, the Keynesian model imposes virtually no analytical discipline upon its users and thereby grants them essentially unrestricted analytical license. So it is not surprising that the debate over Keynes's contribution, and over the extent to which the latter-day Keynesian model preserves it, should continue. But there is another and even more fundamental reason why the debate continues, namely, we have yet to resolve the central question posed by Keynes's assault on received doctrine: Is the *existing* economic system, in any *significant* sense, self-adjusting?

The standard Keynesian model does not address this central question. It merely leaves room for us to analyze concrete problems under all sorts of alternative presumptions about what the answer might be, e.g., that the private economy never shows any endogenous tendency to return to equilibrium, or that it always tends promptly to restore itself to equilibrium following any disturbance. Moreover, the standard model hardly allows us even to frame the central question in a manner that would direct research onto a promising track. The comparative statics of IS–LM constructions has a well-demonstrated capacity for converting questions about adjustment performance (or, if you will, stability) into questions about sundry elasticities in the minds of economists.

These observations do not exhaust what might be said about the Keynesian model's capacity for mischief. But the point is simply that, in our judgment, the standard model is incapable of development in the directions to which the central question requires that we turn our attention. In effect, if we wish to say anything worthwhile about the central question, we must start by averting our eyes from the Keynesian model. Where do we proceed from there?

As of the present time, it appears to us that the question posed by Keynes remains unanswered largely because of the continued failure of economists to provide a coherent account of the manner in which production, consumption, and trading activities of individual economic agents are coordinated in theoretical economic systems that bear a family resemblance to economies of actual record. If this surmise is correct, then what is called for now is either a radical reformulation of existing analytical paradigms or—as would seem clearly preferable from almost any point of view—a fresh interpretation of established ideas. We shall pursue the second of these alternatives, although this procedure is calculated to supply less grist for existing analytical mills than food for further thought.

To provide an alternative frame for macrotheory capable of addressing the coordination question is a formidable task that is unlikely to be solved except by the concerted efforts of many workers. It is also necessarily a long-run task. (Perhaps that is why it never gets done—so many macroeconomists follow Keynes in being almost equally responsive to the pressure of immediate policy issues and to their own long-run mortality.) But it seems quite clear to us where we have to start. A theory capable of describing system behavior as a temporal process, in or out of equilibrium, requires a prior account of *how trade is organized* in the system. Equilibrium, steady-state theory has managed pretty well without such an account. Macroeconomic theory cannot do so. Microeconomic theories of how business and household units behave—of how production and consumption decisions are made—when the system is *not* in equilibrium will have to be predicated on some such account. How we conceptualize the organization of trade, therefore, is a question with priority over numerous other theoretical questions some of which might otherwise be of more interest and of more promise as objects of theoretical ingenuity.

I

Our point of departure is established, general, competitive analysis as set out, for example, in Kenneth J. Arrow and F. H. Hahn's recent account of the subject. It is customary to view this body of theory as an almost literal description of an idealized economy in which the notional economic plans of individual economic agents are costlessly coordinated by a central intelligence unit—the so-called auctioneer. This neo-Walrasian conception of economic organization is sharply at variance with that of its patron saint, Léon Walras. Walras regarded his work as an attempt *partially* to characterize equilibrium states of an ongoing economic system. To suppose that Walras conceived his analysis to constitute a *complete* description even of relevant equilibrium conditions would be an egregious error—as is indicated, among other things, by his explicit denial of any such notion in Lesson 35 of the *Elements*. In effect, modern neo-Walrasian theory starts with the solution to Walras's problem, but then proceeds to ask not whether that solution is acceptable in relation to the problem considered by Walras, but rather whether we can conceive of an economy that is *completely* characterized by equilibrium relations of the kind identified by Walras! The answer to this query—the problem which, so to speak, fits Walras's solution—is, of course, affirmative; for the auctioneer model of standard theory describes just such an economy.

That this particular type of model is unsuitable for analyzing any but *virtual* disequilibria is now generally acknowledged. The question then arises: How might we best proceed to modify standard theory so that it can be used to deal explicitly, at least in principle, with *real* disequilibria? On first thought, one's natural impulse is to eliminate the auctioneer and work instead with models in which individual economic agents engage in trade on a strictly "do it yourself" basis. No doubt that is the direction in which a definitive solution to the problem of economic coordination ultimately must be sought. As of the present time, however, and probably for the near future, second thoughts counsel a more conservative procedure. Specifically, it seems preferable temporarily to continue working with models that postulate the existence of a central coordinator of trading activity, but to jettison

two other assumptions of standard theory: (1) the assumption that
trades take place only at prices that ensure collective consistency of
individual trading plans; and (2) the assumption that trades can be
negotiated and executed at no cost to individuals or society in terms
either of forgone leisure or scarce resources.

Let us suppose, then, that individual agents can engage in trade
only by incurring implicit or explicit search and bargaining costs that
are largely independent of quantities traded. On the basis of otherwise
standard assumptions, it can then be shown that individuals will ab-
stain from consumption and amass positive inventories of tradeable
goods in order to avoid prohibitively heavy costs associated with small-
lot trading at frequent intervals. It can also be shown that, in the
absence of arrangements that permit individuals to trade in any desired amounts at dates of their own choosing, contacts between individuals will be so costly that large potential gains from trade will
remain unexploited. In these circumstances, natural forces of greed
and competition might plausibly be invoked to provide a rationale for
the gradual emergence of merchant traders and organized markets.
In keeping with our earlier decision to stick as closely as possible to
received doctrine, however, we shall proceed instead by simply postulating the establishment by social contract of a central supermarket
in which individual agents may execute at will pairwise trades of any
good for any other good at going rates of exchange determined by a
central *trade coordinator*—the counterpart in our discussion of the familiar *deus ex machina* of the neo-Walrasian auctioneer.

So that individuals may be assumed to be able to trade at dates and
in amounts of their own choosing, we suppose that the trade coordinator starts with sizable inventories of all tradeable goods. So that
operating expenses may be met, and aggregate inventories adjusted
over time to conform with prevailing needs of trade, we suppose
further that the trade coordinator charges a fee on each transaction
or, what comes to the same thing, maintains different rates of exchange on trades of x for y than on trades of y for x. Finally, we
suppose that rates of exchange established by the trade coordinator
are governed by two basic requirements: (1) relative rates of exchange
are varied with a view to maintaining average quantities traded at
levels that will ensure positive holdings of all traded commodities at
virtually every point in time; and (2) differentials between buying and
selling rates are varied so as to aim at a zero long-run average level
of net profit. The first requirement effectively asserts that the trade
negotiator is ultimately responsive to prevailing forces of excess demand; the second is a rough device to ensure that the trade negotiator

acts as if he (or she) had to compete for customers with other shopkeepers.

So much for the introduction to our story, brief though it may be. All we require at this point is a coherent mental portrait—in terms of ideas that are neither entirely unfamiliar nor arrantly offensive to common sense—of an economy in which trade at other than stationary equilibrium prices may be presumed to occur more or less routinely. The model just outlined seems to meet these specifications. Accordingly, we turn now to a quick—in fact, desperately quick—discussion of the existence and stability of equilibrium, which is followed by an even faster romp through related problems associated with the identification of possible and probable sources of coordination failure.

II

The existence of equilibria in our supermarket model can be shown to follow from essentially the same assumptions as ensure the existence of equilibria in standard theory. Broadly speaking, equilibrium requires that rates of exchange be such that average rates of purchase and consumption by individual economic agents equal average rates of production and sale for each commodity, that average inventory holdings of individual agents and of the trade coordinator be maintained at constant levels over time, and that actual inventory holdings of the coordinator be nonnegative at every point in time. The familiar zero-excess-demand conditions of standard theory may be viewed as a subset of these conditions, valid in the special case where sale and purchase flows are continuous and buying and selling rate differentials are arbitrarily small. In any equilibrium situation, "notional" and "active" demands and supplies of individual agents will, of course, coincide. Subject to certain obvious and minor changes in terminology, moreover, all equilibria will be Pareto optimal.

As far as equilibrium situations are concerned, then, our supermarket model may be viewed as a straightforward generalization of standard theory. As in standard theory, so in the present model: goods are traded directly for other goods; i.e., both models portray organized barter economies. In principle, the trade coordinator might deal in all kinds of commodities—employment contracts, futures contracts, leases, rentals, loans, insurance—as well as in spot trading of physical objects. In all cases we should expect the trade coordinator to impose standard *quid pro quo* requirements—i.e., Say's Principle would be strictly observed in all trades. In the case of contracts that call for future performance of specific acts (payment of interest, rent, provision of labor services, etc.) we should expect the coordinator to impose further *accountability conditions* to guard against conscious fraud or unintentional overcommitment by individual economic agents. In the nature of the case, conditions of this sort would be costly to enforce, and all such costs would have to be borne ultimately by individual economic agents. Accordingly, we should expect trade in any but short-term and easily monitored and enforced contracts to be severely limited. In this respect, the present model stands in sharp contrast to certain versions of standard theory.

III

Much more could be said about equilibrium properties of our model, but here the preceding rough and ready observations must suffice. Dealing next with stability, we should begin by remarking that in the context of the present model this issue cannot be discussed in terms simply of trader reactions to price changes and relative speeds of adjustment of prices. The essential question is whether the trade coordinator, acting intelligently and on the basis of information derived from past experience, can manage most of the time to maintain effective control of all inventories so that no individual economic agent is ever denied for very long the right to trade commodities that the trade coordinator normally would handle as a matter of course.

Two considerations merit special notice as factors that would tend to ensure global stability. First—and in contrast with standard theory —price variations may be presumed to be governed not by predetermined velocity coefficients, but rather by reasoned and intelligent decisions of the trade coordinator. Except in circumstances where trader reactions to price variations are both erratic and violent, therefore, it should be possible for the trade coordinator to devise some strategy of price adjustment that would ensure stability. Second—and again in contrast with standard theory—quantities actually traded by individual agents can be directly restricted by the trade coordinator in cases where price adjustments alone do not ensure effective inventory control. Thus, even in exceptional circumstances where global stability might otherwise be a serious problem, departures from equilibrium should be limited in magnitude and bounded in duration. This is not to say that what Leijonhufvud has called "corridor phenomena" are *never* of any consequence; it is merely to say that such phenomena appear to be of no consequence in a world of organized barter.

IV

The possibility of coordination failures obviously depends directly on the stability of disequilibrium adjustment processes and upon the nature and extent of external shocks to which the system is exposed. In our supermarket model, as in standard theory, it is possible to concoct cases in which everything goes wrong; the ideas of economists extend to many things that are not dreamed of in the real world. Unless one is chronically subject to acute bouts of intellectual perversity, however, such cases are not to be taken seriously. On almost any set of reasonable assumptions about the behavior of individual agents and the trade coordinator, coordination failures should be rare or nonexistent in a world of the kind portrayed by the model considered here. To be sure, if a substantial proportion of traded commodities were highly durable capital goods, then serious problems might arise from time to time in coordinating present production of such goods with future demand for their services (i.e., future purchases of consumption goods). Such problems might be avoided if appropriate facilities existed whereby present purchasers of capital goods could contract currently for future sale of consumer goods outputs; but such facilities would be extremely costly to operate, so it would seem highly implausible to suppose that they would in fact be provided by the trade coordinator. Though we cannot rule out stock-flow complications as a possible source of coordination failures, our own impressionistic feeling—Keynes to the contrary notwithstanding —is that this complication *alone* is not of overwhelming significance. More generally, we should argue that, in a world of organized barter in which the coordination of trading activities is completely centralized, there is no serious reason to object to the classical view of economic activity as a thoroughly harmonious concert conducted by Adam Smith's invisible hand.

V

But suppose that some rudimentary monetary and credit complications are introduced into our model. Specifically, suppose that the trade coordinator decides to decentralize exchange activities by establishing distinct trading posts for all but one commodity and designates the exceptional commodity that is tradeable at all posts as *money*. We might then imagine coordination failures to occur from time to time because individual agents develop an irrational passion for cash rather than goods and services. But such failures—commercial crises, as they might be called by a student of eighteenth- and nineteenth-century economic history—would surely be short-lived, for real balance effects would operate with a vengeance in this kind of commodity–money world.

Suppose next, however, that trading specialists assigned to manage various trading posts were permitted to conclude trades on the basis of book credit as well as cash. Then we should expect a significant—and perhaps predominant—proportion of all trades to be made initially on the basis of book credit, cash settlement coming later in accordance with payment rules of the kind with which we are familiar in real life. In this situation, we should have to distinguish clearly between *means of payment*, which would consist of book credit *and* cash, and *means of settlement*, which would be represented by cash alone. In situations of disequilibrium, credit means of payment could expand or contract rapidly at the discretion of individual economic agents, virtually without reference to the short-run availability of means of settlement. Inflation of money prices could occur and be sustained for some time even with a constant stock of cash, and any major interruption in cash flows (an increasingly probable occurrence as means of settlement became an ever smaller fraction of total means of payment) could produce sharp restrictions on trade. This could lead, in turn, to rapid declines in output and employment, and to consequent price deflation, resulting eventually in widespread insolvency among trade specialists as well as bankruptcy of many individual economic agents. In this kind of world, corridor phenomena might well be of major consequence; i.e., sustained and serious coordination failures might occur because insolvency of trade specialists would temporarily eliminate from the economy market homeostats that are essential for effective coordination of the notional economic plans of individual agents.

Of course the world in which we live is not like this at all. But suppose that it were. Or, more plausibly, suppose that our monetary and credit version of the supermarket model were a reasonable first approximation to the world in which we live. The implications are pretty obvious—and not at all reassuring.

VI

Here our story must end for now, although in truth it is hardly begun —for, of course, we have yet to regain a "Keynesian perspective." The theoretical conception of the economic system with which we break off (1) lacks a central information-processing and bill-collecting agency; (2) has, instead, middlemen trying to coordinate production and consumption activities in each output market separately; (3) makes the management of stocks of inventories essential to the coordination of these activities; and (4) has the system potentially subject to commercial crises associated with expansions and contractions of the volume of bank and nonbank commercial credit. All of this might be J. S. Mill or Alfred Marshall. At most, we might stretch our claim to being "with it" to include Knut Wicksell and Ralph Hawtrey.

So what becomes of our intention to provide food for further thought? If there is such a thing as stale food for fresh thought, we can only hope that some readers will derive nourishment from noting that (a) we started from a conceptualization of economic process lodged in "modern" general equilibrium theory, (b) proceeded to complicate matters in what we dare claim to be an obviously desirable and "realistic" direction, and (c) by that route ended up with Mill!

16

A RECONSIDERATION OF THE THEORY OF INFLATION

Recent discussions of inflation are disturbingly reminiscent of similarly topical discussions of unemployment that preceded and followed publication of Keynes's *General Theory of Employment, Interest and Money* in 1936. Now, as then, traditionalists argue that the economy will work best if left to itself. Now, as then, a much larger group of puzzled or simply uncommitted economists question whether private ownership economies can work well without constant governmental prodding. Now, as then, a small but vocal group of radicals contends that such economies cannot work well under any circumstances. Now, as then, finally, debate tends to be carried on largely at cross-purposes because adherents to different camps are unable to agree upon a common framework of analysis as a basis for rational discussion of their differences.

What is disturbing about all this is the melancholy prospect that the outcome of the present inflation debate will be as inconclusive and intellectually unsatisfying as that of the earlier unemployment debate. A different outcome is hardly conceivable unless at some stage discussion is directed away from issues that turn ultimately on implicit differences in method and ideology and is focused instead on issues that are reducible to questions of logic or fact.

If such a redirection were feasible within the framework of presently established theory, surely it would already have taken place some time ago; for whatever else might be said about the Knave of Science, it cannot be claimed that its practitioners are naturally more quarrelsome than those of other disciplines. If this is granted, then what seems to be required is a restatement of established theory that will provide fresh perspective on the manner in which individual economic activities are co-ordinated—or might fail to be co-ordinated—in private ownership economies that bear a family resemblance to economies of actual record.

Anything more ambitious than an outline of such a restatement is out of the question here. The best that might be hoped for in a single paper is to motivate further work by showing that central aspects of a presently confused and controversial literature can be significantly

218

clarified by following a line of inquiry that, if not at all new, represents a clear departure from prevailing modes. Such is my purpose in the pages that follow.

I. BACKGROUND

Inflation is generally acknowledged to be a monetary phenomenon in the trivial sense that the phenomenon manifests itself in a sustained and rapid rise in the general money price level (see Johnson, 1972, 1975). It is possible to quibble about the meaning of the terms 'sustained', 'rapid' and 'general money price level', but these are matters more of terminology than of substance. Serious difficulties arise only when we ask: precisely what forces govern movements in the general level of prices in an ongoing monetary exchange economy?

The theoretically most sophisticated way to approach this question is through general competitive analysis. Here one starts with an unambiguous body of formal knowledge about the circumstances in which the production and consumption plans of a set of individual economic agents will be compatible with associated plans to trade commodities among themselves at rates of exchange that are defined in terms of underlying conditions of taste and technology. Assuming that one of the commodities traded is an asset called 'money' that serves as a common unit of account, one can proceed to prove various theorems about the way in which money rates of exchange will vary in response to alternative postulated changes in underlying conditions. As Patinkin and others have shown, this approach yields—among other things—a modern version of the quantity theory that serves rigorously to validate classical propositions about the invariance of equilibrium values of real magnitudes (including rates of interest) with respect to changes in the nominal quantity of inconvertible paper currency (see, particularly, Patinkin, 1956; Archibald and Lipsey, 1958; Clower and Burstein, 1960). On the basis of common knowledge about the sluggish manner in which underlying conditions of taste and technology normally change, it is then natural to argue that rapid unidirectional movements in all (or most) money prices must be attributable primarily to exogenous changes in the nominal quantity of money.

As recent contributions to the micro-foundations of monetary theory have shown, this approach to the explanation of inflation raises as many questions as it answers (see, especially, Ostroy, 1973; Howitt, 1973; Ostroy and Starr, 1974). Strictly speaking, general competitive analysis, as presently formulated, is descriptive only of *virtual* economic systems; it deals with the formulation of production, consumption and trading plans but it is utterly silent about their execution. This being so, it is difficult to see how the theory can be considered to characterise any but stationary states of an ongoing economy, and even more difficult to see how the commodity designated as 'money' within the theory could be considered to play any role other than that of an analytical *deus ex machina*—a device introduced *ad hoc* into what would otherwise be described as a model of centrally co-ordinated multilateral barter to lend it superficial verisimilitude as a theory of decentralised monetary exchange. Appearances to the contrary notwithstanding, therefore, general competitive analysis—at least as presently formulated—is incapable of providing an intellectually satisfying explanation even of stylised inflationary processes. This is attributable not to any logical weakness in the theory but rather to the fact that its premises are too special to permit the theory to deal explicitly with situations in which—as in real life—commodity trades normally can be carried out routinely at prevailing prices even though individual trading plans are mutually inconsistent. More concretely, the central flaw in established competitive analysis lies in its lack of an acceptable theory of exchange intermediation. The conventional artifice of a 'market authority' or 'auctioneer' serves only to obscure this flaw, not to correct it. The question arises whether an approach less sophisticated than general competitive analysis might be fruitfully utilised to discuss the theory of inflation.

Unfortunately, the class of presently promising alternatives contains just two types of theory, both of which are essentially aggregative variants of general competitive analysis. I refer, of course, to what are commonly referred to as 'monetarist' and 'income–expenditure' theories. It would be possible to deal critically and at length with each of these types, but I doubt that such an exercise would add even marginally to present professional understanding of their shortcomings. Here just a few broad comments are in order.

From a formal point of view, the main difference between monetarist and income–expenditure models is that, in the former, attention is focused on the willingness of economic agents in the aggregate to hold existing money balances while, in the latter, attention is focused on the willingness of separate economic sectors (households, firms, etc.) to equate money expenditure with money income and so maintain existing sectoral money balances constant. Obviously this difference does not amount to a distinction. The two types of theory are distinguished at another level by rather different presumptions about the self-adjusting tendencies of the economic system, but in neither case do the theories furnish any basis for reasoned assessment of the probable factual validity of their maintained hypotheses. The monetarist position is quite clear on this: it rests explicitly on a 'black box' conception of the economic system—what comes out can be predicted only by what goes in. The income–expenditure position is less clear, but it appears to rest on what might be called a 'grab bag' view of the economic system—regardless of what goes in, almost anything might come out! Neither point of view is of any value for circumventing the difficulties associated with the central flaw in their parent theory— the lack of an acceptable theory of exchange intermediation. Where the parent theory is unambiguously silent, its offspring are noisily ambiguous. As far as our understanding of inflationary processes is concerned, there is nothing to choose between them.

II. GENERAL PROCESS ANALYSIS: A SKETCH

In every advanced society the exchange activities of individual economic agents are co-ordinated by a relatively small subset of these same agents who act in a special capacity as brokers and auction agents or as outright dealers in commodities that are regularly produced, consumed or used by members of the community. Thus the arrangement and execution of trades is almost never an independent do-it-yourself affair; on the contrary, most exchange transactions take place within a highly structured framework of market institutions that has evolved gradually out of an interplay of political, social and technological factors with everyday economic forces of greed and competition.

The main outlines of contemporary market arrangements are much the same as those of much earlier times, suggesting that the forces underlying these arrangements have worked continuously and with great power throughout the course of recorded human history. Recent work has clarified the nature of some of these forces (see, particularly, Hicks, 1967; Clower, 1969; Perlman, 1971; Brunner and Meltzer, 1971; Chuchman, 1975; Jones, 1975). For example, it can be shown that market intermediaries—inventory-holding middlemen of various kinds—will find it profitable to operate in any community where fixed costs of trade associated with individual search and bargaining activities are sufficiently great. Similarly, it can be shown that trade specialisation will occur in situations where higher trading volume is accompanied by economies of scale in holding inventories. Monetary exchange—involving arrangements where at least one commodity is used as a common means of payment by virtually all trade intermediaries—can be accounted for in a similar manner, and it is then a fairly straightforward matter to explain the emergence of banks and other loan merchants, the development of trade credit arrangements, the creation of manufacturing concerns, and so on. These problems have been explored extensively elsewhere (for references see Clower, 1975), so I shall not dwell on them further here. For present purposes, it is more to the point to take the existence of prevailing institutions for granted so that attention is focused on the behavioural properties of intermediary economies rather than on their evolution.

Let us begin by considering the special case of a pure commodity–money economy in which each trade intermediary deals with just two goods—one of them the money commodity—and in which all trading is spot (cf. Howitt, 1974). The essential function of intermediaries is to reduce search and bargaining costs to primary agents by providing a 'ready market'. To perform that function, intermediaries must at all times hold inventories of both money and goods and must stand ready to buy and sell at stated prices in such quantities as prospective customers might desire. In a literal sense, prices are administered by intermediaries, while quantities are (within wide limits) administered by customers. In general, however, prices set by intermediaries must be varied from time to time to maintain control of trade inventories. Since customer arrival times are random from the point of view of intermediaries, trade volume over short intervals of time cannot significantly affect price decisions. Prices will tend to vary discontinuously and discretely in response to perceived gaps between desired holdings of goods and money and actual holdings as determined by the average volume of purchases and sales over more or less extended intervals of time.

In this kind of economy, equilibrium requires that prices be uniform among traders of any single good (provided we abstract from transport costs); that rates of return on trade inventories be equal to the rate of return on capital in general; that prices be such that the quantity produced and sold of each non-money commodity is equal, *on average*, to the quantity demanded for purchase and consumed; that each trader's average inventory holdings be constant; that the general money price level be such that net production of the money commodity is zero; and that the total existing stock of money be just equal to the amount demanded to hold for trade or other purposes.

This is already a fairly long list of requirements—and it is by no means complete. In particular, I have omitted all mention of requirements imposed on primary agents. In the situation considered, each primary agent will hold inventories of goods and money, and these must be maintained constant, on average, if equilibrium is to be maintained. In addition all the usual marginal conditions must hold, at least in a stochastic sense, since otherwise the realised trade volume of some intermediaries would vary over time. Obviously formal modelling even of this very special kind of intermediary economy is a complex affair. On the basis of the discussion so far, however, it is possible to say some things about the probable dynamics of motion in such a system—and that is the essential purpose of the present argument. Previously I have called this kind of exercise *general process analysis*. What follows is merely a sketch of ideas that are developed much more fully elsewhere (for example in Clower and Leijonhufvud, 1975, and Leijonhufvud, 1973).

To make matters as simple as possible, suppose that the money commodity—let us call it 'gold' for the time being—serves no purpose in the economy except as a means of payment and store of value. Suppose further that, starting from a state of full equilibrium, the stock of money in the economy proceeds to grow at a steady rate as a result of a technological innovation in gold mining. The first impact will be felt by traders who deal with gold producers; their inventories of goods will decline and their inventories of money will rise. To replenish their inventories, these traders will either purchase goods from other traders or increase prices paid to primary agents or both. One way and another, the effect of the increased money stock will spread gradually throughout the economy—but certainly not at an even pace. There will be long lags in the adjustment of some prices, delayed shifts in the mix of outputs produced by primary agents, changes in consumption patterns because of differing individual price and wealth elasticities of demand, and so on. Eventually, however, the economy will settle down to a steady rate of inflation—not with the same pattern of relative prices as before, or the same patterns of production and consumption, but with patterns that are nevertheless constant over time. One can then envisage a situation where merchants would increase their prices to cover costs, and gold miners produce more, yet obtain a lower standard of living. Price controls might be proposed, causing merchants to increase their prices even more in anticipation.

What actually might happen is that gold miners finally would quit working so hard, prices would stop rising, and after a year or two everyone would find himself in the same position as before, except that pockets and cash registers would contain larger average quantities of gold—and gold miners would have more leisure.

No modern economy is as simple as the one just considered. In real life, few intermediaries act simply as middlemen. Retail merchants set prices to customers but take prices from their suppliers who, in turn, set prices to merchants but take prices from their suppliers—and so on, down the line, until one reaches primary producers, auction markets for farm and fishery products, etc. Most sales occur not spot but future. Orders are placed by merchants on the expectation that price at time of delivery will be similar to price today, but actual transaction prices generally are determined by date of delivery rather than date of order. The great bulk of all payments are made initially in the form of book debits to trade accounts which are settled later with cash or bank transfers. Formal modelling of these and other complications, although possible in principle, poses tasks that are truly mind-boggling. Sooner or later, of course, such modelling must be carried out if we are ever to place ourselves in a position to predict with any accuracy the short-run future behaviour of any actual economy. Meanwhile, it seems purposeful to work out the details of simple models of the kind set out above—though my hunch is that the qualitative behaviour of even very complex systems will not differ significantly from that of the pure commodity–money economy as sketched above.

III. GENERAL PROCESS ANALYSIS: FURTHER DISCUSSION

The account of market structure and performance outlined above is very traditional. It is compatible not only with Marshall's ideas as set out in his *Industry and Trade* (Marshall, 1919, book 2, chaps. 5–8) but also with those of his classical predecessors—Smith, Ricardo, Senior and Mill. It also accords well with views expressed by Marshall's most famous contemporaries—Jevons, Walras, Edgeworth and Walker. Its relation to more recent works should be equally clear. It includes general competitive analysis as a limiting case that is approximately valid for analysing full equilibrium states of a general process economy. As for monetarist and income–expenditure models, these are subsumed in general process analysis under the heading of 'partial, *ad hoc* representations of temporary equilibrium states'.

To be sure, a theory that covers all possible cases may be so general as to be useless (cf. Samuelson, 1947, pp. 7–8). Just as surely, a theory that is grounded on nothing more substantial than intuitive reflection and mathematical convenience is almost certain to be useless regardless of the restrictiveness of its so-called empirical implications. To be worthwhile in any meaningful sense, a theory should be so formulated as to fall somewhere in between these two extremes. I think general process analysis satisfies this condition.

To begin with, it should be evident that, for all *full equilibrium* comparative statics experiments, the empirical implications of general process analysis are qualitatively identical with those of general competitive analysis and related theories. As for other types of comparative statics exercises (for example, 'temporary equilibrium' experiments of the sort that characterise standard IS–LM analysis), general competitive analysis yields ambiguous results, but for a perfectly sensible reason, namely, such experiments deal with *transient states* of a general process model and such states do not fall within the logical purview of comparative statics analysis. Some might regard this as a weakness of general process analysis, but it is more accurately regarded as an indictment of the intellectually shoddy comparative statics exercises that fill modern texts in macroeconomic theory. In this respect, general process analysis deserves to be regarded as a guard against wishful thinking rather than an obstacle to fruitful inquiry.

The strength of general process analysis as a background for empirical inquiry comes out most clearly, however, in dynamical applications. It is customary in standard theories to construct dynamic models in a strictly mechanical fashion so that price adjustments appear to be made by 'unseen forces' rather than by individual economic agents. Given this framework, it is usual to proceed as if the motions of the system were determined once and for all by given structural factors. In the nature of the case, the motions of any given model may be stable or unstable depending on the values assigned to specific parameters. From this it is but a short step to the conclusion that some economies will work well while others will work ill, and it is then difficult to overlook the possibility that the world in which we live has cast up systems that work poorly and stand in need of redesign.

General process analysis rests upon another conception of market organisation and leads to radically different conclusions. In the first place, price as well as quantity adjustments are explicitly associated with conscious decisions of individual economic agents. Market structure and performance characteristics are regarded not as preordained consequences of technical and structural factors but rather as unforeseen and unforeseeable evolutionary consequences of the interaction of behavioural and technological forces. On this view, unstable economic systems, although theoretically conceivable, are not practically viable. Systems that survive over long intervals of calendar time effectively declare themselves to be 'of stable type'. Indeed, an even stronger assertion is warranted: systems that survive need not have a structure that guarantees *asymptotic* stability (i.e., stability in the limit as time tends to infinity), but they must have a structure that guarantees *practical* stability (i.e., strict boundedness of motion over any finite interval of calendar time).

This discussion might be continued at length, but it has been carried far enough already to support the only conclusion that is strictly required for present purposes, namely, the conclusion that general process analysis is in no way less informative or restrictive than standard theories, given comparably restrictive underlying assumptions, but that it differs sharply from standard theories in making us clearly aware of areas of inquiry where additional empirical research is required before we can safely draw any conclusions at all from our theoretical models.

IV. THE PROBLEM OF INFLATION

I began this paper by stressing the need for a common framework of analysis as a basis for rational assessment of the factual validity of alternative views about the nature and control of inflationary processes. I have outlined a framework—general process analysis—that seems to me to go some way towards meeting this need. It is not a framework that will appeal to everyone. It leaves too much open for discussion to appeal to doctrinaires, and it focuses too much attention on messy institutional details to appeal to those who like their theories neat. All the same, in what follows I shall try to show that the framework is of some value as a device for professional communication despite its obvious limitations for other more ambitious purposes.

For the sake of argument, let me begin by supposing that we have to deal with a fiat money economy that is described to a good first approximation by a general process model that defines an asymptotically stable equilibrium motion that is unique up to a proportional transformation of all variables that are denominated in units of money. This means that the classical (Ricardian) quantity theory of the long-run value of money is rigorously valid, i.e., the full equilibrium values of all real magnitudes are independent of the nominal value of the cash base. Other things being equal, it also means that the general money price level depends in the long run only on the cash base. It follows that, except on highly implausible assumptions (e.g., sustained retrogression in resources and technology), an ongoing inflation can always be halted by holding the cash base constant.

This conclusion no doubt will sound like the opening gun in a salute to monetarism. In fact it is nothing of the sort, for to accept the conclusion as a valid statement about the real world commits one to nothing except a belief in the proposition that observed economic events are amenable to prediction in terms of formal theoretical models—a proposition the validity of which is not presently at issue. More pointedly, although cash-base control is a necessary and sufficient condition for long-run control of the general money price level, such control does not imply stability of money prices or anything else in the short run. Of course, this conclusion is also part and parcel of contemporary monetarist thought. But it is a central tenet also of all income–expenditure theories. Up to this point, therefore, we have no grounds for argument.

Proceeding to potentially more contentious matters, let us add detail to our model by supposing that the economy contains a fractional reserve banking system whose deposit obligations are equivalent to cash as means for settling trade debts. Suppose also that trade intermediaries maintain book credit accounts with one another and with other economic agents and that debit entries to these accounts are equivalent to cash as a means of payment. Then the total quantity of money in the economy—which we define as cash outside banks plus deposits transferrable by cheque plus gross accounts payable—is an endogenous variable the value of which is determined by (among other things) the cash base, bank reserve ratios and prevailing payment and settlement practices.

In this kind of economy, just as in one where money consists solely of cash, the full equilibrium general money price level will depend (other things being equal) on the nominal level of the cash base. As before, moreover, cash-base control is not a sufficient condition for short-run stability of prices or related real magnitudes. We then come to the central question of modern inflation theory: is short-run stability in the cash base of minor significance for economic stability, or is rigid adherence to a rule of steady and moderate expansion in the cash base essential to avoid serious economic instability in both the short and the long run?

I have purposely stated this question to avoid direct confrontation either with the view that economic stability depends *solely* on 'spending', or with the view that economic stability depends *solely* on 'money'. Neither position is espoused in this extreme form by any but members of the lunatic fringe of professional economists, though many economists apparently would subscribe to weaker versions of each. As I see matters, however, the issue is not which, if either, of these two alternatives is best suited to guarantee economic stability, but rather whether economic stability is even a remote possibility in the absence of highly responsible cash-base control. The first of these questions is, I submit, undecidable on the basis of present factual and theoretical knowledge, but the second seems to me to admit of a tentative answer within the framework of general process analysis.

Given a model in which (as in real life) trade credit and demand deposits dominate cash as a means of payment, and in which (again as in real life) non-cash means of payment can expand or contract by substantial amounts to meet 'the needs of trade' even when the cash base is constant, it is implausible to suppose that increases in the cash base will in all circumstances induce immediate increases in other means of payment, or that decreases in the cash base will not sometimes induce a sharp reduction in other means of payment by producing a 'liquidity crisis'. Suppose that the model also includes a business sector that produces and uses large quantities of long-lived capital goods. For good measure, add to the model a non-bank financial sector that deals in all varieties of long- and short-term debt. In this kind of system, quite minor random shocks are capable of producing wide swings in production, employment, interest rates and prices, even if all trade debts are settled in cash. If the 'slippage' and 'whiplash' possibilities inherent in a permissive monetary environment are also taken into account, then the stage is set for Wicksellian cumulative processes that work in both directions.

Specifically, suppose that the monetary authority—which we may presume has complete command of the cash base—pursues a general policy of 'leaning against the wind'. If it does not lean hard at the outset of any upward cumulative movement (and how is it to distinguish between random and systematic movements?), the cash base will expand in response to bank demands for additional reserves to support new loans to permit business firms to settle newly contracted trade debts. Prices will rise, interest rates will lag, and the cumulative process will gather momentum. What I am describing is the kind of nightmare that percipient classics associated with the 'real bills' doctrine. The scenario is just as nightmarish if it starts with a downward movement in economic activity. As far as I can see, moreover, only the details of the nightmare are altered if we suppose that the monetary authority pursues no consistent policy but simply 'drifts'.

Of course it is entirely possible that the economy will behave very poorly even if the monetary authority keeps a tight rein on the cash base and thereby forces trade intermediaries and dealers in debts to keep a weather eye at all times on the relation between accounts payable and currently available means of settlement. It is also possible that cumulative movements could be avoided if the monetary authority pursued a consistent policy of 'resisting the wind', except that, in this as in any other situation that involves impossibly delicate judgements, it is difficult to imagine how such a policy could be carried out successfully in practice. However that might be, it seems clear that, other things (specifically, fiscal policy) being equal, any erratic policy stands a good chance of producing needlessly violent ups and downs, or needlessly extended periods of inflation and deflation, or some combination of any or all of these.

V. CONCLUSION

As happens on occasion, the space available for argument falls short of that required to complete it. The rest must be supplied by the reader's imagination—assisted by a few concluding assertions. Earlier I implicitly denied any personal commitment to monetarist doctrine. I now explicitly reaffirm that denial. But historical evidence, common sense, economic intuition and considerations related to the present argument have all combined to lead me to a qualified monetarist position. Specifically, though I would not subscribe to the proposition that all would be well if monetary authorities pursued a policy of steady and moderate expansion in the cash base, I am fully convinced that any other policy is bound to lead to folly in the form either of boom and bust or sustained inflation. Against this, it has been argued that every monetary economy has occasional need for a lender of last resort. That may be so, but this function need not and probably should not be joined with the more routine task of providing a cash base adequate to sustain *normal* settlement requirements.

A final remark and I am done. In Britain it is common even today to hear professional economists insist that monetary policy must be conducted with an eye to 'general credit' conditions rather than to movements in the cash base, and also to hear that the proper way to cure inflation is to adopt an appropriate wages and incomes policy and to combine this with brutal fiscal measures. To my mind, such views reflect willful retreat from reality (cf. Johnson, 1972, pp. 4–21). There is one and only one cure for the present British inflation: firm control of the cash base. To impose such control in present circumstances must inevitably produce heavy if temporary unemployment and other serious dislocations of economic life. Failure to impose such control will inevitably produce exactly the same problems and may well lead to disastrous social consequences as well. There is no need to state the moral, but there is great need to heed it.

REFERENCES

Archibald, G. C. and Lipsey, R. G. (1958). 'Monetary and Value Theory: A Critique of Lange and Patinkin,' *Review of Economic Studies*, XXVI (Oct.) 1–22.

Brunner, K. and Meltzer, A. (1971). 'The Uses of Money: Money in the Theory of an Exchange Economy,' *American Economic Review*, LXI (Mar.) 784–805.

Chuchman, G. (1975). 'A Model of the Evolution of Exchange Processes,' University of Western Ontario, Money Workshop, revised version.

Clower, R. W. (1969), *Monetary Theory: Selected Readings* (Harmondsworth: Penguin Books).

Clower, R. W. (1975).'Reflections on the Keynesian Perplex,' *Zeitschrift für Nationalökonomie* XXXV (July) 1–24.

Clower, R. W. and Burstein, M. L. (1960). 'The Invariance of the Demand for Cash and Other Assets,' *Review of Economic Studies*, XXVIII (Oct.) 32–36.

Clower, R. W. and Leijonhufvud, A. (1975). 'The Co-ordination of Economic Activities: A Keynesian Perspective,' *American Economic Review* (*Proc.*), LXV (May), 182–88.

Hicks, J. R. (1967). *Critical Essays in Monetary Theory* (Oxford: Clarendon Press).

Howitt, P. W. (1973). 'Walras and Monetary Theory,' *Western Economic Journal*, XI (Dec.) 487–99.

Howitt, P. W. (1974). 'Stability and the Quantity Theory,' *Journal of Political Economy*, LXXXII (Jan.–Feb.) 133–40.

Johnson, H. G. (1972). *Inflation and the Monetarist Controversy*, De Vries Lectures (Amsterdam: North-Holland).

Johnson, H. G. (1975). 'The Problem of Inflation,' in *On Economics and Society: Selected Essays* (Chicago and London: Univ. of Chicago Press).

Jones, R. (1976). 'The Origin and Development of Media of Exchange,' *Journal of Political Economy*, LXXXIV (Aug. Pt. I) 757–75.

Leijonhufvud, A. (1973). 'Effective Demand Failures,' *Swedish Economic Journal*, LXXIII (Mar.) 27–48.

Marshall, A. (1919). *Industry and Trade* (London: Macmillan).

Ostroy, J. (1973). 'The Informational Efficiency of Monetary Exchange,' *American Economic Review*, LXIII (Sept.) 597–610.

Ostroy, J. and Starr, R. M. (1974). 'Money and the Decentralisation of Exchange,' *Econometrica*, XLII (Nov.) 1093–1113.

Patinkin, D. (1956). *Money, Interest, and Prices* (Evanston, Ill.: Row Peterson).

Perlman, M. (1971). 'The Roles of Money in the Economy and the Optimum Quantity of Money,' *Econometrica*, XXXVIII (Aug.) 233–52.

Samuelson, P. A. (1947). *Foundations of Economic Analysis* (Cambridge, Mass.: Harvard Univ. Press).

17

THE ANATOMY OF MONETARY THEORY

> It is obvious even to the most ordinary intelligence, that a commodity
> should be given up by its owner in exchange for another more useful to
> him. But that every economic unit in a nation should be ready to exchange
> his goods for little metal disks apparently useless as such, or for documents
> representing the latter, is a procedure so opposed to the ordinary course
> of things [as to seem] downright "mysterious."
> KARL MENGER, "ON THE ORIGIN OF MONEY"[1]

Modern discussions of monetary theory have fairly well demolished
its traditional foundations without so far putting anything definite in
their place. To be sure, some progress towards reconstruction has
been made. In particular, contributions by John R. Hicks (1967),
F. H. Hahn (1973), Karl Brunner and Allen Meltzer, Jack Hirschleifer
and a host of other writers have shown that set-up costs of engaging
in trade must play a central role in any acceptable formal theory of
monetary exchange. Other contributions by Clower (1969), Morris
Perlman, Joel Fried, Joseph Ostroy and R. M. Starr, and Peter Howitt
have suggested that individual holdings of commodity inventories
must also be taken into account. Finally, many writers have argued
that certain physical characteristics of commodities are vital. Thus
some of the ingredients for a reconstruction of the foundations are
not seriously in doubt. What remains to be settled is the manner in
which these and possibly other ingredients might best be combined.

This problem is not likely to be resolved in the near future; at best,
we might hope for an early professional consensus about the way in
which the problem should be approached. My purpose in this paper
is to contribute to the formation of such a consensus by exploring

I am indebted to numerous colleagues for helpful personal discussions about central
ideas in this paper, but especially to Joel Fried and Peter Howitt of the University of
Western Ontario, and to Robert Jones and John Riley of UCLA. As will become clear
in the sequel, all of my thinking in this area has been strongly influenced by recent
work of Professor Hicks, particularly his *Theory of Economic History* (1969) and *Critical
Essays in Monetary Theory* (1967). My debt to other writers, both at UCLA and elsewhere,
is not too inadequately acknowledged, I hope, by citations in the text.

[1] Menger, p. 239. I owe this reference to Robert Jones, whose Brown University
dissertation supplies one possible solution to Menger's "paradox." For a published
version of the argument, see Jones.

rather carefully the roles that transactions costs and other purportedly crucial complications might play in the evolution of monetary exchange arrangements within a simple spot-exchange economy that is initially imagined to be as devoid of explicit empirical features as any standard Arrow–Debreu model.[2]

I

Our first order of business is to state explicitly just what aspects of experience we should want to have "explained" by any theory that claims to provide even a minimally adequate description of a monetary economy. This may be accomplished most conveniently by setting out an agenda of requirements that any such theory should satisfy. On the basis of earlier literature, everyday observation and my own considered professional judgment, I should regard four requirements as mandatory:

(1) The theory should imply that trade is an ongoing process in time rather than a once-for-all affair that ends in the permanent elimination of incentives for further trade.

(2) The theory should imply that, on average over any finite time interval, each individual holds positive stocks of all goods that are regularly traded.

(3) The theory should imply that the bulk of all trades occur not through essentially random pairing of individuals who happen to share a double coincidence of wants, but rather through systematic pairing of specialist with nonspecialist traders in a relatively small number of organized, continuously operating markets.

(4) The theory should imply that at least one and at most a few distinctive "money" commodities are transferred (or promised for future delivery) by one party to another in virtually all exchange transactions.

The rationale of each of these conditions will become clear as we proceed.

II

Directing inquiry now to our central theme—the logical anatomy of monetary theory—let us start by imagining a Patinkinesque community of self-interested individuals each of whom receives "like manna

---

[2] For extensive discussion and references see A. M. Ulph and D. T. Ulph.

from heaven" a predetermined quantity per time unit of one or more durable goods that may be consumed directly, traded for other commodities, or held for future consumption or trade. Suppose also that each individual is a natural source of labor services that can be consumed directly (as "leisure" or as inputs in household "production") or contracted for sale to other individuals. Given these assumptions, received theory informs us that potential gains from trade will exist if different individuals have different preferences or endowments. Let us assume that this proviso is satisfied. Then, depending on the magnitude and distribution of potential gains, trades will almost certainly occur. What we can validly say about the volume and pattern of trading activity will then depend on just what story we choose to tell about the manner in which individual trading plans are conceived and executed.[3]

At this stage, of course, we have almost unlimited room for maneuver. Our basic model includes certain necessary elements of an acceptable theory of monetary exchange, namely, objects to be traded, agents to trade these objects, and incentives for agents to interact so that actual trades occur. But it lacks all elements that might be or have been adduced by various writers as necessary conditions for monetary exchange. Our next task, therefore, is to add further content to our model.

III

Let us proceed by asking, first, what additional assumptions should be included in our argument to ensure satisfaction of the first of the requirements listed earlier, i.e., the requirement that trading activity should occur as an ongoing process in calendar time?

At first glance, the answer to the question might seem to be, "none at all," since our basic model is explicitly formulated as a stock-flow system in which potential gains from trade are sustained over time by the continuous receipt of fresh commodity endowments by individual traders. As Roy Radner, Hahn and others have shown,[4] however, even outwardly "essential" sequence models may turn out to be logically equivalent to "nonessential" sequence models of the Arrow–Debreu type in which trading contracts are concluded at just one instant in calendar time. The source of this equivalence is significant; it lies in the twin assumptions that traders are inhumanly

---

[3] This theme is most elegantly elaborated in papers by E. C. H. Veendorp, J. M. Ostroy, Allan Feldman, P. J. Madden, and R. A. Jones.

[4] Cf. Radner; Hahn, pp. 230–34; Ulph and Ulph, pp. 365–67.

prescient and that trading contracts and arrangements for future delivery of commodities can be negotiated at zero cost. If either or both of these restrictions are dropped, the first of our requirements can be easily satisfied by almost any stock-flow model.[5]

Let us drop both restrictions; more precisely, let us suppose that individuals view future endowment flows as probable rather than certain, and also that individuals can negotiate trades only by engaging in extensive search and bargaining activities. Then our model will satisfy our first requirement. Will it also satisfy the second; i.e., can we assert that each individual will hold positive average stocks of all goods that are regularly traded?

Again, the answer would appear at first thought to be in the affirmative. For it is easy to show that if search, bargaining and other trade-related activities impose set-up costs on individuals in the form of foregone leisure or consumption or both, then individuals will engage in trade, if at all, only at discrete points rather than continuously in time; hence, each individual will hold, at one moment of time or another, positive stocks of all traded goods.[6] What we have to show, however, is not that holdings of stocks will occasionally be positive, but rather that average holdings over any finite time interval will be positive.

To avoid tacitly assuming what we seek to prove, let us suppose that we have to deal with an individual who wants to trade a good X for another good Y, but discovers to his horror that no other individual is willing to trade X or Y for anything but a third good, say, Z. In this case the individual will either not trade at all, or he will first sell X for Z and then use Z to purchase Y. Unless units of Z are less costly to store than units of either X or Y, however, the individual will (if rational) combine every sale of X or Z with a nearly simultaneous purchase of Y with Z, which implies that average holdings of units of Z will be arbitrarily close to zero. Thus storage costs as well as set-up costs apparently must be invoked to ensure that our model satisfies the second requirement listed earlier. Actually, this is too strong. If search and bargaining costs are substantial relative to potential gains from trade, then indirect trades will be infrequent or nonexistent, in which case storage costs will be irrelevant. But there is also another possibility. If individuals regard future endowment flows as merely probable rather than certain, we should expect many or even most

[5] Strictly speaking, pure stock models fail this test; but such models are seldom used except to discuss special aspects of the logistics of exchange, for which purpose they are invaluable (cf. Ostroy).

[6] See Hirshleifer, pp. 138–41, for an especially clear exposition.

traders to hold precautionary balances of some goods as a hedge against possible real-income reductions, and such balances would consist predominantly of goods with relatively low costs of storage. If such holdings are widespread and are concentrated in a few goods that are held by virtually all individuals, then it may well cost less time and effort for an individual to trade X for one of these goods, and then go on to purchase Y, than to trade X for Y directly. In this situation, therefore, our argument goes through as stated initially: i.e., storage as well as transactions costs must be invoked to ensure satisfaction of our second requirement.

IV

The third requirement in our agenda—that the bulk of all trades should occur in organized markets—appears not to have been noticed in earlier work or, as seems more likely, has simply been taken for granted.[7] However that may be, the oversight is crucial; for as we shall see later, the existence of organized markets appears to be almost a precondition for monetary exchange. But our immediate task is just to explain how, on our present assumptions, organized markets might evolve in response to the working of natural economic forces.

If potential gains from trade were large and widely distributed across individuals and commodities, trading activity might be substantial even in a community without organized markets; but if search and bargaining costs were at all significant, vast areas of potential gain would never be explored. In the latter case, as George Stigler has observed,[8] there would exist "powerful inducements"—namely, widespread profit opportunities—for some individuals to localize trade by establishing "ready markets" for commonly traded goods in which other individuals could routinely execute certain designated pairwise trades at dates and in quantities of their own choosing.

Powerful inducements notwithstanding, we should not expect many individuals to act as specialist traders. To establish a ready market and attract enough customers to earn a profit that would make the activity worthwhile, an individual would have to:

(1) accumulate inventories of a wide variety of commonly traded goods;

---

[7] This is reflected in the common use of the word "money" to refer to a complex of ideas that would be more accurately rendered by using the term "organized markets." For more on this, see below, note 11.

[8] Stigler, pp. 218–19.

(2) offer to trade at rates of exchange more attractive than average rates which individuals could normally expect to obtain on short notice by trading with other nonspecialists;
(3) maintain a spread between "buy" and "sell" rates that would encourage volume trading and discourage competition by other specialists, yet yield a real income sufficient to offset operating costs;
(4) earn a rate of return on average holdings of trade inventories at least equal to his rate of time discount.

Casual introspection suggests that these conditions would dissuade any but the most thrifty, foresighted, diligent, energetic, sagacious and enterprising individuals[9] from setting up shop as trade specialists. But specialist traders could never be common in any case; for if they tended in that direction, competition among them would reduce trading spreads to the point where only those specialists with relatively low rates of time discount would choose to survive.

I need not emphasize the social benefits that flow from the existence of organized markets. The trouble and effort that would otherwise be incurred in the conduct of the most ordinary business of life has been a favorite theme of writers on money since the time of Aristotle.[10] What does merit emphasis is that these benefits do not depend logically on the use of special "money" commodities as media of exchange. The literature of monetary economics—again from Aristotle on—is replete with instances in which writers have inadvertently used the word "money" as if it were synonymous with the phrase "organized markets."[11] Historically, of course, "money" and "markets" have generally coexisted, but that connection is one of fact rather than logic. Confused understanding of this point is, I conjecture, a major reason why monetary theory has for so long remained one of the least settled branches of formal economic analysis. As we have just seen, it is easy to explain how organized markets arise from the working of natural economic forces; there is no mystery here, except perhaps Adam Smith's "instinct to truck and barter." What is not easy to explain is how the organization of such markets tends always to take a highly specialized form that permits us objectively to assert that certain ob-

[9] This list is lifted, of course, from various places in A. Marshall's *Principles of Economics*.
[10] See A. E. Monroe, p. 17, for Aristotle's contribution, and J. H. McCulloch, pp. 1–2, for a particularly lucid modern version of the same story.
[11] This usually occurs as soon as a writer has (with little difficulty) pointed out the costs of simple barter and passed on to consider other cases, for the only other cases that ever seem to come to mind are those that involve fully monetized market exchange. For an explicit account of other conceivable cases, see Clower and Axel Leijonhufvud, pp. 184–85.

jects (or "documents representing the latter") play a distinctive role as "money." That, of course, is the task set for us by the fourth and final item on our agenda.

V

Given the individualist behavior assumptions of standard theory, we have no option but to suppose that monetary exchange will emerge, if at all, only if that way of organizing trading activity is clearly advantageous either to specialist traders or to nonspecialist traders and is disadvantageous to neither.

Can it be shown that a typical specialist will have reason to require that customers give or receive units of a few designated "money" commodities in exchange for all other goods? The answer appears to be in the negative; for although it is known that economies of scale may be achieved by concentrating inventories in relatively high-volume lines of activity,[12] it can be shown that the elimination of one commodity from a specialist trader's list of "tradeable goods" will necessarily reduce trading volume in one or more other commodities that remain on the list—which works in the wrong direction. Indeed, granted that inventory holdings are a potential source of scale economies, and ignoring such considerations as costs of travel and transport and diseconomies in the operation of large-scale markets, the logic of our analysis leads us to conclude that the only permanently viable form of market organization would be one in which a single specialist trader—presumably one with a very low rate of time discount and a very keen eye for profit—provided the only ready market in the entire community. This form of organization would also be socially optimal in the usual efficiency sense since, with all trading activity concentrated in a single market, potential economies of scale in inventory holdings could be exploited to the fullest possible extent.

This line of argument does not demonstrate that a monetary form of market organization would be disadvantageous to specialist traders. However, it strongly suggests that no specialist trader would find it worthwhile to initiate moves in that direction. What about nonspecialist traders? Have they any incentive voluntarily to restrict their dealings to a relatively small subset of the set of all pairwise trades that specialist traders in the aggregate would be able and willing to handle?

Again, the answer appears to be in the negative. For why should any individual who wishes to trade, say, X for Y, proceed instead first

---

[12] See Kenneth Arrow, S. Karlin and Herbert Scarf, pp. 7–8.

to trade X for another commodity Z, and then to trade Z for Y, particularly if it is always possible to trade X directly for Y with less time and effort? On closer inspection, however, this argument is seen to beg the question, for it rests on the tacit assumption that an individual who wishes to trade one good for another also wants to acquire the second good *immediately*. To appreciate why this might not always (or even usually) be so, suppose that an individual's only endowment flow consists of units of a good X, and that all units of this good are sooner or later used to finance purchases of a variety of other goods— Y, Z, A, B, ..., etc. Then, as has been shown in recent work on the demand for trade inventories and the timing of exchange transactions,[13] the individual will—except in very special cases—minimize total trade-related costs by purchasing many or even most consumption goods at dates that differ significantly from those at which he sells units of X. To be sure, units of at least one consumption good must necessarily be acquired every time units of X are sold. But suppose that X is typically traded in large-size lots in exchange for just one other good—any good will do. Then units of this other good can later be used to purchase yet other commodities in various lot sizes and at various dates to conform with cost and other considerations that underlie the individual's choice of transaction dates for different goods. So we conclude that individuals will quite generally choose to carry out two transactions to go from X to Y, even though only one transaction is ever strictly necessary.[14]

The last result resolves our central problem; for now we have only to recall our earlier discussion of conditions in which certain commodities would be held and used for transactions purposes to arrive at an obvious and compelling reason why nonspecialist traders might voluntarily restrict themselves to selected pairwise trades, namely, storage costs. If there exists some commodity that is already a common object of exchange and which has distinctly lower storage costs than all or most other commodities, a rational individual will choose to acquire or dispose of units of this good in virtually all exchange transactions. Moreover, since different individuals are unlikely to differ much in their perception of the relative costs of storing different

[13] See Herschel Grossman and Andrew Policano for discussion and references; also Clower and Howitt.

[14] An obvious exception would occur if "time taken to go to market" greatly outweighed all other trade-related costs, since in this case an individual would "bunch" sales of endowment goods with purchases of goods for consumption, thereby minimizing the number of trips to market. History provides a possible example of this in dealings of the general merchant of pioneer times with trapper and farmer customers. See also Lars Jonung for some fascinating comments on Swedish experience.

commodities, it follows that nonspecialist traders as a group will choose to conclude most transactions with one or a few goods which will thus come to play a distinctive role as "common media of exchange" and "temporary abodes of purchasing power."[15] If one of these goods is not just inexpensive to store but is also easy to identify, handle, partition, count, hide and transport (Did someone shout "Gold"?), then that good will almost surely dominate all others as a means of payment in spot transactions. But in that case, and perhaps even under weaker conditions, specialist traders will have no incentive to maintain direct pairwise trading of every variety of commodity. Ready markets that deal exclusively with selected commodity lines (groceries, hardware, clothing, meats, black puddings, etc.) will be at least as viable as more general markets, among other reasons because inventory economies of scale can be exploited fully in such markets with relatively small stocks of trade capital. But there is no need to carry the story further; we have already established a satisfactory rationale for the existence and ubiquity of monetary exchange.

VI

My conclusion can be brief. The preceding analysis indicates that just two main factors, namely, costs of negotiating exchange transactions and certain physical characteristics of commodities, have to be taken into account to establish *necessary* conditions for monetary exchange to emerge in an otherwise strictly Arrow–Debreu economy. *Sufficient* conditions cannot be stated, except in very general terms, because these depend in an essential way on the precise character of individual preferences, on the size and distribution of endowment flows, on the magnitude of search and bargaining costs, and on the technology of market management. Thus our results are not in any sense final or complete; at best they might be said to clarify just how much still remains to be done if we are to make theoretical sense of money.

---

[15] If costs of search and bargaining were relatively unimportant, organized markets would not be viable; but the preceding argument would still provide a rationale for individuals to hold and use certain kinds of goods as temporary abodes of purchasing power. Such behavior would probably not be common, however, because the insignificance of transactions costs would encourage frequent sales of small-size lots of endowment goods in direct exchange for goods to be consumed, which would make storage costs a minor factor in the choice of trading dates. An external observer of such an economy would be unlikely, therefore, to see any pattern in the pairing of traded commodities. These patterns become blindingly obvious only in economies where most trades occur in organized markets.

REFERENCES

Kenneth J. Arrow, S. Karlin and Herbert Scarf, *Studies in the Mathematical Theory of Inventory and Production*, Stanford, Calif. 1958.

Karl Brunner and Allen Meltzer, "The Uses of Money: Money in the Theory of an Exchange Economy," *Amer. Econ. Rev.*, Dec. 1971, 61, 784–805.

Robert W. Clower, *Monetary Theory: Selected Readings*, London 1969.

—— and Peter W. Howitt, "Money, Credit and the Timing of Transactions," UCLA Discussion Paper 72, June 1976.

—— and Axel Leijonhufvud, "The Coordination of Economic Activities: A Keynesian Perspective," *Amer. Econ. Rev. Proc.*, May 1975, 65, 182–88.

A. M. Feldman, "Bilateral Trading Processes, Pairwise Optimality and Pareto Optimality," *Rev. Econ. Stud.*, Oct. 1973, 39, 463–74.

Joel Fried, "Money, Exchange and Growth," *Economic Inquiry*, Sept. 1973, 11, 285–301.

Herschel I. Grossman and Andrew J. Policano, "Money Balances, Commodity Inventories, and Inflationary Expectations," *J. Polit. Econ.*, Dec. 1975, 83, 1,093–1,112.

F. H. Hahn, "Foundations of Monetary Theory," in *Essays on Modern Economics*, M. Parkin, ed., London 1973, 230–42.

John R. Hicks, "A Suggestion for Simplifying the Theory of Money," *Economica*, Feb. 1935, 2, 1–19.

——, *Critical Essays in Monetary Theory*, Oxford 1967.

——, *A Theory of Economic History*, London 1969.

Jack Hirshleifer, "Exchange Theory: The Missing Chapter," *Western Econ. J.*, June 1973, 11, 129–46.

Peter W. Howitt, "Stability and the Quantity Theory," *J. Polit. Econ.*, Jan.–Feb. 1974, 82, 133–51.

Robert A. Jones, "The Origin and Development of Media of Exchange," *J. Polit. Econ.*, Aug. 1976, 84, 757–75.

Lars Jonung, "The Behavior of Velocity in Sweden, 1871–1913," UCLA Workshop in Monetary Economics Discussion Paper, May 1976.

P. J. Madden, "Efficient Sequences of Non-Monetary Exchange," *Rev. Econ. Stud.*, Oct. 1975, 42, 581–96.

A. Marshall, *Principles of Economics*, 8th ed., New York 1890.

J. H. McCulloch, *Money and Inflation*, New York 1975.

Karl Menger, "On the Origin of Money," *Economic Journal*, June 1892, 2, 239–55.

A. E. Monroe, *Early Economic Thought*, Cambridge, Mass. 1927.

J. M. Ostroy, "The Informational Efficiency of Monetary Exchange," *Amer. Econ. Rev.*, Sept. 1973, 63, 597–610.

—— and R. M. Starr, "Money and the Decentralization of Exchange," *Econometrica*, Oct. 1974, 42, 1,093–1,113.

Morris Perlman, "The Roles of Money in an Economy and the Optimum Quantity of Money," *Economica*, Aug. 1971, 38, 233–52.

Roy Radner, "Competitive Equilibrium under Uncertainty," *Econometrica*, Jan. 1968, 38, 31–58.

George J. Stigler, "The Economics of Information," *J. Polit. Econ.*, Mar. 1961, 69, 213–25.

A. M. Ulph and D. T. Ulph, "Transactions Costs in General Equilibrium Theory: A Survey," *Economica*, Nov. 1975, 42, 355–72.

E. C. H. Veendorp, "General Equilibrium Theory for a Barter Economy," *Western Econ. J. (Economic Inquiry)*, Mar. 1970, 8, 1–23.

18

THE GENESIS AND CONTROL OF INFLATION

"It can be maintained without exaggeration that most modern economists ... with the exception of the small group ... who in spite of everything still adhere to the quantity theory, lack any real, logically worked out theory of the value of money and its causes, a circumstance which has not of course had a particularly beneficial effect on modern discussion of these questions."
KNUT WICKSELL, 1898

Economists have been a frequent target for public ridicule in recent years because of their apparent inability to arrive at any kind of consensus about the proper way to deal with modern problems of inflation. Popular opinion clearly holds that economists generally are at least as perplexed as the public at large. This might be countered with Mr. Bumble's famous line: "If that is what the public thinks, sir, then the public is an ass." But that response would satisfy no one, not even those who made it. In truth economists *are* divided in their views about real-world inflationary processes, but—and this is more to the point—they are by no means as divided as most outsiders seem to believe. My purpose in the present paper is to elaborate upon this theme.

I. A REVIEW OF THEORIES

It is generally acknowledged that inflation is a monetary phenomenon in the literal sense that it manifests itself in a continuing rise in all or most money prices.[1] On the basis of first principles such as are taught in most elementary economics courses, it can be argued that inflation must be a monetary phenomenon in a much deeper sense as well; for if all money prices are rising, this means that the rate of exchange between two "composite commodities," namely "goods" and "money," is falling, which surely means that the supply of one "commodity" is rising in relation to the other. But this proposition hardly carries one beyond the London *Economist*'s famous phrase: "Inflation is a situation in which too much money is chasing too few goods."

Outward simplicity may, and in this case does, cloak inward com-

---

[1] Cf. Johnson (1975), p. 197.

plexity. First there is the question: What is money? Second there is the question: What determines its quantity and rate of change? Third there is the question: How much money would be just enough? Fourth there is the question: Supposing we know what inflation is, what do we do about it? None of these issues can be discussed unambiguously except in the context of a coherent conception of the nature and performance characteristics of a monetary exchange economy. The last issue cannot be discussed purposefully except in the context of a theory of monetary exchange that appears to have definite empirical validity. It is in relation to these two requirements that serious difficulties arise, for up to the present time economists have been unable to agree upon a common theoretical framework for rational discussion of their outward differences.

The closest approximation to a common theoretical framework is provided by general competitive analysis, but its value for other than academic purposes is severely limited. As recent work by Hicks, Hahn, Ostroy and others has shown,[2] the premises of general competitive analysis are too restrictive to accommodate such elementary facts of experience as trade at other than equilibrium prices and decentralized market arrangements in which certain commodities play a special role as generally accepted means of payment. It is possible to massage the theory into a form that permits it superficially to deal with these and related phenomena, but in the process it is necessary to do such violence to accepted standards of scientific procedure that the theory loses all logical force. Strictly speaking, general competitive analysis is open to just two possible interpretations: it is descriptive either of an ongoing economy in a state of full equilibrium or of a virtual exchange economy in which production, consumption and trading plans are never executed except in a state of full equilibrium. On either interpretation the theory is quite unsuited to deal explicitly with disequilibrium adjustment processes in a world where economic plans are at least partially executed in virtually any and all circumstances.

Two other so-called theories have acquired a certain following among professional economists, namely, income–expenditure theories suggested by Keynes's *General Theory* and "modern" quantity theories suggested by Friedman's influential writings. I say "so-called" because it seems to me that no instance of either of these types satisfies minimal standards of logical coherence as a description of the disequilibrium behaviour of any economic system.

Income–expenditure theorists start with the trivial proposition that

[2] See especially Hicks (1967), Hahn (1973), Ostroy (1973), Ostroy and Starr (1974).

an economy cannot be in equilibrium unless aggregate income is equal to planned aggregate expenditure. From there they proceed in an *ad hoc* and largely arbitrary fashion to discuss the determinants of planned expenditure on the presumption that this is the dog that mainly wags the aggregate income tail. An experienced and sensible economist can play this game endlessly without ever stating a patently foolish conclusion, but the game is also played by inexperienced and foolish economists—with results that serve to discredit not only economists but their discipline. As a matter of logic, income–expenditure theories are *incompletely specified* variants of general competitive analysis. As such they do not deserve serious consideration as a basis for any but cocktail-party conversation of the problem of inflation.

As for modern quantity theorists, they start with the trivial proposition that an economy cannot be in equilibrium unless prices are such that the quantity of means of payment that economic agents wish to hold is equal to the quantity actually in existence. Following a route that is as *ad hoc* and nearly as arbitrary as that followed by income–expenditure theorists, quantity theorists then discuss the determinants of the stock of money on the presumption that prices must move to bring the real value of this stock into equality with the *real* demand for money. Again, we have to deal with theories that are incompletely specified variants of general competitive analysis. In the hands of an expert—a category that includes Professor Friedman as a top-ranking outlier—this type of theory can be made to seem powerful despite its lack of logical underpinnings. But not all economists are experts, so modern quantity theories are ultimately of no more use than income–expenditure theories as a basis for rational discussion of inflationary processes.

The preceding animadversions may well raise doubts about the validity of my central theme. In light of these comments, how can it be argued that economists are less divided in their views about inflation than is popularly supposed? The answer is that none of the theories subjected to criticism above is logically invalid; each is simply incomplete, hopelessly ambiguous, or lacking in empirical relevance. Viewed from the perspective of a more general theory, however, all of them may well be seen to offer useful insights into the problem of inflation. That will be my contention.

II. TOWARDS A MORE GENERAL THEORY

To make theoretical sense of elementary facts of experience in an ongoing economy, we must first dispense with the notion that individual economic activities are coordinated by a fictitious "auctioneer" or—what comes to much the same thing—by vaguely specified "forces of supply and demand." In real life, economic plans are formulated and carried out within the framework of a complicated structure of market institutions that have evolved gradually out of an interplay of political, social and technological factors with everyday economic forces of greed and competition. The detailed characteristics of these institutions vary considerably from one economy to another and also from one market to another within any given economy. In every economy, and in all markets, however, we find that the day-to-day coordination of economic activities is carried out by highly visible exchange intermediaries—economic agents who act in a specialized capacity as brokers and auction agents or as outright dealers in various commodities that are produced and consumed in any considerable volume within the community. Thus the performance characteristics of an economy, although dependent in the final analysis upon the actions of individual producers and consumers, are determined in the first instance by the actions of exchange intermediaries. For it is these intermediaries who set and vary prices and who maintain buffer stocks of commodities so that trades can be executed routinely by other agents regardless of current levels of production and consumption. It is on the behaviour of intermediaries, therefore, that we must focus primary attention if we wish to explain how an economy works, or might fail to work, in circumstances that approximate those of real life.

A full account of the theory of an intermediary economy—of what has elsewhere been called *general process analysis*[3]—is out of the question here. In any case, all that we require is a broad sketch of certain fundamental ideas that have a direct bearing on the problem of inflation. In the immediately ensuing discussion, therefore, I shall deal with a simple, special instance of general process analysis, namely, the case of a pure commodity–money economy in which each exchange intermediary deals with just two goods—one of them the money commodity—and in which all trading is spot.[4]

The essential function of intermediaries is to reduce search and bargaining costs to prospective customers by providing a ready market for goods at prices that, on average, are better for both buyers and sellers than could be obtained in quick trades by direct barter. To perform that function effectively, intermediaries must at all times hold inventories of both money and goods and must stand ready to buy or sell at stated prices in such quantities as prospective customers

---

[3] See Clower (1975), pp. 4 ff.
[4] See Howitt (1974) for a formal model of such an economy.

might desire. To pay expenses and earn a profit, intermediaries must of course charge a brokerage fee on each transaction or maintain a differential between buying and selling prices.

In a literal sense, prices are administered by intermediaries while quantities are (within wide limits) administered by customers. In general, however, prices set by intermediaries must be varied from time to time to maintain control of trade inventories. Since customer arrival times are random variables from the point of view of intermediaries, trade volume over short intervals of time cannot significantly affect pricing decisions. Price will tend to vary discontinuously and discretely in response to perceived gaps between desired and actual holdings of goods and money as determined by the average volume of purchases and sales over more or less extended intervals of time. It is worth remarking, in particular, that conventional concepts of market demand and supply play no direct role in price adjustment: indeed, it hardly makes sense to speak of "market" demands and supplies except in relation to *average* purchases and sales of a commodity as experienced by intermediaries over finite intervals of calendar time. The operative forces governing price movements are notional excess *stock* demands as seen by intermediaries, and the magnitude of these forces cannot be inferred from a knowledge of prevailing levels of production and consumption.[5]

By its very nature, an intermediary economy is unlikely to respond to changing conditions of production or consumption except with lags that appear outwardly to be both long and variable. No single intermediary sees anything more than a small part of the economy, and even that small part is seen only indistinctly because each intermediary typically will be competing for customers with many others. On first thought, then, one might suppose that an intermediary economy would be inherently unstable. Certainly in standard theory, where the stability of any given model depends in an essential way upon the values assigned to particular slope and speed-of-adjustment parameters, we should be inclined to regard a system with long and variable lags as potentially very unstable. In general process analysis, however, price and quantity adjustments are explicitly associated with conscious and purposeful decisions of individual economic agents. Market performance characteristics are therefore to be regarded not as preordained consequences of technical and structural factors but rather as the end product of a complicated evolutionary process that permanently eliminates certain organizational arrangements because they do not work

---

[5] Cf. Clower (1975), p. 16.

and provisionally tolerates the survival of other arrangements because they have worked.[6] On this view, unstable economic systems, although theoretically conceivable, are not likely to be observed since they do not have survival value. Systems that survive over long intervals of calendar time effectively declare themselves to be "of stable type." Indeed, an even stronger assertion appears to be warranted: systems that survive need not have a structure that guarantees *asymptotic* stability (i.e., stability in the limit as time tends to infinity) but they must have a structure that ensures *practical* stability (i.e., strict boundedness of motion over any finite interval of calendar time).

Under what conditions can stationary equilibrium occur in an intermediary economy? Evidently we require that preferences and technology be given, or at least constant in a stochastic sense, since systematic changes in these factors clearly would lead ultimately to changes in prices and in quantities produced and consumed. If the economy is one in which the quantity of the money commodity is determined exogenously (e.g., by nature or by some kind of monetary authority), constancy of this quantity would also be required as an essential background condition. Taking these conditions as satisfied, we should then have to add various other requirements. Specifically, prices set by intermediaries would have to be uniform for any single good (abstracting from transport costs); rates of return on trade inventories would have to be equal to comparable rates of return on production capital; prices would have to be such that the quantity produced and sold of each good was equal, *on average*, to the quantity demanded for purchase and consumed; each individual intermediary's average inventory of money and goods would have to be constant; and the general level of money prices would have to be such that the total existing stock of money was just equal to the amount demanded to hold for trade purposes.

This is already a fairly long list of requirements, and it is by no means complete. In particular, I have so far said nothing about requirements imposed on agents who are not intermediaries. In the model considered here, each producer and consumer will hold inventories of goods and money to avoid prohibitively heavy transaction costs associated with frequent trading in small lots. These inventories must be maintained at constant levels, on average, if equilibrium is to occur. In addition, all the usual marginal conditions must hold, at least in a stochastic sense, since otherwise the realized trade volume of some intermediaries would vary over time. In the present context, however, it hardly makes sense to talk about "efficiency" or "opti-

---

[6] Cf. Marshall (1913), pp. 139–141.

mality," even in equilibrium, for we are dealing with a system in which possibly very large quantities of resources are devoted to trade and this fact, plus the essentially social character of prevailing market arrangements, makes it impossible to establish any definite benchmark of optimality or efficiency. Equilibrium is efficient in a practical sense if it generally permits individuals to carry out production and consumption plans as scheduled and so serves effectively to ensure the coordination of economic activities.[7] In particular, equilibrium does not necessarily involve full employment of labor or other resources in any absolute sense; a certain amount of slackness may be regarded as not only "normal" but also efficient.

This discussion might be extended in a variety of directions. On this occasion, however, a few generalizing reflections must suffice. Obviously no actual economy is as simple as the one just considered. In real life, few intermediaries act simply as middlemen. Most operate also as business firms and so act in one capacity as intermediaries in the purchase of labor services and in another capacity as intermediaries in the sale of finished products. Thus retail merchants set prices to consumers and to prospective employees but take prices from their suppliers who, in turn, set prices to merchants and to their employees but take prices from their suppliers—and so on, down the line, until one reaches primary producers, auction markets for farm and fishery products, etc. Most sales occur not spot but future. Orders are placed by merchants on the expectation that price at time of delivery will be similar to price today, but actual transaction prices generally are determined by date of final manufacture or delivery rather than date of order. The great bulk of all payments are made initially in the form of book debits to trade accounts that are later settled with cash or bank transfers, which means that the "money supply" is largely endogenous even though the cash base is rigidly fixed by factors outside the control of individual economic agents.

Formal modelling of these and other complications, although clearly possible in principle, poses conceptual and mathematical problems that are truly mind-boggling. Sooner or later, of course, such modelling must be carried out if we are ever to place ourselves in a position to predict with any accuracy the short-run future behavior of any actual economy. Meanwhile we must probably be satisfied with recognizably rough-and-ready models with simple structures. These will have obvious limitations, even if they are fully elaborated and set out in a form that satisfies modern standards of rigor and precision. Still, it is my hunch that the qualitative behavior of even very complex

---

[7] Cf. Leijonhufvud (1973), pp. 29–30; Clower (1975), pp. 8–9.

systems will not differ significantly from that of the simple pure commodity–money economy considered above. However that may be, I propose now to use this simple model—with suitable modifications— to take a fresh look at the problem of inflation.

III. INFLATION: A GENERAL PROCESS PERSPECTIVE

The account of general process analysis set out above is thoroughly traditional. It is compatible not only with Marshall's ideas as presented in *Industry and Trade*[8] but also with those of his classical predecessors— Smith, Ricardo, Senior and John Stuart Mill. It also accords well with views expressed by Marshall's most distinguished contemporaries— Jevons, Walras, Edgeworth and Walker. Its relation to more recent work should be equally clear. It includes general competitive analysis as a limiting case that is approximately valid for analyzing full equilibrium states of a general process model. As for monetarist and income–expenditure models, these are subsumed in general process analysis under the heading of "partial, *ad hoc* representations of temporary equilibrium states."

Now, consider a moderately generalized version of a pure commodity–money model in which we continue to suppose that all trading is spot but in which we also allow for fractional-reserve private banking so that "money" now includes bank deposits as well as cash. Let us further suppose that the cash commodity—let us call it "gold" for the time being—serves no purpose in the economy except as a means of payment and store of value. In full equilibrium, the ratio of cash to bank deposits will be constant, markets will clear on average so that aggregate income will equal aggregate expenditure, and existing demands for money (cash and deposits) will be equal, on average, to the existing stock. Starting from this kind of situation, how might a sustained rise in the money prices of all commodities be generated and, given that such an inflationary process occurs, how might the process be "explained" by adherents to different theoretical positions?

Only two possible sources of inflation make any sense at all in these circumstances, and one of them makes too little sense to merit more than passing mention. The uninteresting possibility is that there might be a general retrogression in technology or a progressively increasing reluctance to work that produces a sustained and general decrease in the output of goods. Such a commodity inflation—with an essentially constant stock of money—is certainly conceivable, but we can hardly regard it as a possibility that deserves serious consideration. No mod-

[8] See especially Marshall (1919), Book 2, Chapters 5–8.

ern economy is likely to experience anything of this sort, though in some situations (e.g., present-day Britain), something similar may occur as a consequence of inflationary movements arising originally from another source, and this could seriously exacerbate other tendencies making for a rapid increase in the general money price level.

The more relevant possibility, of course, is a change in initial conditions that leads to a sustained positive rate of increase in the stock of money. This might come from two main sources: a change in technology that makes gold substantially cheaper to produce (this would include the discovery of new sources, as during the fifteenth and sixteenth centuries, as well as the discovery of new extraction processes as at the end of the nineteenth century); or debasement of the coinage by government. Both possibilities are of some interest, if only for historical reasons. The second, however, is of special concern because it corresponds exactly to modern situations in which the cash base consists of fiat money rather than gold.

Let us note in passing that it makes no sense at all to think of inflation as a consequence of a rise in the velocity of money. Such a rise might occur, but it would at worst produce a once-over increase in money prices, not a continuing inflation. A prolonged rise in money prices could be caused by changes in banking practice (more generally, by changes in credit arrangements) that served gradually to increase the ratio of deposits to cash; but this would be most unlikely to produce a rapid rate of increase in prices, and it is doubtful if the rise would be sustained for very long in any case. As for a steady increase in government spending financed either by taxes or by borrowing (with no change in the cash base), we can affirm categorically that this might produce a temporary increase in some or even most prices but it could not in any circumstances produce a continuing rise in the general level of money prices. So we return to the case of a debasement of the coinage: i.e., governmentally generated increases in the cash base.

Suppose that the government (or monetary authority) proceeds to increase the cash base at a steady rate. It will matter very little whether this occurs through government purchases of private or public debt or through government purchases of goods and services. In either case, the first impact will be felt by intermediaries (bond brokers or merchants), whose inventories of commodities will decline and whose inventories of cash will rise. To replenish their commodity inventories, these intermediaries will turn to other intermediaries or to primary agents, or both, and within a short time prices paid by intermediaries will increase (i.e., market rates of interest will fall and prices of goods will rise). As the stock of cash continues to rise, bank loans and deposits will expand, trade generally will appear to be picking up, and so the effect of the increasing money stock gradually will spread through the economy—but certainly not at an even pace. There will be long lags in the adjustment of some prices, delayed shifts in the mix of outputs produced by primary agents, changes in consumption patterns because of different individual price and wealth elasticities of demand, and so forth. Eventually, however, the economy will settle down to a steady rate of inflation—not with the same pattern of relative prices as before, or the same patterns of production and consumption, but with patterns that are nevertheless constant over time.[9]

One can then imagine various explanations being offered for the rise in prices that is actually being observed. One school will point out that prices are governed by the relation between expenditure and income and will note, correctly, that government deficits continue to keep pace with the rise in prices. Another school will point more directly to the source of the problem by drawing attention to the rise in the aggregate money stock. These explanations obviously come to much the same thing. A third school, however, will see something quite different, namely, that prices are rising *because* costs are rising. This view will be applauded by intermediaries, who will naturally view price increases by themselves not as a means of making higher profits but rather as a way to avoid serious losses—which requires that they increase sale prices in step with the prices they have to pay for new supplies. If this superficial explanation of the inflation is accepted— and in real life it invariably *is* accepted by perhaps most people—then someone will suggest that inflation can be halted by fixing costs—a wages and income policy—and from that point onward unreason might well become the order of the day. Unfortunately, no actual inflation ever proceeds at a steady pace. I say "unfortunately" because if that were not so, it would be a simple matter for any sensible person to point out the stupidity of a cost-push explanation of inflation. Actual inflations—even sustained and rapid ones—always proceed by fits and starts. Because of this the operations of intermediaries as coordinators of economic activity are thrown into a more or less constant state of turmoil. Inventories of goods are always either too low or too high. Price increases are introduced at some times in anticipation of increased demands that do not materialize, while at other times price increases are delayed and sudden shortages then occur because demands suddenly increase. No outside observer can make sense of price movements. Depending on prevailing levels of inventories in relation

---

[9] On this, see Varian (1976).

to desired holdings, prices can rise even when stocks are increasing (flow excess demand negative) and remain constant or decline even when stocks are declining (flow excess demand positive). The velocity of money undergoes odd and erratic movements; the ratio of deposits to cash reserves also behaves unpredictably. Money movements appear to be generated by changes in real activity rather than the other way around. Search activity increases as price relationships become ever more chaotic. Resources are unemployed because owners do not wish to commit them too quickly in one direction lest commitment in another direction should shortly turn out to be more desirable. In short, economic "laws" appear to break down. In fact, what breaks down is the capacity of intermediaries effectively to coordinate economic activities. It is one thing to operate in the face of mere ignorance—this is the usual situation of any intermediary. Plain ignorance can be dealt with in normal circumstances by operating on the assumption that tomorrow will be something like the average of experience over the past week or month or year. But when ignorance is compounded with Knightian uncertainty and the past becomes an essentially worthless guide to the future, intermediaries cannot follow conventional rules and stay in business. The behaviour of intermediaries then appears to become—and may in fact be—both erratic and unpredictable, and their ability to serve effectively as coordinators of economic activity is diminished accordingly.

In the course of the preceding argument I have slipped almost without noticing it from a discussion of the genesis of inflation into a discussion of the rather different problem of control. Before turning complete attention to the latter topic, however, I should like to remark that I see no serious division of opinion among economists over the issue of the genesis of inflationary processes. The general public may be confused in this regard, but no reasonably competent economist doubts that inflations actually experienced in modern times are attributable to government dictated or government tolerated increases in the cash base. It is another question whether in the absence of variations in the cash base modern economies would always be well behaved. Perhaps they would still experience periodic ups and downs, credit crises, and all the other ills that used to be discussed in books about "the business cycle." That in no way affects the validity of the proposition that continued, rapid inflation is possible only if the cash base is permitted continually to increase. So one can be a "monetarist" in a Humean sense, as I most certainly am and as almost all other economists probably are, without in any way being a Monetarist in the Chicago School sense.

IV. INFLATION: THE PROBLEM OF CONTROL

The problem of bringing an ongoing inflation under control without seriously disrupting existing patterns of economic activity would evidently be fairly difficult even in a spot economy of the kind considered in the preceding discussion. Any sudden reduction in the rate of increase in the cash base would have much the same effect as would a sudden reduction in the absolute level of the cash base in a stationary economy. Matters would be more complicated in an inflationary world, however, because a change in government policy would itself introduce a new element of uncertainty into an already uncertain situation. Still, it seems clear that a policy of gradually reducing the rate of increase of the cash base, if it were firmly adhered to, would work out reasonably well in a world of spot exchange.

It is an altogether different question whether the same type of policy would work well in an economy where a major part of current activity is concerned with the production and use of long-lived capital goods. In this case, even moderate reductions in the rate of increase in the cash base might trigger large declines in production and employment and so set in motion processes of contraction that would seriously disrupt the normal working of the economic system. The main danger here is that the reduction in employment might be followed by a reduction in household holdings of liquid assets to a level where large numbers of families were unable to express an effective money demand for food and clothing and other necessities of life. In real life, the crucial factor that determines whether markets adjust easily to changing circumstances is the distribution of money and other buffer stocks throughout the economic system. Significant changes in this distribution can seriously interfere with the ability of primary agents to signal demands for goods to intermediaries and this, in turn, can lead intermediaries to emit distorted or noisy signals to producers, leading to further unfavorable changes in the distribution of liquid assets by creating further declines in employment.

In my view, the only way to guard against the dangers just mentioned is to broaden significantly the coverage of typical unemployment insurance programs. Ideally, such programs should even cover the self-employed, for in any policy of inflation control a substantial number of small-scale enterprises are almost certain to be forced into bankruptcy and their operators will then almost certainly join the ranks of the unemployed. Provided that adequate provision is made to ensure that no large segment of the population is ever left completely without resources (a proviso that most definitely *was not satisfied* in the U.S. during the early 1930s), I see no reason to suppose that a policy of gradual reduction in the rate of increase in the cash base would produce sustained disruption of any economy.

But of course there is a hitch even here. In the wake of the Keynesian Revolution, most governments in the world have taken upon themselves responsibility for maintaining "full employment." The one thing that cannot be avoided in any policy that aims at bringing inflation under control is shifts in demand and consequent increases—perhaps substantial increases—in levels of unemployment. As a practical matter, therefore, it may well be doubted whether any policy that aims simultaneously at full or even high employment and the gradual elimination of an ongoing inflation can be carried out successfully. One goal or the other simply must be sacrificed.

To me it seems clear which goal ought to go. Those who argue that full employment must take precedence over any and all other considerations seem to me to place too much weight on the value of human sweat for its own sake. By all means we should ensure that those who can't find work should continue to eat and even enjoy a certain amount of fun and leisure; but to guarantee everyone continual work as well as continual pay is an act of utter folly, for it inevitably carries with it a threat of direct and piecemeal intervention in economic affairs that can only work to inhibit the transition of the economy from a state of rapid to a state of moderate or zero inflation.

V. A CONCLUDING COMMENT

I began this paper by remarking that economists are by no means as divided in their views about the genesis and control of inflation as is popularly supposed. The body of the paper does little directly to support this claim. Still, I think it will be generally acknowledged that the only way to avoid inflation is to avoid any but moderate and steady increases in the cash base. As for the problem of inflation control, that remains a disputed issue—and rightly so; for in truth economists stand together here only in being generally unable to say anything definite about the probable short-run effects of any specific set of policy actions.

REFERENCES

Clower, R. W., "Reflections on the Keynesian Perplex," *Zeitschrift für Nationalökonomie*, 35, July 1975, 1–24. Reprinted as ch. 14 of this volume.

Hahn, F. H., "Foundations of Monetary Theory," *Essays on Modern Economics*, M. Parkin (ed.), London: Longmans, 1973, 230–242.

Hicks, J. R., *Critical Essays in Monetary Theory*, Oxford: Clarendon 1967.

Howitt, P.W., "Stability and the Quantity Theory," *Journal of Political Economy*, 82, Jan./Feb. 1974, 133–140.

Johnson, H. G., "The Problem of Inflation," in *On Economics and Society: Selected Essays*, Chicago and London: U. of Chicago Press, 1975.

Leijonhufvud, A., "Effective Demand Failures," *Swedish Economic Journal*, 73, 1973, 27–48.

Marshall, A., *Economics of Industry*, London: Macmillan, 1913.

Marshall, A., *Industry and Trade*, London: Macmillan, 1919.

Ostroy, J., "The Informational Efficiency of Monetary Exchange," *American Economic Review*, 63, September 1973, 597–610.

Ostroy, J. and Starr, R. M., "Money and the Decentralization of Exchange," *Econometrica*, 42, November 1974, 1093–1113.

Varian, H., "On Balanced Inflation," *Economic Inquiry*, 14, March 1976, 45–51.

PART V

AFTERWORD

19

MONEY AND MARKETS

Professor Walker has kindly invited me to write an afterword so that
(to paraphrase his suggestions) I might have an opportunity both to
reflect on my earlier work and to express some thoughts about contemporary trends in monetary economics. To be candid (as one feels
bound to be in the privacy of an afterword), I did not find the first
suggestion appealing. I recall Joan Robinson once saying (in reference
to her book on imperfect competition), "I'm so glad I wrote it, because
that way I didn't have to read it." I thought her remark amusing at
the time; now I know she meant it. The second suggestion was more
tempting. I should have recalled my mother saying, "Don't go looking
for arguments." I ignored her then; I now think it wasn't bad advice.
But all this is by the way. What follows may not be quite what Walker
demanded, nor quite what I set out to supply, but I trust that in most
respects it is responsive to the invitation that called it forth.

I. DOUBTS ABOUT ORTHODOXY

My "doubts about orthodoxy," as Walker describes them, occurred
long before I knew any economics. What others may see as an intellectual development, I know to be a personality trait. My first serious
reading in economics was Keynes's *General Theory*, which I found
fascinating not because I understood much of it (though I thought I
understood all of it at the time), but rather because of Keynes's ir-
reverent yet graceful style. So I wrote an undergraduate thesis in
which I mimicked Keynes and slashed away at contemporary writers
who struck me as defenders of orthodox theory. When shortly thereafter I studied under John Hicks at Oxford and learned what orthodox theory was actually about, I took a mental vow to moderate my
tone in later writings. I also cast about for more promising targets to
attack, but by then Keynesian economics had developed its own orthodoxy, so I did not have far to look. I don't deny that my writings
display a certain intellectual coherence, nor that a logical progression
links my later with my earlier work; how else should it be for one to
whom economics is more a way of life than a way to make a living?
But it would be disingenuous to deny that much of my work is some-

what iconoclastic. Considering the areas in which I have tended to concentrate—monetary theory and macroeconomics—some of this is surely justified. For the rest, I gladly admit to an ingrained distrust of "authority."

Professor Walker infers from my published writings that the early 1960s were a crucial period in my intellectual development. His inference is surely correct, but behind each of my papers from that period lies a personal story that perhaps is also worth telling. In professional publications as in marriages, things are not always as they seem on the surface.

The "Keynes and the Classics" essay (Chapter 1) is a revised version of a much longer paper on Keynesian microdynamics that made use of various mechanical price and quantity adjustment rules that I thought were plausible but for which I could provide little economic motivation. The paper yielded some results that were sharply at variance with conventional multimarket stability analysis, so I was delighted with it. But my delight was short-lived, for the paper was expeditiously rejected by the *Journal of Political Economy* as "intriguing but unpersuasive." Then as now I could see no special virtue in the excess-demand adjustment rules of established theory. I knew too much about economic organization to imagine that the prices of more than a handful of commodities were determined on a day-to-day basis by impersonal market forces, but I could not construct a coherent account of the logistics of trade that would support my use of non-conventional adjustment rules. So I put such questions on my mental back burner, and sent an appropriately expurgated version of the essay to the *Quarterly Journal of Economics*. The published paper barely hints at the perplexing problems that were the centerpiece of the original analysis. Even less does it reveal my frustration at being unable to resolve them.

The question of price and quantity adjustment rules is mentioned obliquely but then sidestepped once more in my note on classical monetary theory (Chapter 2). On the surface, this essay does little more than clarify the then- (and perhaps still-) prevalent confusion between "temporary" and "full" equilibrium supply and demand functions. It was designed also to clear up some other loose ends in Patinkin's work (thus it is closely related to my 1960 paper with Burstein, reproduced here as Chapter 11). I like the paper as a whole, partly because it is craftily (*sic!*) executed, but mainly because it reveals so clearly the intellectual emptiness of quantity theory accounts of short-run adjustment processes. The paper may strike some as a regression toward orthodoxy, but the careful reader will rightly view the interpretative passages in the middle of the paper as mildly sarcastic reminders of the utter silence of established theory on price and quantity adjustment issues about which it ought to make at least some noises.

Judging from the literature it has spawned, my most influential single work is "The Keynesian Counter-Revolution" (Chapter 3). There is a certain irony in this, because it was probably the easiest of all my papers to write. But justice will be served. Many of my "followers" have since gone off in directions different from mine, so I'm more a bugler for the rear echelons than the leader of an army (I shall say more of this later).

The "Counter-Revolution" paper has a curious history, some of which is worth recounting. It owes its existence to a letter I received in January 1962 inviting me (very belatedly) to present a paper on "The Role of Money in General Equilibrium Theory" at an International Economic Association conference to be held in France during April of the same year. The invitation reached me in Liberia, where I was then laboring with some other economists to alter prevailing conceptions of that country as "the white man's grave"; so, to put it mildly, I was ecstatic—even though the deadline for finished drafts was just three weeks away. I put aside all other work and settled down to write, but nothing wrote; my hand was willing, but my head refused to work. The reason was simple: I could think of nothing to say about money and general equilibrium that had not already been said, most of it by Patinkin (and Patinkin was to be my discussant!). After a week of agonizing, I considered withdrawing from the conference—for all of ten seconds. Instead, recalling an exchange between Hicks and Patinkin in the *Economic Journal* some five years earlier to which I thought I had something to add, I switched my topic to "Keynes and General Equilibrium Theory." An hour later I had an introduction. A day later I had another title: the one the paper now bears. Ten days later, slightly dazed, I put a finished draft in the mail; the paper seemed almost to have written itself.

Two days before the conference convened, I met Frank Hahn in London and we exchanged papers. With uncharacteristic modesty (perhaps he was merely being jocular) he told me that his contribution—on some problems of proving the existence of equilibrium in a money economy—was "a trivial thing, of no importance." I expressed sympathy, and told him that my contribution, by contrast, was "a major breakthrough." When we met the next morning, I told him I had read his paper and that it was indeed of no importance, to which he replied: "That's all right, neither is yours." Of course his paper was brilliant—and mine grew on him with the passage of time.

I shall postpone comment on the argument of the "Counter-Revolution" paper and reactions to it, except for one extended remark. The paper does not take issue with the price adjustment rules of established theory, nor with the presumption that all prices (including wage rates) are freely flexible. So in no obvious respect does it anticipate later work with fix-price models. The novelty of the paper lies in its demonstration that the "notional" excess demands of established theory may not be operative in disequilibrium. It is another question whether effective demands of the kind defined in the paper can usefully be regarded as operative in the same circumstances. I claimed nothing of the kind in the paper, nor do I support such a claim now. On the contrary, my view is that the entire issue is moot, because the adjustment rules of established theory cannot plausibly be regarded as useful ingredients for a fruitful theory of disequilibrium economics.

"Monetary History and Positive Economics" (Chapter 4) was more fun to read than to write. When I was invited to review Milton Friedman and Anna Schwartz's *A Monetary History of the United States, 1867–1960* for the *Journal of Economic History*, I accepted with alacrity, partly because I was flattered, but mainly because it gave me a much-desired opportunity to take some shots at the non-Keynesian "opposition." (I wasn't quite sure to what other camp I belonged, but I was sure it wasn't Friedman's!) I then knew Friedman only slightly, and Anna Schwartz not at all, and though I had a grudging admiration for Friedman's book on the consumption function, the rest of his writings left me angry or unmoved. All in all, therefore, I was disposed to give Friedman and his coauthor a hard time before I had even seen a copy of their book. Nor did my attitude change after my first or second pass through the volume; on the contrary, I had by then compiled a list of "targets for attack" that was nearly fifty pages long. But knowing Friedman's reputation as a debater, I decided to go once more through the entire book, this time very carefully, to search for passages that might cause my otherwise deadly shots to ricochet back at me. When I was done, I had nearly fifty pages of crossed-out "targets" and a completely ungrudging admiration for the book and both its authors.

The published review was a surprise to my friends. In all candor, it was even more of a surprise to me. In part, of course, my about-face was simply a quiet tribute to the scholarship of Friedman and Schwartz. More important, it marked my personal emancipation from more than fifteen years of intellectually debilitating ideological bias against the Chicago school. Chicago is one of the few centers of economic study where the existence of organized arrangements for coordinating economic activities—"markets" in common parlance—has always been regarded as a problem to be investigated rather than, as at most other schools, an independent presupposition of economic analysis. Thus it is in keeping with the Chicago tradition to inquire into the self-organizing capabilities of a private enterprise economy, which seems to me precisely the direction that one must take if one hopes successfully to question the price-adjustment rules of neo-Walrasian theory. Before my encounter with Friedman and Schwartz, my mind was resistant to this line of research; after the encounter, it was at least open to persuasion.

I don't think my "emancipation" had any immediate effect upon my thinking, though the strong methodological motif of the review might suggest otherwise. My views on method were not then, nor are they now, at all doctrinaire. In describing myself as a neo-Walrasian (see the Editor's Introduction), I meant mainly to contrast my outlook with that of the inductivist, black-box, curve-fitting school of theorists to which Friedman was popularly supposed to belong. Probably I should also have dissociated myself from the empty-box brand of neo-Walrasianism that had already drawn my fire in the "Counter-Revolution," but the English version of that essay was still in process, and I saw no point in raising an issue that was not germane to my immediate task. So I chose instead to distance myself indirectly by paying the methodology of positive economics rather more than its due.

II. TOWARD GENERAL PROCESS ANALYSIS

The papers in Parts II and III document my transition from conventional theory to general process analysis: from thinking of markets as vaguely synonymous with "impersonal forces of demand and supply" to thinking of them concretely as specialized trading institutions, organized and operated by economic agents for the purpose of coordinating, for a profit, the economic activities of other agents. The content and thrust of the various papers is masterfully characterized by Walker in his Introduction. I shall continue to confine my reflections, therefore, to matters that lie behind or beyond the published papers.

Economics is less obviously a young man's game than mathematics, but I doubt that many economists have had a really new idea after the age of thirty-five. I must confess that, one way or another, everything I've done in the second half of my life reminds me (at least retrospectively) of something I did or thought about earlier. This is especially true of my papers on money, which are full of rearranged ideas, some drawn from earlier published work on unrelated subjects, others from ruminations that earlier came to nothing. Some of what is original in them is a matter more of emphasis and perspective than of fundamental insight. Indeed, what struck me most when rereading these papers was not their content (though I confess I enjoyed some of it) but their style, which reflects a strategy of argument that underlies all of my work.

I have always thought that the essential art of economics, as of any other science (or of literary fiction, for that matter) is to tell a good story in a persuasive way. No doubt this leaves a good many things (some might think too many) to individual taste; for what is deemed "good" depends on one's perception of what is important, interesting, and likely to interest or amuse others, and what is deemed persuasive depends as much on prevailing fashions in argument as on established canons of logic. Still, most of us would agree that to be "good" a story must deal with recognizable subject matter. That is why so much of economics is essentially topical, and also why so-called seminal contributions typically contain as much motivating material as formal analysis. Even more strongly, most of us would agree that to be persuasive a story must be conceptually coherent; in other words, the actors in the story and the actions they are assumed to perform must make sense, both taken in isolation and when considered as a whole. That is why we frown on ad hoc argument, and also why, despite sometimes serious flaws in logic, the works of great economists never seem to lose their savor.

To me, as perhaps to most economists, conceptual coherence is ultimately a matter of intuition: Given some initial thought experiment that serves to motivate a model, the question is not just whether the model describes salient aspects of the experiment in a logically satisfactory way, but also whether the model does so without implying other consequences that seem intuitively at odds with the same underlying thought experiment. To put the matter another way: *The model is not the message; the message is always more than the model.*

The central role that the principle of conceptual coherence plays in my work is perhaps brought out most clearly by the story that goes with my "Reconsideration of the Microfoundations of Monetary Theory" (Chapter 5). This paper has had a surprisingly favorable reception, considering its limited scope and accomplishments. I have the impression, however, that most readers have seen it as the beginning of a series of papers on money rather than a continuation of my earlier work on Keynesian economics. In fact, I can't think offhand of any writer who has linked the formal model in the "Reconsideration" with the dual-decision model of the "Counter-Revolution"; yet, in truth, the two models are simply alternative formalizations of a single thought experiment. Indeed, the dichotomized budget constraint model of the "Reconsideration" not only portrays the thought experiment of the "Counter-Revolution" more accurately in a logical sense than does the dual-decision setup, it also expresses a point of view that is more appealing to common sense. Let me explain.

The thought experiment that underlies the dual-decision model is set out at the beginning of Section VI of the "Counter-Revolution" paper (Chapter 3). There I contemplate an individual who, for some reason, finds that his realized money income will not support his desired money expenditures. I then argue that such an individual must sooner or later consider ways to economize, since he cannot convert mere offers to work into effective (money) purchasing power. I might have left it at that, or I might have argued that a person who is unable to sell as much as desired today would, if rational, treat that fact as relevant information in forming a reasonable expectation of his earnings tomorrow, an expectation that, in turn, would affect his expenditure plans for tomorrow. This last thought experiment, correctly modeled, would have introduced realized money income into individual excess-demand functions as a loose proxy for expected future earnings, thereby resolving my immediate problem (which was to cast doubt on the universal relevance of conventionally defined demand functions). But I was after something more, something that at one stroke not only would put realized earnings into the demand functions, but also would establish a clean separation in the choice constraints between current plans to buy and current plans to sell. How to do this was not obvious, at least not to me. Though suggested by my reading of Keynes, the formal model finally adopted was literally an act of desperation, and it could be improved, both descriptively and analytically. Its main deficiency is that to some degree it conveys a false impression of what I meant to say (and, if I remember correctly, of what I thought I was saying). But that was perhaps just as well; a model that more accurately portrayed my underlying thought experiment might well have been less effective for making my central point.

I can't recall being aware of a hiatus in the "Counter-Revolution" argument until some years later when, during a year of research leave, I tried to introduce the dual-decision hypothesis into an otherwise conventional model of price dynamics. It quickly became apparent that, taken literally, the constraints of the dual-decision model were

"too tight"; they made sense only if one viewed expenditures and
earnings as averages over an interval of time rather than as instantaneous rates of flow. Furthermore, the model implied the direct
dependence of effective demands not just on prices but also on quantities exchanged of each and every commodity. To say anything about
the dynamics of effective demand, one would thus have to add to the
usual price-adjustment equations an extra and highly complex array
of rationing rules that would specify just which agents transacted
precisely what quantities of each commodity in every conceivable state
of the economic system. It seemed a bit excessive to impose this new
burden on an already overworked "invisible hand." In any case, unlike
the technically more gifted economists who later trod much the same
path, I was unable to formalize any but trivial rationing schemes. So,
defeated by this line of inquiry, I gave up and went back to rethink
the problem.

In the mid-1960s, the monetarist movement was just gathering steam,
so "money" was a central topic of conversation and controversy. I was
involved in these discussions, along with everyone else, but I soon
became impatient with what I heard and read—and said—because
neither I nor anyone else seemed to have any idea how one might
distinguish analytically between money and other commodities, much
less how one might construct a formal model in which just one commodity (or a few) could be shown to play a role similar to that assigned
to money in every text on money and banking. Somehow these concerns entered into my rethinking of the dual-decision hypothesis (or
perhaps it was the other way around!). In any event, the result was
the dichotomized budget constraint model of the "Reconsideration."
Realized income did not appear explicitly in the new demand functions, but it did appear with a lag via the money stock variable, which
implied that a sustained excess of expenditure over income would
produce an eventual reduction in planned expenditures. So the new
model not only accurately conveyed the message contained in my
original thought experiment, it also linked disequilibrium analysis
with monetary theory in a conceptually coherent and intellectually
satisfying way.

As for the dual-decision hypothesis, I gave it up, for the reasons
indicated, long before the "Reconsideration" appeared (and also before the "Counter-Revolution" was published). Imagine my astonish-
ment when a virtually distinct branch of economic theory began to
develop from the dual-decision hypothesis and from the surprisingly
similar (but, to my mind, even less coherent) Patinkin model of constrained supply. I refer, of course, to the fix-price models of Barro

and Grossman, Dreze, Negishi, Grandmont, Benassy, Malinvaud, Varian, and other writers. Although I am an acknowledged "grandfather" of all these "babies," I disowned them at the 1980 Aix-en-Provence World Conference of the Econometric Society as "monsters" begotten by a father (the dual-decision process) whose paternity I admitted but whose character I deplored. I then gave my blessing to other babies— a motley lot, except for their distinctively Marshallian grins—describing them as well-formed offspring of a fraternal twin of the father whose babies I had just disowned. The audience was puzzled by my remarks, and I can't say I blame them. What was obvious to me was not only not obvious but not even true for most of my listeners. The fix-price literature had by then developed its own impetus and analytical uses, quite apart from the source (or sources) that originally inspired it. So, while I do not myself regard this line of inquiry as particularly promising, neither would I now defend my earlier condemnation of it.

As mentioned earlier, the "Reconsideration" was originally conceived as an extension of the "Counter-Revolution" paper. In the writing, however, other matters intruded—so much so, indeed, that the original conception dropped out of sight. What was left was a model of household choice in a money economy that raised more questions than it answered. Specifically, the model implied that the choice alternatives confronting households were more restrictive in a money than in a barter economy, which meant that monetary exchange is less efficient than barter exchange, contrary to both common sense and two hundred years of conventional wisdom. Something obviously was wrong, but what? Not the model: If trading activity were costless, as was tacitly assumed in the model, then no agent would voluntarily accede to any restriction on direct pairwise trades; hence, monetary exchange as defined by the model would simply not occur. Thus I was driven by the logic of the model (more accurately, by the principle of conceptual coherence) to inquire into an area that I had hitherto ignored: the logistics and costs of individual trading in a world without organized markets.

The results of my inquiries are reported sequentially—in ever greater detail and with increasing precision—in the papers reprinted here as Chapters 6–10 and 13. Since they represent stages in the development of a new outlook on the analysis of the economy, and since they were each written in response to outside demands rather than as independent research papers, it is hardly surprising that the ideas put forward in them appear somewhat unfinished. Eventually, however, those ideas coalesced into a well-focused research program: general

process analysis, the main outlines of which are set forth in "Reflections on the Keynesian Perplex" (Chapter 14) and further elaborated
in other papers in Part IV of this volume.

III. CONTEMPORARY PERSPECTIVES

One does not have to be a compulsive reader of the professional
journals to recognize that monetary theory has been a relatively in-
active field since the middle to late 1970s. Activity in the more topical
field of monetary economics has meanwhile quickened and intensified, reflecting prevailing pressures to "say something relevant" about
current problems of unemployment and inflation. This is an unfortunate state of affairs. Monetary theory turned quiescent just as its
accomplishments had set the stage for constructive rethinking of conventional theories of market behavior, so no such rethinking has occurred. On the contrary, monetary economics has continued to develop
in its customary fashion as a seat-of-the-pants discipline that stumbles
blindly from one real-world problem to the next without drawing
from or adding to the accumulated stock of fundamental economic
knowledge.

Why have modern developments in monetary theory been so generally overlooked or ignored in the recent literature on monetary
economics and macroeconomics? The explanation lies, I suspect, in
the fact that these developments occurred in the context of a longstanding intellectual problem the significance of which was generally
regarded as problematical at best. Specifically, the problem was to
account for the use of intrinsically worthless objects as common media
of exchange. The solution proffered by modern research (see Chapter
17) runs in terms of transactions costs and the physical characteristics
of commodities, complications that are ignored in conventional theory. The validity of this solution appears to have been generally acknowledged by specialists in monetary theory; what previously had
been the central problem of traditional monetary theory thus became
a non-issue for all practical purposes. For most economists, however,
including the authors of leading modern texts in money and banking,
this solution meant little or nothing. The problem it resolved was a
source of concern only to fastidious theorists who felt uneasy about
putting money into models where it didn't seem to fit. A more important question, first posed clearly by Keynes in the *General Theory*,
was whether conventional wisdom about the self-adjusting capabilities
of the economic system could survive the construction of an intellectually satisfying theory of monetary exchange. When monetary theory

returned an apparently affirmative answer to this question, at least in a limited class of models for which an immediate answer was possible, most economists simply left matters there. No longer uncomfortable about putting money into their models, they returned to "business as usual" and devoted themselves to more pressing problems: unemployment, inflation, supply shocks, stagflation, *et hoc genus omne.*

Now, the real significance of modern work in monetary theory extends well beyond any single specialty. The hallmark of conventional models of value and monetary theory is that rules of price and quantity adjustment that govern market interactions are routinely devised and just as routinely imposed without explicit (if, indeed, any) reference to their consistency with the more fundamental notions of self-interest that are assumed to determine the production and consumption decisions of individuals. By contrast, modern research in monetary theory indicates that, to account for the very existence of monetary exchange, we must presume that the organization of trading arrangements—and hence, the specification of price and quantity adjustment rules governing market interactions—is undertaken by agents within the economic system, and so is responsive to the same forces of greed and competition as operate in other spheres of economic activity.

The implications of this inconvenient finding can, of course, be overlooked or ignored without fear of logical contradiction, but conceptual coherence and hopes for an empirically fruitful reconstruction of established theory are at stake. To ignore those implications consciously is, I suggest, to acknowledge that one cares less about the subject matter of economics than about intellectual games. So, to be charitable, I presume that the "business as usual" school is presently operating in a state of unfortunate ignorance rather than studied neglect.

However that may be, the consequences are serious. The economics profession is currently divided as never before on theoretical fundamentals as well as on policy issues. There is no way that these divergences of opinion can be brought to a head, much less resolved, unless attention is somehow focused on the general problem of the self-organizing and self-adjusting capabilities of a decentralized production and exchange economy. These issues cannot be addressed within the framework of conventional equilibrium theory or variants of it because that theory either presumes that the economy requires no organization (the coordination of economic activities is costless) or that its organization is established by an external agent (the neo-

Walrasian auctioneer) whose costs, if any, do not count. Given either of these hypotheses, conventional theory allows us to address the self-adjustment question, but to what purpose is then unclear. The performance characteristics of "toy" models that command neither widespread professional nor popular respect are, I suggest, neither here nor there; to work with such models at all is simply to evade the central problem.

Consider, for example, the kinds of models used by those who are generally considered (and consider themselves) to be Keynesians—James Tobin being perhaps the most notable member of this group. The standard construction here is one or another kind of IS–LM construction. Some are very simple, some are very elaborate, but all are at bottom variants of the temporary general equilibrium model set out in Hicks's *Value and Capital*. In the nature of the case, these constructions have no immediate empirical implications. They can be made to produce such implications only if they are padded out with various ad hoc restrictions suggested by casual empirical observation or econometric research: Phillips curves, Okun's law, adaptive expectations, mark-up pricing, implicit labor contracts, and so on. Inevitably, few of these devices survive the march of time. Invented to explain one set of facts, they are sooner or later contradicted by some new turn of events. But the basic models survive, because they are impervious to empirical or theoretical criticism. They are not so much wrong as fraudulent, because they promise what they cannot deliver, namely, rational understanding of major forces governing movements in aggregate income, employment, and prices.

The case of the monetarist branch of the "business as usual" school is no better. Like the Keynesians, the monetarists base themselves squarely on general equilibrium analysis, but upon a much vaguer version than anything to be found in the modern literature. Like the Keynesians, who assume without serious argument that the economic system generally doesn't work, the monetarists presume for equally poor reasons that the economic system always works almost perfectly. The monetarists have but one solid string in their bow. They argue, correctly, that in a money economy with determinate prices there must be some monetary magnitude that, if appropriately fixed, will ultimately put a slow anchor on upward movements in the general price level. But the monetarists then compromise the usefulness of this string by encrusting it with a large collection of contentious empirical hypotheses that are dredged up from the historical record. Their policy shots are correspondingly inaccurate and unreliable. Moreover, though the monetarists originally gained notoriety as opponents of the Keynesians, the passage of time has brought the two camps ever closer together. They are united by a common belief in ad hoc methods and a common unwillingness to reexamine the analytical preconceptions from which their arguments proceed. From the monetarists as from the Keynesians, therefore, we can expect to see much more of what we have already seen, and nothing that significantly advances our understanding of the world in which we live.

The currently most prominent branch of the "business as usual" school is the new classical economics of Lucas, Sargent, Wallace, and Barro. In some respects, the new classical economics is more accurately regarded as a throwback to pre-Keynesian modes of analysis than as a modernist extension of monetarism; its uncompromising reliance on conventional market-clearance presumptions and on the rational expectations hypothesis (the stochastic equivalent of perfect foresight) is almost quaintly anachronistic. Its analytical procedures, however, are anything but antiquated; indeed, observing the new classical economists in action, encumbered as they are by self-imposed methodological constraints, one is reminded of nothing so much as a world-class hurdler performing his specialty with both legs tied together. It is an awesome sight, but very unreal.

To be fair to the new classical economists one must recognize the narrow focus of their research. It is directed almost exclusively at devising a parsimonious theoretical explanation of business fluctuations. The explanations start with conventional market-clearing assumptions, which can be justified as logical implications of individual maximizing behavior in a world where transactions are costless. The Muthian hypothesis of rational expectations has obvious merit in this same context; indeed, for this case it might be regarded as a straightforward implication of what I have earlier called the principle of conceptual coherence. As numerous critics of rational expectations models have shown, one can imagine worlds in which rational expectations are anything but reasonable. In those cases, the rational expectations hypothesis looks more like a technical gimmick than a model-building principle. That is nevertheless not an effective criticism of the hypothesis as it is actually used by the new classical economists. A more pertinent criticism, it seems to me, is that to account for observed business fluctuations the new classical economists must somehow introduce autoregressive exogenous shocks into their equilibrium models. This is accomplished by supposing that the monetary authorities are irresponsible, and that monetary disturbances are propagated asymmetrically, and with occasional lags, through the rest of the economic system. Of course, this explanation is simply a *deus ex machina*. One cannot introduce these kinds of complications into an otherwise pristine new classical economic model without doing violence to the principle of conceptual coherence. The major objection to the new classical economics is much more straightforward; namely, that it equates theoretical progress with improved econometric performance of theoretical models rather than with enhanced understanding of the way in which decentralized economic systems work.

This brings me back to my starting point. I have argued that the approaches of the Keynesians, monetarists, and new classical economists to monetary theory and macroeconomics will get us exactly nowhere because each is founded, one way or another, on the conventional but empirically fallacious assumption that the coordination of economic activities is costless. Now, I do not deny that rational analysis of unreal worlds can yield results that are of immense practical importance; the examples of Newtonian physics and classical hydrodynamics are obvious cases in point. Nevertheless, for some purposes, such as the fruitful study of particle physics and supersonic flight, models based on radically different assumptions are essential. Similarly, while no one would wish to dispute either the intellectual or the practical merit of established value theory, neither can one doubt that for some purposes, such as the fruitful analysis of ongoing processes of monetary exchange, models of a very different kind may be required. My contention is that they are.

INDEX

Alchian, A., 199n51
Ando, A., 76n32
Archibald, G., 45n16, 138, 140
  on classical economics, 27
Aristotle, 236
Arrow, K., 211
  neo-Walrasian literature, 202n59
Arrow–Debreu models, 232, 233, 239
auctioneer, 211, 244–5, 269–70

bargaining costs, 239
Barro, R., 166n1
barter economy, 83, 84, 95, 161
  like money economy, 31n7
  transactions costs in, 98
  see also monetary economy
barter, organized, 214–15
Baumol, W., 45n16, 134n9
bonds, 139
  demand for, 139
  income from, 141
Brunner, K., 107n2, 231
budget equation, 82–3, 147
bunching costs, 170, 178, 179–80
Burstein, M., 196n39
Bushaw, D., 45n15, 45n16, 144n14, 167

Cambridge money equation, 32
Carroll, L., 187
cash balances
  cost of holding, 127
  demand for, 138–9
  Patinkin, D., 139
cash base, 248, 250
Churchman, G., 199n51
classical economics
  dichotomy, 27
  economic policy, 160
  full employment, 24
  monetary theory, 28–33
  recessions, 160
commodity–money economy, 222, 245
competitive analysis, 211, 243
  for analyzing equilibrium, 249
  comparative statics, 225
  inflation in, 220

money in, 220
  virtual systems, 219
consumption function, 51
coordination of economic activities, 218, 245
  costless, 127, 272
  failures, 213, 215
  intermediaries, 252
corridor phenomena, 214, 216
costs of trading, see trading costs, search costs, set-up costs, transactions costs
credit, 109n9

Davidson, P., 193n28
debits to trade accounts, 224, 248
Debreu, G., neo-Walrasian literature, 202n59
deflation, 159–60
demand and supply
  aggregate, 158–9
  household, 36
  labor, 21–3
demand functions
  assets as variable in, 45–6
  see also excess demand
disequilibrium transactions, 39, 43, 44
Domar, E., 25n11
dual-decision hypothesis, 48–53, 261–2, 265, 266–7
Duesenberry, J., 25n11
dynamic system, 141–3

economic history, 66
economic system as self-regulating, 268–9
equilibrium, 39
  efficiency of, 248
  in holding of cash, 127
excess demand, 82
  disequilibrium, 53–5
  individual, 152
  see also Say's principle
exchange
  coordination of, 221
  equilibrium of, 213
  intermediaries, 245

273